Mimesis and Reason

Mimesis and Reason

Habermas's Political Philosophy

GREGG DANIEL MILLER

SUNY PRESS

Cover photo by Gregg Daniel Miller

Published by State University of New York Press, Albany

Printed in the United States of America

For information, contact State University of New York Press, Albany, NY
www.sunypress.edu

Production by Kelli W. LeRoux
Marketing by Anne M. Valentine

Library of Congress Cataloging-in-Publication Data

Miller, Gregg Daniel, 1967–
Mimesis and reason : Habermas's political philosophy / Gregg Daniel Miller.
p. cm.
Includes bibliographical references and index.
ISBN 978-1-4384-3739-2 (hardcover : alk. paper)
ISBN 978-1-4384-3740-8 (pbk. : alk. paper)
1. Political science—Philosophy. 2. Habermas, Jürgen—Political and social views. I. Title.

JA71.M458 2011
320.01—dc22 2011004019

10 9 8 7 6 5 4 3 2 1

Contents

Preface

Under the broad rubric of modernity, postmodernity, and the democratic imaginary in a postsocialist age, a certain set of normative questions—together with the question of whether normativity can be asserted at all—motivates the studies of many political theorists and philosophers working today: What secular sensibility can govern the legitimate exercise of power in the modern age? Can any particular political body in an age of pluralism have confidence that its moral values are born of more than historical inertia but less than pure will to power? I will take up these questions in providing an assessment and reconstruction of a particular theory of communication found in the writings of Jürgen Habermas.

In doing so, I will work toward refiguring critical theory's self-conception where, presently, a theory of communication is understood to provide a merely procedural account of communication deployed for the purpose of testing the normative validity of speech-acts. Against the conception of communicative action as a principally negative pursuit, I will argue that critical theory needs (and, to a great degree, already has) a theory of reaching understanding that entails not only the *testing* of the *manner* of raising validity claims, but in addition, incorporates within it resources to appreciate how the scene of communicating is a vital experience that alters persons so engaged in conversation. This duality of the scene of speech—its negative testing function, and its positive, productive one—has important, cautionary implications for claims concerning the way that the democratic form of conversation is supposed to protect the moral character of its process. It is better, I argue, for critical theory to squarely confront the fundamentally *illiberal* phenomenology of reaching understanding, an event that esoterically partakes of the mimetic tradition of affective experience as much as it exoterically embraces the rationalist, Enlightenment tradition.

In his major work, *The Theory of Communicative Action*, and in his subsequent development of a discourse ethics, Habermas has aimed to disclose certain moral intentions posited as always already at work in communication under conditions of modernity, where *communication itself* offers up the promise of moral engagement in a secular, democratic, postmetaphysical age. It is to the structure of language and the practice of communication that Habermas has turned, for *if* in modernity the rationality of action cannot pretend to a correspondence with an extra-mundane referent (e.g., God's plan), *then* the use of reason, which is to say, *logos* in action, has only itself to fall back on: The practice of language itself must offer up the moral norms that it takes for its own guide. Under the name of "communicative rationality," Habermas has developed this intuition concerning the productive dialectic between norms and action through an engagement with and consolidation among eclectic theories of language, truth, morality, and action that answers pragmatically to the requirements of democratic mores.

The text that follows addresses both Habermas's principal achievements and shortcomings in an attempt to *reconstruct* his theory of communicative action. In tracing Habermas's *positive* contribution concerning the *way* in which participants are bound to one another in communicative action, I will examine his appropriations and reworkings of themes and concepts from various philosophers and theorists, principally, Theodor Adorno, Plato, George Herbert Mead, and Walter Benjamin. This panel of thinkers represents Habermas's sounding board for developing his theory of the experience of understanding in the process of communication.

In an extended examination of his intellectual sources, I will show that root and branch Habermas's theory of reason is haunted by its constitutive other—the concept of *mimesis*.[1] Wherever one looks in his massive published output, reason appears either in opposition to mimesis or as a formulation aimed at succeeding and replacing mimesis. Although Habermas is far from unaware of the significance of mimesis posed *against* his theory of communicative action, he never explicitly probes how consequential an examination of mimesis and communicative action together might prove to be *for* communicative action.

To the contrary, Habermas's explicit approach (especially in his later work on discourse ethics) has been to sacrifice mimesis to the benefit of the *formal* and *procedural* aspect of communication. Indeed, Habermas has been criticized as overly proceduralist, but I believe this criticism is unfounded, and principally true only to the extent that it applies to Habermas's own *positioning* of his theory. The substance of his theory is another matter, for the *binding* power of communication falls out of any depiction of communicative action as merely abstract procedure. What remains underdeveloped in Habermas's self-accounting is the specific nature in which a *critical* theory of communication can rely on a modern normativity *in determinate relation with* the way that communication binds people to one another politically.

What must be pursued in thinking communication, mimesis and normativity together are potential tensions or misalignments between the rationality of the *process* of argument and its mimetic *mode*.

This is not, of course, to say that we can forego a theory of argumentative procedure. A theory of argumentative procedure is necessary to articulate the democratic norm to which communicative action answers, but as I shall argue, the legitimacy of power in the modern age concerns not only the giving and taking of reasons in argument. In the course of coming to understanding in argument, participants come to be affectively engaged with one another; conversation itself produces the affect that binds together speakers. The centrality of affective engagement to a concept of understanding, I will argue, shifts the burden of Habermas's program from talk of procedure *against* affect to an examination of *how* and *to what extent* affective engagement is either dependent on or is indifferent to matters of right procedure. If affective engagement takes on a cognitive character, then the merely preparatory conceptual opposition between affect and logos must be transcended in the figure of communicative action.

If talking and arguing have nothing but a critical function, a testing function, then there is little hope that the right practice of communication can address what Habermas has diagnosed, following Max Weber, as modernity's most significant problem, the depletion of meaning in the modern lifeworld. What must be further developed in theoretical terms is the *positive* and *productive* force of communicative action which, when understood properly, must be asserted as communicative action's *illiberal* underside. Only in thinking about the positive, productive character of communicative action can we take seriously the affirmative answer Habermas presumably wishes to give to his rhetorical question "whether or not the social integrative powers of the religious tradition shaken by enlightenment can find an equivalent in the unifying, consensus-creating power of reason" (Habermas 1985c, 197).[2] The necessary, but neglected other side of communication—its action, its communicative power—has been underplayed for good reason, for it poses a significant challenge to the *moral status* of the critical intent behind the characterization of communicative action as structurally democratic. It then becomes a question *for us* as to whether and in what way the two aspects of communicative action, its critical and creative energies, interact. I aim to articulate how the ambivalent relation between the critical and creative aspects of communicative action comes to the fore in two conjoined aspects of the practice of communication: in the context of Habermas's theory of the self and in the world-disclosing aspect of language.

A theory of the self and of intersubjectivity is the necessary correlate to Habermas's attempt at developing a theory of communication as the basis for moral action, for the worth of communication as a moral force lies not only in the nature of *what* is discussed but in the effect discussion has on participants. Habermas's theoretical work on the nature of the self, however, has taken two incompatible directions, a problem that needs to be addressed for any successful reconstruction of his theory. On the one hand, in his more liberal moments, Habermas asserts the inviolability of autonomous speaking subjects, asserting an autonomy that presides over, above, and outside of the force of their communications. He argues that the procedure of communicative action allows for a speaker on his or her own to realize the unforced force of the better argument, to offer a rational yes/no position on proffered validity claims. Such a yes/no response could function normatively for his model of autonomy only if it were to remain insulated from compelling or seductive rhetoric. This Kantian model of the self as an autonomous evaluator of validity claims is put into question, however, by Habermas's alternative theory of the self derived from the interactionist model of George Herbert Mead.

Following Mead, Habermas posits that every ego has an *intersubjective core*. Certainly, the model of an intersubjective ego-core does not in any obvious way subtend a theory of self as an autonomous evaluator of validity claims. How is an intersubjective self to act autonomously? Is this not a contradiction in terms? Indeed, *who* is the subject of autonomy where every ego is constitutively intersubjective? Who is the proper subject of communicative action, and who is the who motivated by reasons? Resting on the answer to these questions is the very nature of communicative action, whether it can operate as a truly political principle, forming political actors and binding them together, or whether communicative action is to remain a merely instrumental tool, a force akin to Max Weber's notion of domination, with a strategic aspect but without a truly communicative one.

On its face the latter instrumental position would vitiate Habermas's intent for his theory. If the theory of communicative action anchors a paradigm shift from a subject-centered reason to an intersubjective reason (Habermas 1987b, lecture XI), then more likely, autonomy (i.e., the power of subjects to bind themselves morally,) is preserved only when communicative action *fails*. Autonomy would be construed a failure because the *way* in which communicative action operates does not intend to preserve one's already constituted ego. To the contrary, acting communicatively puts one's self at risk, or better, it acts on the multiple strands that constitute the self, toward a reordering, a renarrativizing of oneself in context. If communicative action is to carry the hopes of democratic theory, then it must pose democratic *participation* as a potentially transformative experience.[3] The *effect* of communicative action may confirm what and how one already thinks and believes, but only as a result of the self-decentering demanded by thoughtful interaction. What makes communicative action special for modern thought is that it enacts in a particularly democratic manner the figure of self-expansion, of collaborative learning, of creating new understandings achieved with another about a subject matter. The temporality of this experience would seem to belie the contemplative stillness that autonomy requires. The intersubjective practice of communicative rationality is a far cry from that which posits autonomous selves monologically evaluating validity claims.

In this sense, then, we must put a question mark over Habermas's demand that the *moral* status of communicative action rests on a strong distinction between external compulsion (from the seductive rhetoric of another) and internal motivation (by the unforced force of good reasons). If the identity of the self is understood as decentered from the start, then the distinction that sets off *moral* persuasion from illegitimate force, motivation from compulsion, can be made only from the *observer's* position (so as to taxonomically distinguish communicative from strategic language use). From the *participants'* points of view, however, the *experience* of communicative action proper does not admit such a distinction. Understanding entails attention to what is being understood *with* the other. In attempting to understand, our defenses are down, or better, we consider ourselves within our line of defenses, and so we are open to what is being said. Habermas's conceptual schema, the quartet of fundamental concepts—the subjective and the intersubjective, the instrumental and the communicative—*slide,* as it were, under the experience of communicative action, altering the ground on which such categorical separations could be maintained, that ground being the self in itself *as* open to the (disclosing arguments of the) other.

Habermas's model of communicative action posits that every speaker participating in communicative action to occupy virtually and at once all of the subject positions in speech—speaker, hearer, participant-observer, as denoted in the three pronouns of speech, I, you and s/he or they (the "generalized other"). Is this expansive, internally extensive figure of the self plausible? Just what is the *experience* of this specific decentering of the self in communication? Does the experience afford the moral distinction between legitimate and illegitimate persuasion? Are the *formal* pronouns of speech sufficient defense against their virtual transcendence necessary for understanding to take place? In sum, does the world-disclosing power of communicative action, which requires the destabilizing of prior understandings and the subject positions that language *formally* protects, cede the moral symmetry in the structure of communicative action for purposes of producing new understanding?

To correct Habermas, a proper theory of subjectivity *under* the priority of intersubjectivity in communicative action will require a genealogical study of the relation between reason and mimesis in order to trace the emergence of the so-called unforced force of the better argument—that magical, moving center around which the whole spiral twists, which bridges and binds discussants in agreement, and which posits in turn the identity of speaking subjects. Communicative rationality must own up to its mimetic heritage if the paradigm of intersubjective agreement is to fully supplant individualism's reliance on the concept of autonomy and the philosophy of consciousness as the principal approach to understanding action and judgment in a secular, postmetaphysical world.

Acknowledgments

This book is the product of many years of study, teaching, and listening. It would not exist were it not for the ongoing work of many scholars fascinated with competing accounts and theories of power, language, morality, justice, aesthetics, and the relations across and between these domains. The question of relevance is typically self-evident for members of this community, but it does not always translate well to others, and so it is to this community, first, that I offer my thanks, for where legitimacy may be taken for granted, the real work may proceed.

Many of the revisions were written not in a university setting but in a parallel society of moms and their babies in whose company I struggled against sleep deprivation and the demands of necessity simply to hold a thought and to write a sentence worth reading. I thank them all for their friendship, the baby-swapping and trust that allowed each of us to carry on with our work knowing our little persons would be no worse for wear on return. I wish to thank especially Rose Tatlow, Katie Stelter Belisle, Audrey Freudenberg, the staff at the Learning Tree Montessori preschool, and my son Moses, who is not a baby anymore.

I also have quite obviously benefited, as a member of the reading public, from the scholarship of Jürgen Habermas. The primacy of the question of intersubjectivity in political theory would not have arisen for me were it not for his work.

Influential, too, have been conversations too numerous to mention with teachers and students, friends, colleagues, strangers, and family, all of whom have made their mark directly or indirectly. I want to thank, in particular, the students of Brooklyn College, Lewis & Clark College, the University of Washington Seattle and Tacoma campuses, and Western Washington University, whose genuine enthusiasm for the themes addressed here showed me that political theory remains a powerful mode of both criticism and positive formulation of our personal and collective aims, as well as delivering a guide for our methods and styles of engagement, judgment, and action.

I wish to especially thank those whom, in their professional capacities, have listened to, read and/or commented on earlier drafts of these chapters at meetings of the Western Political Science Association, the American Political Science Association, the Midwest Political Science Association, and a conference on Action and Identity sponsored by the Philosophy Department of SUNY, Stony Brook. I also wish to thank the anonymous reviewers at SUNY Press, as well as Michael Rinella, Jane Bunker, Andrew Kenyon, and Kelli Williams-LeRoux for their support of the manuscript. The professionalization of our discipline has many drawbacks on the kind and pace of output. Its positive effect, however, is to draw typically isolated scholars into a community of like-minded strangers who care about similar issues.

Education is dangerous in part because of the tremendous disconnect between what goes in and what comes out. My various teachers have shaped this book in ways they would not necessarily recognize or endorse, although it would not exist without them. For good or ill, they represent for me the model of scholarship and deep commitment to the enterprise of intellectual work. I have tried to emulate them, whatever failings the present text may have. In this respect, let me mention, at the University of Chicago, John Padgett and Mark Hansen; and, formerly of the American University, Şerif Mardin and Nick Onuf. At the University of Washington, Christine Di Stefano, Jamie Mayerfeld, Nancy Hartsock, and Mikkel Borch-Jacobsen have given me their unflagging support. Without them, this book would have never appeared. Formerly of the University of Washington, and now of the University of Dubuque, my thanks and admiration go out to John Stewart. I also wish to thank in memoriam Ken Hoover who was very kind to share beer and conversation during my teaching stint at Western Washington University. He is missed.

Various colleagues and friends who have helped in large ways and small include Paul Axelrod, Paul Fotsch, Jim Bohman, John Fritzman, Curtis Johnson, Matthias Lutz-Bachman, Lennie Feldman, Sarah Pralle, Theresa Zimmerman, Mort Schoolman, Brian Danoff, Liesl Haas, Gordon Babst, John E. Barnes, Ellis Goldberg, Steve Hanson, Talia Oren, Maggie Sullivan, Andy Sabl, Jen Seltz, Niall O'Murchu, and Kenny Lawson.

I also wish to recognize the faculty of the recently formed Philosophy, Politics and Economics group at the University of Washington, Tacoma among whom I have been fortunate to be present at the founding: Michael Forman, Katie Baird, Amos Nasciamento, Turan Kayogolu, and Charles Williams.

My greatest personal debt goes to my spouse, Anjali Grant. Her confidence in me, unwarranted as it is, has thereby sustained me.

Introduction

Those in earnest over the modern narrowing of human interests to economic interests must revisit such basic processes as meaning-making in communication to help think past a narrowly instrumental and interest-based account of human activity and the political. Jürgen Habermas's conception of critical theory extends the scope of critique deeper than and beyond questions of political economy to consider those conditions of the production of meaning that foreground any question concerning the deliberate distribution of resources.[1] It is one of Habermas's singular contributions to have brought philosophy's *linguistic turn* to critical theory, that is, to have drawn attention to language and communication as a medium and mode of interaction and power, of domination both legitimate and not.

Habermas's normative theory attempts to defend an ideal of understanding that satisfies the deep epistemological challenges of the linguistic turn in philosophy with respect to a positive valuation of modernity's value-pluralism. Although Habermas consistently emphasizes the universal ambitions of his theory of communicative action—that the democratic structure of ideal speech can act as a normative counterfactual for all speech events aimed at understanding, and that the deep structure of speech holds the power to dissolve and transcend any merely conventional value—his attention to the complex differentiation of modernity forces a shift in the nature of how universal theory can be conceived, the implications of which are still being worked out.[2]

The main thrust of Habermas's normative project is to refigure the concept of reason as a force aiding the constitution of just ends. Communicative rationality is the centerpiece of a paradigm shift away from reason narrowly construed as a subjective faculty of instrumental, means–end calculation. A concept of subjective, calculative reason remains essential, of course, for when we want to think about how humans come to decisions *efficiently*, but questions of efficiency beg a theory of the constitution of that which is to be efficiently arranged. Do we wish to deny *a priori* the applicability of the status of *rational* to all but those purposive decisions and actions taken by self-interested actors to satisfy pre-established goals? If not, then how shall we characterize a modern, postsubjectivist practice of reason, one that is neither so narrow that it ceases to help in addressing the most fundamental of political questions—who are we, and what ought we to do?—nor so full, as in Hegel's view of Reason, that it subsumes and determines all answers in advance?

If a *reasonable* politics does not merely denote the procedure by which political actors make tradeoffs among competing interests, but also helps to produce those interests in the first place, then how might we articulate a concept of reason, or rather, a practice of reasoning, which contributes to the positive making of good decisions? If a classical notion of politics remains relevant—politics as participation in community—then how is the identity of the *we* that makes decisions implicated in the *reasonable* expression of and development of *our* political will? Can the common employ of reason inspire political solidarity, and is *this* solidarity reasonable? Can political solidarities derive from within themselves answers to the demands of a reason sprung from their own process of working themselves out? Is there any other alternative?

Toward forcing a basic shift in our collective thinking about the nature of reason in advocating a *paradigm shift* from subjective reason to communicative reason, Habermas conceives of communicative rationality as: (a) intersubjective, not subjective; (b) an achievement rather than an endowment; (c) an experience arrived at and rearrived at through the action of discussion; (d) an experience whose principle basis is articulated speech in public rather than privately held thoughts or feelings; (e) answering to a set of moral preconditions figured as governing the event of understanding, rather than answering to either an underarticulated, intuitive moral sense or a moral sense overspecified by dogma; and (f) producing and validating claims in a process of coming to understanding, rather than mirroring or corresponding to objective truth.

In brief, Habermas's concept of communicative action aims to overcome subjectively individualistic and metaphysical accounts of reason so as to locate a specifically *communicative* rationality as an emergent aspect of human interaction—of intersubjectivity—one that is in need of constant renewal, and therefore subject to continuous testing and reinvigoration in its application and revision. In these terms, communicative rationality is therefore *political* insofar as it produces and reproduces the commitments necessary for communal solidarity. Importantly for Habermas, the process of communicative action also is normatively consonant with a *democratic* ethos in that the procedural norms governing the practice of coming to understanding imply adherence to a principle that demands that communicative outcomes can be considered just only if all relevant actors have a chance to participate in the discussion. In such a discussion, participants must be free to raise any issue deemed necessary to advance their views, thus laying the basis for self-critique insofar as any commitment produced in public communication, by virtue of that fact, must be open to further collective scrutiny.

Habermas stands against those who tend to recode *moral* adjudication as a covert expression of a will to power. Some argue that a clash of ultimate values, inspired by competing desires and oriented toward incommensurable end points, could not, by virtue of the nature of the disputes, uncover solutions except by force, by power.[3] This notion of ethical (Kuhnian) incommensurability, however, preempts with theory that which might be bridged by reasoned engagement in practice. It also tends to homogenize views within culture groups where a more differentiated view of culture would in its very formulation allow for more points of productive intercultural contact.[4] Communicative rationality lends itself normatively as a model for the deliberate, just pursuit of political engagement because its mode of practice does not in advance decide that the plurality of cultural resources for moral engagement are incommensurable. Indeed, as Habermas suggests, "[c]ommunicative action provides the medium for the reproduction of lifeworlds, . . . because in coming to an understanding about something in the world, actors are at the same time taking part in interactions through which they develop, confirm, and renew their memberships in social groups and their own identities" (1984, 337, 1987a, 138). Communicative actions can nourish the ground for the sake of which norms matter, for the sake of which we bring critical judgment to bear on our beliefs and practices. Habermas's positing of this "reproductive" function implies the hope not merely for a conservative hanging on to cultural values, but their active renewal and, where necessary, supercedure through the collective work of articulate reassessment, and this critical work presumes a plurality of cultural values not in principal already hived off into impenetrable warring factions.

Notwithstanding its ambitions and in light of its intended virtues, Habermas's theory stands in need of fundamental clarification and reconstruction. Habermas's *discourse ethics*[5] depends on producing and reinforcing a notion of *moral autonomy* that stands at odds with the epistemological premise of communicative action: Habermas's discourse morality aims to be universalist, offering up a content-free procedure for moral engagement, but the speaking subjects to whom it applies, who employ it, cannot but derive knowledge—self-knowledge as well as knowledge of others and of things/events in the world—from a position of their own situatedness, their own historicality, which is to say, from a context that overflows and thereby enframes and emplots any subject-position. The historicity of the latter would seem to disallow the avowed neutrality of the former. This at least apparent contradiction in Habermas's theory—one easily ignored in transcendental moral theories that dismiss all-too-human variation as inessential to the moral problematic, but that self-styled *post*metaphysical theories like Habermas's must address directly—is how we also might describe political philosophy's modern dilemma, that of rescuing the possibility for a universalist philosophy in a world that we recognize as populated by peoples who, thankfully, are inassimilable to a single, coherent, universalist philosophy.

Indeed, the question arises as to whether we can anymore ally universalism with morality, or if these two orientations have become fundamentally opposed to one another. Can political philosophy accommodate itself to difference on these terms? Habermas manifestly aims to salvage the universality of moral judgment, but this gesture can be made plausible not with a thinned-out *range* of applicability for universality (as he surmises [1993a, 91]), but with a reinterpretation of what it means to think and act postmetaphysically. The prioritizing of intersubjectivity that Habermas effects with his theory of communicative action has yet to find its place in Habermas's discourse ethics. This is due to the inadequate notion of autonomy that Habermas had effectively superseded with his theory of communicative action, but has unfortunately brought back round in his discourse ethics.

The issue of autonomy comes into sharper focus when we consider the issue of motivation. Why should communicative action motivate its participants to do the right thing? A procedural model alone cannot produce an account of what might motivate persons to take it up as their own. Habermas's exoteric insistence on proceduralism *should* preempt the need to squarely address psychological theories of commitment or desire (which might complement or threaten rational procedure), but his claim worked out in his theory of communicative action—that subjects engage with the world at three levels (the subjective, the intersubjective, and the objective)—undermines Habermas's apparent commitment to proceduralism. A theory of procedure alone would find its natural correlate in autonomous will-formation except for the power of communicative action to produce not autonomous individuals but persons in a fuller sense. Without such a power, communicative action as a theory and as a practice is drained of its practical significance.

This disconnect between a relational theory of persons in the world and a theory of procedure that might govern action becomes egregious when Habermas addresses the issue of free will in the exercise of moral action. In adopting the notion of free will and subjective agency, Habermas's account appears to leave undercontextualized the decision to act morally, where he follows a certain reading of Kant's notion of free will. Indeed for issues of moral decision, Habermas seemingly has taken a step back behind his intersubjectivism to the philosophy of consciousness.[6] Habermas writes that "[w]ith Kant, we refer to the capacity for binding one's own will on the basis of moral insight as freedom of will (*Willensfreiheit*), or autonomy" (1998d, 311). Habermas is saying precisely that an *autonomous* ego submits to moral insight, that is, to a moral respect for the other. To be sure, Habermas introduces an intersubjective element, for he says that "in the various practical self-relations [by which he means in this passage *moral* reflection] I, as a first person, adopt the second-person perspective in which interlocutors—that is, other participants in [moral] discourses—focus on my expressions." But *who* is this ego who "adopts the second-person perspective"? Is it the same autonomous ego with the intersubjective core? By and large, Habermas leaves unreconciled his separate discussions of autonomous egos and intersubjective egos. As necessary to his theory of communicative action is the latter concept, the former is to his discourse ethics.

We can intuit why Habermas tacitly resists an effort to weaken or enlarge the notion of an ego's free will, for were he to think the subject of autonomy as fundamentally intersubjective, then doubt would be cast on precisely the *universalist, moral* aspect of discourse morality. If, for example, an autonomous self is thought of as always already a bundle of personal obligations, heteronomous to itself, then questions of moral validity could not be answered by referring to a decontextualized purity presumed to be distilled from the mixture that subjects are. Such a purity could only be a fantasy unless the internal heteronomy of selves were fundamentally irrelevant, the object of moral contemplation but not the subject. Can moral theory survive the demise of the autonomous subject? If so, it can only be through a rethinking of morality not as transcending the world we are in and the obligations that form us, but as detectable and operative as a bias of the interiority of this condition and these relations. Indeed, problematic for a strictly individualist and cognitive account of moral autonomy is *constitutive* desire[7] or any other form of affective tie that cannot but inflect a subject's experience of rational autonomy.

How shall we characterize the way in which reason *bonds* humans to their commitments, to their agreements, and to one another? Is it only pain, a sublime pain even, as Nietzsche (1967, 61–62) suggests, that produces humans with the power to keep their promises? What of laughter or humor as the bonding agent of mutual understanding?[8] Habermas strictly separates strategic talk that *compels* from reason that *motivates*. To think clearly about the nature of affective motivation, affective constitution, we should consult the resources of Romanticism. Since the advent of Romanticism, it is *aesthetic theory* that commands the province of human sensibility and affective power. From Habermas's perspective, to affirm the affective power of communication risks the normative certainties of reason. Viewed otherwise, however, we might ask whether it is precisely the affective power of communication that not only demands moral action to begin with, but more importantly, provides the necessary glue to make reasons stick? In his exoteric formulations, Habermas unfortunately has expelled from the interior working of communicative action the force central to aesthetic theory, a charitable consideration of which might contribute to a better rendering of the relationship between motivation and a theory of reason. It also might help us to think through not only a postsubjectivistic account of reason but a postsubjectivistic account of affect. Theories of reason would benefit by reconsidering their necessary intersection with and mutual dependency on aesthetic theory.

With that set of initial observations and questions behind us, let me summarize: The task of my text will be to negotiate a passage across the reason–aesthetic divide as it operates in Habermas's project, for the future of critical theory depends on pushing past the conceptual divisions between knowing and acting, being and becoming. I will perform this task by reengaging the sources of Habermas's theories—principally, Theodor Adorno, Plato, George Herbert Mead, and Walter Benjamin—by putting to them the question not only of the validity of Habermas's appropriations of their work, respectively, but also to consider how their treatment of the reason–aesthetic divide has manifested itself overtly or covertly in Habermas's theory of communicative action. I will, in the end, offer a *reconstruction* of communicative action, in the sense that through my analysis we might cast new light on the normative goals that Habermas has set for critical theory. We shall find, however, that in my reconstruction of communicative action, I will challenge Habermas's self-explication of communicative action as rationalist and universalist, to the point where certain goals dear to Habermas's conception of the project of Enlightenment will appear as unrecognizable, and not merely more distant than ever, but rather, as products of category mistakes, and therefore false goals, the kind that Habermas and critical theory would do well to leave behind.

The principal conceptual distinction that underlies Habermas's theory of communicative rationality is that between rationality and mimesis. It will fall to Chapter 1 to take some initial steps in underlining the conceptual importance of the opposition between rationality and mimesis, to establish some of the principal insights of the Frankfurt School from which Habermas takes his most immediate inspiration on questions of reason and aesthetics, and to suggest that we should not take at face value Habermas exoteric employ of the division between reason and mimesis. Chapter 2 pursues in a genealogical mode the imbrication of mimesis and rationality in Plato, with and against whom Habermas thinks through his postmetaphysical concept of rationality. Chapter 3 looks to the nature of the communicating subject, for the moral structure of communication must answer to a particular theory of the subject who speaks. Habermas's source for his theory of the subject—as possessing an intersubjective core—is the American pragmatist George Herbert Mead, and Mead too, as we shall see, explicitly frames his theory of linguistic intersubjectivity against mimetic experience. Chapter 4 completes the investigation in taking up the question of the mimetic experience of language as developed by Walter Benjamin and appropriated by Habermas as the "unforced force of reason."

Chapter 1

Reason and Mimesis

> To represent the mimesis it supplanted, the concept has no other way than to adopt something mimetic in its own conduct, without abandoning itself.
>
> —Theodor Adorno (*Negative Dialectics* 15)

Habermas's theory of communicative action proceeds in a self-consciously postmetaphysical way, which is to say, it insists that we cannot but think and act politically *without* the confidence of an extra-worldly source of validation for those activities, and that we must always be on guard that our most cherished convictions, and even the seemingly most prosaic—our view of reality, for instance—may be inadequate and in need of sometimes mind-altering correction. We do not judge the *adequacy* of our convictions on a scale that measures a right correspondence between our utterances and fixed referents in the world, nor can we rely on a supposed correspondence between our moral convictions and an eternal moral order. We may judge our convictions adequate or inadequate only with reference to the normative horizon of the world in which we live and act, and this demands a historical self-understanding, a critical reflection combined with a hermeneutics.[1] The fundamental principles of truth, morality, and any method that determines adequacy must become cognizant that cognition itself cannot reproduce an objective image of the world, but always already takes its form and direction from the politically contested activity of historically situated meaning-making.[2] Old-fashioned "consciousness-raising" must remain on the table, for political purposes, but neither (to mix metaphors) as a stepchild to political economy, nor any longer naively in thrall to a narrative of turning false consciousness to true. Instead of revealing what is already good and true, we postmetaphysical moderns are fated to agonize over our convictions and how they stack up against those of others, and how, in our world of Weberian value-pluralism, a normative political science might endeavor to think about how to adjudicate among competing claims answering to different notions of the good. A postmetaphysics brings the politics of interpretation front and center. This does not lead to wholesale relativism, for reasons addressed later, but it does mean that analysts and observers cannot pretend to exclude themselves from the court of opinion, because *that*, for good or ill, is what court there is, and the moral–political task is to discern better from worse from within this twilight world of opinion.[3]

I. The Postmetaphysical Condition of Reason

In the demise of a viable socialist vision, a normatively democratic view fills the horizon of our contemporary moral–political imaginary, and this democratic form of political decision-making proves a fine homology for the premises of postmetaphysics. Following self-assertively in the tradition of Enlightenment, Habermas lays the possibility of a secular morality under conditions of an advanced, democratic capitalism based on the character of *reason*. Value-pluralism does not trump the necessity of mutual coordination and understanding; it is, rather, the enabling condition of understanding. Reason does not illuminate reality per se, but rather, the reality *for those to whom it belongs*. The peculiar illumination that reason provides comes in the form of articulate *reasons*, reasons that can be accepted or rejected on the basis of common understanding. The deepening of understanding comes through the practice of reasoning-in-common, and the reality that reasons illuminate is the discursive reality of being-in-common. We might call this process becoming-in-common. Thus, any theory of reason requires a concomitant understanding of the social solidarity and common understandings and commitments that underwrite its truth-value, while preserving and even inciting a critical capacity for self-reflection, to determine better from worse, progress from regression. For Habermas, "we must distinguish between the social fact that a norm is intersubjectively recognized and its worthiness to be recognized" (1990, 61).

Why must a democratic theory turn to reason, and why a reason that self-consciously asks itself to split the difference between historicism and reflection rather than answer to metaphysical adequation? Contemporary critiques of Reason's traditional conceits of foundationalism and metaphysics have worked to undermine confidence in the secular validity of any kind of extra-worldly authority, and have contributed to a (largely beneficial) suspicion over the supposed neutrality or objectivity of this-worldly injunctions made in the human sciences to explain or interpret events or experiences.[4] It no longer suffices for political theory to depict Reason as John Locke did, as a faculty implanted universally by God to ensure that humans realize the objective demands of a moral order—particularly as Locke did, by grounding moral reason in the constellation of property, productivity, and appropriation by possessive individuals.[5] For "us," right reason is hardly a neutral mirroring of God's will such that in mastering nature we sanctify ourselves as righteous, laboring beings. We know in particular that a modern political economy is structured in ways that do not answer to any realization of collective reason on this model, nor does Locke's model have any more powerful claim to make on us than the claims of those other groups and practices, and indeed, the natural environment, sacrificed on the altar of productivity.

Any epistemological filter like *reason* does not neutrally discover the facts of our bearing in the world, but rather every epistemology has a determinate hand in the production of what it "sees," and indeed, it begs the question of whether "seeing" is the proper metaphor: better perhaps is "grasping," "listening to," "dialoguing with," "playing with," "participating in," or "snuggling up to." The moral force of reasoned judgments is always relative to the mode of understanding and the epistemological horizon within which its standards may be applied, and it requires a political sensibility—a sensitivity to power and justice that directs the course of self-reflection. On this account, Locke's worldview is no less reasonable, but all the more obviously motivated, on its own terms, by an *extra*-rational sentiment that betrays the best impulses of Lockean liberalism.[6] And its status as *political* makes Habermas's theory of communicative action, too, a *political* innovation, and not merely a *discovery* of a form of reason that was somehow missed by every theorist and philosopher prior to him. But Habermas *knows* of the politicality of his intervention: The paradigm shift Habermas is trying to force, in a shift we might think of as taking us from early modernity to late, Albrecht Wellmer has called "a postrationalist theory of reason." It reflects a self-critical awareness not only of the rational elements in reason, the moral promise inherent in the structure of the linguistic character of reason, but also the romantic elements internal to its bearing that motivate its operation. This is the double promise of communicative rationality, as a reflective resource and an activity of social solidarity.

I would resist, however, those like Lyotard who argue that reason is simply a catchword couched in an implausible meta-narrative, the sheen on a lens through which the analyst insists everyone look, a lens that doubtless and insidiously validates the analyst's perspective. This claim goes too far, I would argue, for to *a priori* conflate knowledge with illegitimate power answers the question of the possibility of moral judgment before it gets asked. If we imagine humans as storytellers above all, then Lyotard, who surely tells his own meta-stories (of the course of literature and science, for example), athough correct to criticize the strong claims of objectivity made by some, sits actually quite close to Habermas's attempt to account for a reason that does not exist *a priori* but rather emerges in the doing.[8] The particular hope for a utopian future of brotherhood, sisterhood, or humanity must be relegated to failed grand narratives of the past; our task is not to vanquish power, but rather to effectively constrain and enable it for uses deemed by right procedure to be just and worthy, and to understand (with Foucault and Weber) the ways in which the exercise of power affects all within its purview. Not all subject-producing or subject-effacing power stands already guilty. The point is that, within the question of moral judgment, we must raise claims, ask questions, and remain open in our efforts to theorize the political, to the possibility of hearing new voices singing new music, as Nietzsche would say.

Skepticism concerning the ill use of conceptual power raised by Lyotard's epistemological perspectivalism *is* significant for questioning whether reason in fact remains the relevant cipher for thinking through competing claims to moral validity. However, the "strong contextualist" supposition of multiple, distinct language games, each with its own rules and norms, and answering to incommensurable versions of the good,[8] does nothing to release us from the moral demands inherent within every language game, the fact of which stimulates us to become multilingual, able to speak of moral demands immanent to each perspective, and which stimulates also the need to locate some way of thinking about how and when to privilege the terms of one language game over the rest in given situations. Attention to difference—in terms of the modes of experience, of expression, of culture, of communication, of moral bearing, and of the mode of being itself—is crucial in testing any reliable account of a reason that still can hope to be held to account for its oldest function, that of standing in for what is truly human in our ethos.

For to speak of the epistemological condition of modernity, "reason" today can be posited legitimately only in a wholly different sense than in linking our judgments to a permanent, transcendent, and unconditional moral order. The distinction between accident and essence in our moral thinking must give way to appreciating fully the scope in which without an anchor in essence, the formerly abjected category of accident, of heterology, now becomes all we have to go on—and it is both less and more heterogenous to itself than formerly understood. A hermeneutics of experience and an analytic discourse demanding active participation by those affected is all moral thinkers have to wager with when sifting through the competing claims among constellations of value-pluralism, which points to the political task accorded to reason: A democratic sensibility forms its core, and this democratic deliberation essentially is open-ended in terms of its substantive outcomes. As Habermas puts it in its *negative* form:

> The potential of unleashed *communicative* freedoms does contain an anarchistic core. The institutions of any democratic government must live off this core if they are to be effective in guaranteeing equal liberties for all. (1996a, xl)

This anarchic core at the heart of communicative freedom, unrestricted communicative action, as we shall see over the course of this investigation, is in truth a *mimetic* core, and in this sense a core posited as anarchic can at the same time be *constitutive* of any cultural solidarity. It serves a *negative* function, as a dissolvent, but it also can do the work typically attributed to a certain style of *aesthetic* thinking usually set off from traditional theories of morality: to innovate the values that motivate us to adhere to a cultural community, and to criticize it.[9]

We can thankfully give up the sense of reason as an immediate mirroring in speech and thought of the natural order of reality.[10] Our confidence is gone in this sort of narrative insofar as pluralism requires secular adjudication, and disputes will not be satisfied by a dogmatic position that claims to successfully mime an ordered reality. One cannot know that one's reasons mime reality, nor can one know that reality is ordered in the way our concepts would imply. This is not just a skepticism. It is the character of modern instability, a perpetual openness that is the condition for the making of meaningful judgments. Reason does not articulate reality as such but reality for us. Reason is always historical reason, a mode of as well as a product of world-building.[11]

The consequences of this humility and reasonableness, as it were, are not as some fear. The anxious scare-slogan that "nothing is real, so everything is permitted" finds justification only against a background of faith that absolute certainty was ever possible. With the end of this shibboleth, nihilism loses its force to intimidate, for reason does not aspire to the demands of an absolute order, but rather presupposes that reasonableness emerges as a normative counterfactual only against our ineliminable historicity and linguisticality. Objectivity still has meaning but within the bounds of knowledge that can be discursively redeemed. For "it is part of the grammar of the expression 'knowing' that everything we know can be criticized and justified" (Habermas 1998d, 312). Separable from but analogous to this notion of "epistemic rationality," a modern morality must invoke reason, and not, say, authenticity, because it is the rhetoric of reason's *reflexivity* that can motivate adherents to its cause. As Habermas himself argues, a postmetaphysical thinking cannot answer the question, "Why be moral?"—but neither does this question truly present itself from within a postmetaphysical framework: "moral convictions do not allow themselves to be overridden without resistance . . . ; this is shown by the bad conscience that 'plagues' us when we act against our better judgment" (1992h, 239, 1998a, 35). This resistance arises, unbidden as it were, because for Habermas (revaluating Nietzsche's account of the genealogy of morals), a modern moral intuition cannot avoid reflexivity. Such a modern morality would, then, take on the character of the best of aesthetic theories, for it would in the same gesture negate and create: The self-reflection of morality carries the potential to generate an authentic social solidarity as inherently self-reflexive.

II. Mimesis

Traditionally *mimesis*[12] has anchored two overlapping traditions, one anthropological/ psychological and the other having to do with the representational arts.[13] As the basis of an anthropology, mimesis means *making oneself similar*, or *speaking in the voice of another*, or *acting as another would act*, as in mimicry.[14] Both Plato and Aristotle considered imitation a basic human activity, found in child's play, but by no means shed in the human passage to maturity. Mimesis answers to a noncognitive mode of bringing difference into identity, to effect similarity in action. Let a child imitate a storm, or an adult a citizen.

In the arts, mimesis characterizes the somewhat mysterious relationship between original and copy—as in representational painting—but it applies as well as to the activity of theatrical actors on a stage (again: *speaking in the voice of another*, or *enacting a role*), in the making of music, where music may convey the affective aspects of human character, or dance, as in the homeopathic rituals of disciplined, rhythmic motion to effect an exorcism of a possession by the Corybantes.[15] Mimesis, however, is also used to indicate the imitation of nature, where what is imitated is no object but the power to create *as* nature creates, which is to say, an artist mimes the power of creativity itself.

Part of the contemporary attraction to the concept of mimesis is that as a catchword it is sufficiently indeterminate such that, successfully counterposed to its equally hoary, but also contentiously debated counterpart, reason, it offers an alternative to our culture's overreliance on explanations of interest-based, volunteeristic, and ultimately private rational choice. Mimesis could prove a viable basis on which to think about how interests are formed and transformed, one that characterizes the intersubjective microprocesses of the social constitution of the human subject and community rather then bracketing our political thinking until only after we assume a givenness of identity and interests.

For illustrative purposes, we might briefly consider the centrality of mimesis to the process of political foundation in an early text in political philosophy's modern canon, Thomas Hobbes's *Leviathan*. In his introduction, Hobbes declares provocatively that in founding political order, humans imitate nature, understood as the creative artistry of God. Hobbes opens up his grand text this way:

> Nature (the art whereby God hath made and governs the world) is by the *art* of man, as in many other things, so in this also imitated, that it can make an artificial animal. . . . *Art* goes yet further, imitating that rational and most excellent work of nature, *man*. For by art is created that great LEVIATHAN called a COMMONWEALTH, or STATE (in Latin CIVITAS), which is but an artificial man . . . in which the *sovereignty* is an artificial soul; . . . the *magistrates* and other *officers* of judicature and execution, artificial *joints*; *reward* and *punishment* . . . are the *nerves* . . . ; the *wealth* and *riches* of all the particular members are the *strength*; *salus populi* (the people's safety) its *business*; *counsellors*, by whom all things needful for it to know are suggested unto it, are the *memory*; *equity* and *laws* an artificial *reason* and *will*; *concord*, *health*; *sedition*, *sickness*, and *civil war*, *death*. Lastly, the *pacts* and *covenants* by which the parts of this body politic were at first made, set together, and united, resemble that *fiat*, or the *let us make man*, pronounced by God in the creation. (1994, 3–4)

Let's be clear. Hobbes here is saying that the human invention of politics is like God's creation of humans. God's art finds its parallel in the human art of creating political order, and political order is nothing other than the representation of the unity of all citizens combined into a single body which they themselves belong to by virtue of their co-production of it. Citizens are like Gods insofar as creating politics imitates God's creative power. Furthermore, Leviathan is nothing foreign to its creators; it is rather an artificial reproduction of their own natural bodies, but amplified, and disciplined in terms of specific functions, with each particular citizen performing a duty that *is* the political body's internal workings. The imitation of God's power instaurs Leviathan, and the imitation occurs via "*pacts* and *covenants* . . . which . . . resemble that *fiat*, or the *let us make man*, pronounced by God in the creation." It is the *resemblance* to God's power that empowers the fiat to bind citizens together as one. Mimetic power produces the mimetic polis constituted by mimetic citizens.

Some readers have placed Hobbes in the *rationalist* tradition of politics for his notion that political order is founded on a social contract[16]: Rational agreement in the form of binding contracts guaranteed by the sovereign's authority, so the argument goes, tames persons' self-regarding behavior, thereby steering a polity clear of the otherwise mutually destructive and inevitable war of all against all. This one-sided, juridical explanation of what produces and maintains political order fails to take into account Hobbes's insistence on the mimetic aspect of the original production of politics. We might be better off saying that the instantiation of political unity by way of explicit Covenants, that is, through propositional speech, culminating in the virtual, although consensual, performative speech act, "I promise to join, . . ." does not make rational but only *gives articulate form to the nonpropositional communion* that takes place in the deliberate founding.

As Hobbes says, political founding is rather like "that *fiat*, or the *let us make man*, pronounced by God in the creation." This shift *within* the field of performative speech acts, from promise to fiat, occurs by sleight of hand; agency silently shifts from the proto-citizens who promise to join to Leviathan who then refracts the promise as a command. The original fiat, the so-called social contract is then *received* like a command that brooks no disobedience. As one cannot choose to disallow God from creating you, neither can one disallow the instantiation of State, or at least so goes the Hobbesian fantasy, but also Hobbes's perceived need for *more* than mere words to bind politically. The guarantee of order and obedience lies in the gesture to accept the fiat *as if it were* given prior to one's own utterance of it, as if one were merely echoing the command, obeying it, and belonging to it. The avowal of obedience that instantiates and constitutes government, in Hobbes's narrative, becomes the *mimetic semblance* of the nonpropositional event, and not the rational basis of it.[17]

Alternatively, we could open up the analysis, for there *is* debate between mimetic and rationalist accounts of political founding: Hobbes employs *both* rhetorics, that of reason and of mimesis. My limited point here is that for Hobbes, the passage out of the state of nature is plausibly described as a mimetic origin ritual.[18] That the ritual takes the form of a contract articulates but not does lessen the force of mimetic identification. As Hobbes (109) puts it, "This is more than consent, or concord; it is a real unity of them all, in one and the same person, . . . [that] *Mortal God*,"

Leviathan. Even at the origin of the so-called rationalist tradition, mimesis proves central and perhaps even unavoidable.[19]

In fact, the two mimetic traditions, anthropological and aesthetic, are first coordinated in Plato's political philosophy—which may have served in this as Hobbes's model, not to mention Rousseau's[20]—which is to say, mimesis is first and foremost a *political philosopher's* attempt at naming an affective power which is amenable to rational manipulation, but a power ultimately resistant within this mode of thinking to the stable identity classical political philosophy prefers.[21] Mimesis is posed as the unavoidable counterpart to identity-reason, and in this sense in Hobbes, mimesis is what reason attempts to stabilize, an imagined disorder by way of a ritualized mimesis. The Hobbesian making of political order rests not only on the mimetic communion of many bodies into a single body (in chap 17), but also on the preparatory work in constructing proto-citizens who come to speak the same language and define their inner-most appetites and aversions in precisely the same ways, which is the force of Hobbes's scientific and mechanistic depiction of human nature in chaps. 1 through 15. "Read thy self!" Hobbes urges (4), and he's sure you will read in yourself exactly what *he* writes down as a universal adequation of sense-experience. If we do *today* sense the reverberations of truth in his definitions, this does not confirm the eternal truth of Hobbes's position. To the contrary, the question this poses for us is how is it that a Hobbesian sensibility has been absorbed into our common sense, our culture, our feelings?[22]

Hobbes's *out of the state of nature story* represents an attempt to mimetically transform his readers so that "we" will employ the same words for the same meanings, and to order our array of sentiment and political obedience along the lines Hobbes has already decided would most capably discipline his reading public At one level, he produces and thereby incites the need for order and the collective fear of disorder, but above all else, he underlines the necessity of a political solidarity arising from a shared mimetic origin story. Philosopher Hobbes wishes to be that fulcrum that pivots chaos to order, that orients the state's internal mimesis, and the extent to which he succeeds is the extent to which we study and internalize his work, its aesthetic intervention in our self- and social understanding.

If, however, we thematize his *rhetoric* of mimesis as an object of study, we institute a rupture of sorts from the mimetic snare. Do we then become disinterested spectators, reading Hobbes but inured to his rhetoric? Conversely, we might ask: In our redoubling on the figure of mimesis in the study of it, do we engage in a homeopathic therapy as a form of subversive mimesis? Or, do we simply perpetuate Hobbes's solution to the rational/ mimetic political question? Must we, as Richard Rorty says of obsolete worldviews, simply leave Hobbesian mimesis behind?

We should take note in the above discussion of all the variability subtended by the notion of *imitation*, for it indicates that, first of all, imitation is hardly mere copying, and it is also not quite as single-minded as "the representation of reality," the subtitle of Eric Auerbach's great book of literary criticism, *Mimesis*. Within political philosophy, *mimesis* is figured as bringing persons, objects or processes into similarity, and not necessarily according to any ulterior or anterior logic beyond the power of similarity itself, though an ulterior or anterior reconstructive narrative or logic can lend coherence to the process. The hope and fear of patriots, alarmists, and revolutionaries alike is a totalizing mimetic power that enthralls, as in a cult or a crowd, and in so doing, preempts questions of legitimacy. The ambiguity of mimesis bears with it political and moral dilemmas.

For some, rational, autonomous action indicates a cognitive and mindful exercise of freedom and independent judgment, whereas, in contrast, mimetic action indicates mindless or instinctual copying, a herd mentality. In particular, aesthetic mimesis is lauded or defamed for possessing the audience, robbing them of judgment by way of inciting them to excited behavior right-minded citizens would otherwise avoid. Aesthetic mimesis also has been held up for its educative function in molding audiences in the stamp of beneficial images of wholesome virtue, or at least, in a necessary solidarity on the model of a political *body* as in Hobbes. Thus, the affective power of mimesis is typically understood as threatening to defenders of the autonomous subject, but quite heartening to those for whom the production of a common sense or a General Will requires far more than mere calculative reason for motivation and loyalty.

On this score, defenders of rationality, such as Habermas, often are held to sound *conservative* noises even though they may ally with critical or progressive movements (e.g., Western Marxism), because in the Romantic tradition, but especially after the reception of Nietzsche, Adorno, and then Foucault, reason itself has been held as a culprit of bad faith. Bad faith, it is argued, because although claimed as a tool for progressive emancipation, rationality, in the same process that draws us from the darkness of our myths, operates by subjecting *all* ultimate aims to an acidic scrutiny those aims can't possibly resist. Thus, in the strong, Nietzschean version of this argument, emancipation is achieved only at the expense of making irrational those aims that had motivated the drive for emancipation in the first place.

At the limit of this trend, some contemporary skeptics of rationality offer up a highly indeterminate defense of "others," a generalized responsibility for the unknown or nonidentical.[23] Countering the force of a confident but totalizing reason, these theorists advocate indeterminability and a fundamental pluralism not only as a condition for reason, but also as a guiding ethic and a telos of openness (if the latter formulation may be allowed). The bare existence of another is to signal a moral demand that we recognize that others exist in excess of what we make of them. Thus, in a perversion of our usual expectations, rationality is held responsible for coercing indiscriminate identity and closure where, to the contrary, mimesis signals a fundamental openness and ontic difference, implying a gap across which is felt a moral duty of respect and an attitude of wonder for otherness in general, or as in Levinas's work, the paradoxical formulation of otherness in its opaque specificity—the face.

Distinguishing mimesis from reason in political philosophy remains in this way plausible only insofar as mimesis answers to an other-than-rational aspect of human sociation and aesthetic response.[24] This dispute certainly orients much of contemporary political theory, and indeed, has been vital for political thinking in some form or other on two accounts. First, because, to paraphrase Rousseau (1973), more than rational law is necessary to solidify a polis. (Why? Because the validity of laws can't answer only to calculative considerations of self-preservation, lest we disobey when the laws prove inconvenient. Thus, we must respect and even *love* the laws, so this argument goes, such that calculative thinking is oriented by a *raison d'etre* rather than supplanting it.) Alternatively, for those (like Adorno) *critical* of a libidinal model of political identification, aesthetic theory under the star of mimesis offers a negating power, subversive to unreflected affective ties, where affect is always tempted to corruption by a cynical reason. Mimesis conceived of as a distantiating process can supplement a reason that alone would be insufficient to motivate citizens to break through false consciousness. Thus, a homeopathic remedy presents itself, a true mimesis acting to subvert false. Which raises the question: Can a subversive mimesis in aesthetic activity destabilize philosophy's hijacking of mimesis for politics?[25]

All of this to the side for the moment, it is vital to realize that these late debates on the open or closed character of reason or mimesis, are, as it were, already present at the origin. What Plato (1997c, 607b) called already an "ancient quarrel," the dispute between political philosophy and aesthetic activity is *governed*—a term to be used loosely—by a common mode of power, namely, mimesis. A political thinking *that wishes for itself legitimacy* finds itself compelled to put power into the service of morality, or at least an ethical solidarity, while at the same time, in finding its right orientation and expression, employing mimesis for aesthetic production and affective response. Art and politics, then, are *competitors* in aim and method for the hearts and minds of citizens: hence their antagonism and their *secret complicity*.[26] Mimesis serves as the process that coordinates the activity of belonging and boundary making together with the dissolution of loyalties and orientations; it connects notions of the beautiful and of the sublime (i.e., modes of aesthetic reception) with questions of identity and identification, and is implicated in the process of constructing a legitimate political order that answers to principles themselves only apparently opposed to mimetic power.

This is what Plato understood long ago (see Chapter 2), and so he advocated the extreme measure of banishing the mimetic poets from his ideal Republic while reserving for himself and for philosophy a *proper* mimesis for the good of the polis, or at least for philosophy's control of the polis. The political struggle for the control of mimesis between philosophy and the poets establishes the antagonistic backdrop against which Adorno finds hope for resistance in art, and why Habermas has such an ambivalent relation to mimesis, why he tries to suppress it, like Plato, and indeed, in the German tradition of sublation, to transform it.

III. Mimesis Against Disenchantment

The separation of politics and art that Plato's Socrates advocates in *Republic* already represents the outcome of a political battle, one that Adorno hopes to reinitiate with his concept of mimesis. And mimesis seems the appropriate point of attack because Plato aimed his anti-aesthetics squarely and specifically at mimetic poets. In Plato's view, poetic mimesis competes with philosophers for the souls of citizens. Plato's myths advocate for citizens a turning toward justice, against the poets who, he claims, merely reproduce in their stories a chaotic world in its appearance. A discipline of spirit promises political restraint, but a poetic conception of the world, complains Plato, merely fuels a chaotic freedom, ugly and irrational because self-contradicting, inwardly and outwardly in turmoil. Plato's judgment that poets corrupt is predicated on the view that citizens will take up as their self-image those myths released into society by society's great storytellers. So the *Republic* itself represents a meta-political gambit: The exoteric political question of "who should rule?" is transformed into the esoteric "who shall be society's storytellers?" The *Republic* entire must be read as presenting a poetic image in competition with poets proper.[27]

Plato's hope for victory rests on the asymmetries in the concepts that organize his philosophy: reason–myth, order–chaos, reality–appearance, beauty and its other—and each side of these conceptual dyads are overlain atop actual protagonists in political struggle. In these asymmetries, mimetic poets are forced (within Plato's argument) to the abjected side of disorder, unreason, ugliness, and immorality. We might say, in the language of deconstruction, that art and its partisans represent the constitutive other of politics, at least from the perspective of philosophy. Hence, mimetic poets are dismissed as unworthy candidates for citizenship, and more importantly, unworthy to assume the role of educating citizens to their own self-knowledge.

Adorno takes up the challenge posed by Plato's aesthetic–political gambit: Adorno will accept for his own guide mimesis over truth, yet a particular variant of mimesis which he figures as *prior* to its construction as merely oppositional to reason. His positive re-evaluation of mimesis emerges out of a dissatisfaction with the failure of Enlightenment's reason to deliver a better world, and in particular, the notion that Nazi experience could be recognized not only as irrational, but, terrifyingly, as a rationality without moral compass. In this light it would not be enough for critical theory to simply urge more *reason*; rather, a conceptual other is needed that would unflinchingly stand opposed to brutality, which could show up the brutality harbored within reason. An analysis at the level of basic politico-philosophic concepts was required.

Adorno today is best known for, with Max Horkheimer, the deeply pessimistic assessment of Reason in their co-authored *Dialectic of Enlightenment* of 1944. Within Western Marxism, this provocative text seemingly drew to a close a certain kind of emancipatory hope.[28] Where Orthodox Marxism had narrowed its emancipatory energies to economic materialism, the circle around Max Horkheimer, and what became the Frankfurt School, deliberately aimed to widen the scope of materialism. Horkheimer in 1937 argued that a strict economism held within it an unacknowledged normative *deficit*:

> [I]f in the present state of society economy is the master of man and therefore the lever by which he is to be moved to change, in the future men must themselves determine all their relationships in the face of natural necessities. Economics in isolation will therefore not provide the norm by which the community of men is to be measured. This is also true for the period of transition in which politics will win a new independence from the economy. . . . [T]hus even the character of the transition remains indeterminate. (1972, 249)

With the proletariat's loss of stature as the predetermined revolutionary class,[29] Horkheimer here signals the need for a new set of possibilities that locates material resistance elsewhere, which answers to norms situated beyond the old economism, and which reformulates the character of "transition," that is, of political revolution. Far from advocating an antimaterialist idealism,[30] Horkheimer saw that cultural forms and basic theoretical concepts that traditionally were understood to stand outside of a material political economy needed to be reconceptualized as *internal* to the material basis of life.[31] The moving forces of social change would then find their home in a necessary relation to economic thinking, but would not be reduced at the normative or practical level to economic laws (of material accumulation, distribution, production, and exchange). The resources for political resistance and change would reside not merely (and not even necessarily) at the level of economy but at the level of *meaning*.

As McCarthy puts it, the early critical theorists aimed to uncover a "normative surplus of meaning that critical theorists can draw upon in seeking to transcend and transform the limits of their situations. In short, the dialectical critique of reason is 'internal' rather than 'total' " (1993, 143).[32] This meant that the Frankfurt School proposed anew a return to the old ethical questions of political philosophy, those concerning a life worth living, but with the demand that questions of truth and value were to have a necessarily *historical* existence, and would act positively toward social and political change. This was a cultural-philosophic historical materialism, an approach that remains consistent across successive generations of the Frankfurt School.

During and after World War II, early optimism gave way to pessimism, as evidenced by Horkheimer and Adorno's *Dialectic of Enlightenment*. In this new phase of their thinking, they argued that reason had surrendered its emancipatory potential.[33] Culture and cultural consumers, politics and citizenship, family and intimate relations all had undergone a sweeping transformation. Reason in the age of science, capital, and mass politics took now for its orienting norm the total mastery of nature and man; the underside of technical mastery was, elaborating on Max Weber's thesis of 1919, the *disenchantment* of the world.[34]

According to this *disenchantment thesis*, experimental method and the logic of capital reduce all matter to component parts, all value to the coin of the realm—all facts and social relations are made manipulable, exchangeable, reproducible, and hence meaningless in and of themselves, but also dislocating, in that human individuation is severed from any embeddedness in a meaningful whole. Reason reduced to a calculative thinking suppresses not only the magical animating spirit of nature, but also represses the free instinctual life that might animate social bonds and self-relations. Although the primacy of technical mastery and capital (read: Enlightenment) might have succeeded in exorcizing the animistic demons of traditional culture, religious dogma, and political Absolutism, it succeeded all too well, leaving Bourgeois science/culture empty of that which might orient notions of a life worth living outside of economism. The means of life have subverted the ends of life.

As one commentator concisely remarks: Adorno and Horkheimer's concept of a vicious *dialectic* of Enlightenment posits "a mismatch between the aims and ideals of enlightenment, and its method of progressive demythologisation. Progressive demythologisation has yielded disenchantment but not liberation" (J. Bernstein 1999, 315). Thus, any faith in reason becomes unreasonable, a dogma, a re-mythologization. Like the archaic snake that eats itself, Enlightenment's own success consumes itself. Nazism, fascism, and anti-Semitism are not deviations from Enlightenment but Enlightenment's culmination, degraded moments of solidarity already signaled in reason's own disenchantment principle.[35] The most atrocious barbarisms are made possible by elevating all means to ends, debasing value by brute mastery. Enlightenment thinking reverts to myth, and myth to barbarism.

Against this assessment of modernity, what hope remains for the original intentions of Enlightenment, the possibility of freedom from dogma, alleviation from natural and social ills, autonomous action for moral purposes, a positive solidarity that does not immolate its members? We might expect that the pessimism in Horkheimer and Adorno's *Dialectic* saturates all hope as instrumental rationality infects all reason. But this is not the case. Their analysis of the self-subversion of Enlightenment carries with it *mimesis* as its shadow, its origin, not quite its opposite, but Enlightenment's object, that which Enlightenment would, if it could, order, arrange and master.[36] "Mimesis" sounds a muted and half-forgotten but still *optimistic* tone in that it signals a force both primitive and irrational, prior to and resistant to the encroachment of full-on modernity.

To lay out what is at stake in a debate between Habermas's communicative rationality and Adorno's mimesis requires at least a provisional definition of mimesis for Adorno. Although mimesis in general notoriously evades definition, as we already have glimpsed, and Adorno is anything but willing to pin mimesis down to a single function, we might cautiously say that in Adorno's work, *mimesis* has two central nodes: The first figures mimesis as a relation between humans and nature characterized by an overlapping force field of imitation, negation, appropriation and creation. The second node finds that same force field (e.g., imitation, negation, appropriation, and creation) operative in describing and evaluating the proper function of art in society. With respect to both of these nodes, human practices are understood by the analyst, with *mimesis* in his or her tool bag of concepts, as to whether they are active or passive, cognizant or inspired, aiming at freedom or necessity, acting to open up possibility or as a cog in capitalism's grinding wheel. In this list of dyads, Adorno favors the mimesis that expands degrees of freedom, although mimesis as a process by no means always acts in this direction. Furthermore, mimesis itself undergoes a history of enlightenment, so an older, archaic, cultic mimetic activity, for example, falls under a different kind of critique than mimesis in modern culture. The attraction for Adorno to mimesis is precisely its variability—it inherently resists what capitalism and its regime of reason would otherwise thoroughly determine as identities suitable for contributions within the bourgeois order. Hence, on the surface of the debate at least, reason aims at identity and the activity of identifying, where mimesis aims at indeterminability, polymorphism and the nonidentical.

Horkheimer and Adorno's respect for the inherent virtue of polymorphism and the nonidentical—in a word, the protean—in *The Dialectic of Enlightenment* takes the form of natural or animistic pantomimesis. In their schematic version of the history of modern consciousness, human understanding progresses in three stages, from magical to mythic/epic to modern/scientific self-understanding. The first period, the magical period, is characterized by mimesis with nature or with cultic spirits. In their words:

> On the magical plane, dream and image were not mere signs for the thing in question, but were bound up with it by similarity or names. The relation is one not of intention but of relatedness. Like science, magic pursues aims, but seeks to achieve them by mimesis—not by progressively distancing itself from the object. (1969, 11)

Mimesis signifies a fundamental *continuity* among things in the world and our knowledge of them. Knowledge may emerge from inhabiting this continuity, but knowledge always is already a degeneration of the relation, because distancing alienates the knower from what may be known. Likewise, conscious imitation of nature defies the spirit of mimesis insofar as consciousness requires a reflective distance between subject and object as a condition of its possibility: "Space is absolute alienation. When men try to become like nature they harden themselves against it" (180).

A true mimesis with nature, that is, a nonintentional mimesis, is *pantomimetic* in that nature is always nonidentical with itself, and therefore the assimilation of a self to nonidentical nature or to many cultic gods dissolves the self into its heterogenous context. They explain, "The shaman's rites were directed to the wind, the rain, the serpent without, or the demon in the sick man, but not to materials or specimens. Magic was not ordered by one, identical spirit: it changed like the cultic masks that were supposed to accord with the various spirits" (9). Even cultic magic, however, already points to the fully administered society: To harness the natural imitation of gods or nature is to already subject nature and God to a purposiveness that would control mimesis rather than let it make manifest the relatedness of humans and nature.[37] Where Plato's gambit for the Philosopher's mimesis is directed to a single source of inspiration, the harmonious otherworldly Forms, Horkheimer and Adorno's natural pantomimesis describes a prior and more primitive notion of submission and self-loss, one that stands prior to the advent of a self-conscious reflective thinking with its ethos of scientific control over the wild forces of nature without and within. This natural mimesis lives on in the human body's own "archaic schemata" (180): burps, farts, stiff joints, the fear that stands hair on end. All that which eludes the ego's self-control rehearses the primal knowledge that instrumental rationality has not suffused all of the world and all of ourselves. A natural mimesis too lives on in certain unconscious social impulses, those "infectious gestures of direct contacts suppressed by civilization, for instance, touch, soothing, snuggling up, coaxing" (182).

Nevertheless, their scheme is *tragic* in its structure: The possibility for mimetic solidarity is forever preempted by a consciousness that, as it develops through the civilizing process, removes itself from the nature that it is, even as it wishes to bridge this self-imposed gap. (This agonizing progression echoes Rousseau's depiction of the civilizing process in his *Second Discourse*.) In this way, the subject–object epistemology of science operates as a mode of domination employed by moderns on nature, on each other, and with a Nietzschean sting, on the self, denatured in the process of becoming self-conscious.[38]

With his counter-concept mimesis, Adorno sets out to show that a *normative* state of a nondominative relation between humans and nature—and by analogy among humans and within human nature itself—can motivate us to challenge and resist the seemingly all pervasive logic of scientific rationality, particularly as modernity's reason plays slave to imperatives of capital accumulation and a cynical politics that misreads human needs as functional necessities of the economy. Mimesis is the action in the event of contact between others on which and through which a healthy uncertainty offers the promise that life has not been already satisfied and reduced to a relation of dead objects in a calculus of mastery.

Counterposed to the Baconian demand that humans should master nature, mimesis as a mode of contact and engagement indicates a more primitive and less determinate relation, one that is marked by awe, respect and supplication, but also, to the contrary, productive of an affective bringing-close, which moves humans toward the rhythms of nature, however dissonant.[39] If Enlightenment reason aims to analyze and organize nature for instrumental ends, then mimesis at least allows for the generosity and terror of nature—within the natural world as well as human nature—to speak in its own voice. It is a voice that holds itself out as indecipherable and unavoidable.

The mimesis that appears in Adorno's *Dialectic of Enlightenment* is a primitive, anthropological power, mimicry, anticipates its later incarnation as aesthetic mimesis. These *two* mimetic forces, archaic and modern, reveal something permanent, although historically contingent, which can oppose reason's inherently political demand for identity among that which it orders. The Platonic philosopher's dogma, to subject art to political judgment, silently makes the *prior* political move to separate art from politics, thereby sterilizing for Adorno what makes art *art*. One alternative to this wholly degraded, depoliticized art, which Adorno does *not* adopt, is a reconciliatory art—that by which we represent ourselves to ourselves, what Hans-Georg Gadamer (1989, 48) has referred to, following Hegel, as satisfying the *human* purpose of art: self-knowledge (which not incidentally aims to answer the Delphic Command, "Know thyself!"). This consoling art, for Adorno, is the conservative flip side to what he in fact advocates, a *disruptive* or *subversive* art, with a power to negate, which flexes a sovereignty whose "ubiquitous potential represents . . . the penetration of an irresolvable crisis" (Menke 1998, 252).[40]

The perception that mimesis holds this promise of *resistance* to a dominant order takes place for Adorno not in just any art, but in the uncompromising, enigmatic, most useless and painful art that challenges the bourgeois self-conceit that comfort is the same as freedom, pleasure the same as happiness, order the same as health, tidiness the same as truth.[41] In fact, for Adorno we might even label as "art" any artifact or practice that strikes us as occupying this position of resistance, whether performed by so-called artists as art or not. Art that purposively tries to be art betrays its own concept, and so for Adorno, a true art only can *indirectly* serve to orient a way of thinking about social relations, because the artistic process in works of the highest caliber represents not an homage to object fetishism but rather is a true mimesis *of mimesis*: It manages to bring us into the light of a pure creativity.[42] The highest art, in Adorno's estimation, has as its paradoxical effect to represent the nonidentical in a mode of becoming that is its perpetual absence, its perpetual promise, like the messiah, never quite here but here nonetheless *as a promise* if you work to accept it as such. Artistic activity figured as a mimetic practice imitates no thing but rather the impulse of that which motivates humans to do art, which is, to be free.[43] It is, in Hegelian language, the tremor of spirit self-actualized, although not as a totality that totalizes, but rather, as a shard remaining from a whole long-ago shattered but still vibrant with light, still vibrating with the force of the infinite.

And this hope for art is *social* insofar as it acts as a negative, normative end of human activity, which is to say directly: preserve the other insofar as the existence of others offers the promise of self-transcendence, of a society other to and better than one's own. The norm is *negative* insofar as it does not prescribe regulative rules for conduct, but rather the opposite, it presents a *way* in which interaction, or perhaps action *simple*, takes place in the absence of rules that constrain and repress. A primitive mimesis resounds in modernist art insofar as, in new form, it signals for humanity a better future freed from the cul-de-sac of Enlightenment rationality.[44]

Politics competes with art and aims to control it, to monopolize mimesis, because it knows that art *both* reconciles and negates, forms and dissolves; is conservative and progressive, reactionary and utopian: In a word, the promise and threat of art is captured in its sovereignty over the world, its apparent other-worldliness brought home, and so it can redeem, but it also can show the lie to power. In the working out of mimesis, then, we get neither a sovereignty of politics nor of art; rather, each takes hold of the other, in practice and also in the matter of judgment. Politics recognizes that a subversive art can resist the comfortable place that it would make for it (in a submissive pedagogic form, or a degraded, autonomous one), and by analogy, offer a "becoming otherwise" for the progressive spirit Adorno endorses. Art in its malleability, however, also is eminently suitable for corruption and inauthenticity.

For Adorno, emancipation *from reason* requires mimesis in that, dialectically speaking, only a logic of de-differentiation *and* an ethos of "identification with" can counter the global tendency of reason's slide toward total differentiation and "identification of." Art must avoid an inauthentic autonomy, and instead achieve an autonomy won through active negation of that which it would work through. Reason, reification, and the alienation of subjects and nature close off the possibility for authentic, nonviolent reconciliation. Reason operates on this model, whereas mimesis subverts it. Mimesis opens up this latter possibility. In this sense, Adorno's definition of mimesis differs from the abjected notion in Plato. It is, in fact, Adorno's intention to invoke a mimesis both before and beyond Greek thinking, for "[r]ationality in general is the demythologization of modes of mimetic behavior."[45]

To conclude here, one can read Adorno's specific sense of mimesis as an entwinement of two impulses, one aesthetic and the other moral: Mimesis might yield a moral and eminently human principle insofar as mimesis binds participants without thereby overwhelming them, giving each an appreciation for what the other's existence represents—the possibility of a better life—and so a duty, however self-regarding, to preserve the other. Mimesis might yield an *aesthetic* principle insofar as mimesis can create a sensibility of a nondominative solidarity—*feelings* of togetherness that make togetherness valuable and a good, but that, again, do not consume the other but exist only insofar as the other exceeds one's apperception.

Under conditions of advanced capitalism, aesthetic practice holds out the promise that this respect for the nonidentical may still find an octave in which to register its power in the world. For Adorno, mimesis stands against the tide of disenchantment.

IV. Mimesis as Re-Enchantment?

Given the discussion just presented, a depiction of mimesis as productive of an open and engaged solidarity, one might wonder what inspires the vituperative condemnation in Habermas's repeated attacks[46] on Adorno's mimesis.

In the paradigm shift to postmetaphysical thinking, a shift that links moral reason to communicative action, Habermas explicitly steers his course against Theodor Adorno's abyssal critique of reason *and* Adorno's counterthrust, the advocacy of Enlightenment's counter-concept, *mimesis*. Where Adorno's pessimism and optimism both defy modernity's faith in Reason, Habermas insists that the critique of reason has proceeded for too long without reflecting on its own normative presuppositions of critique. He identifies a fundamental weakness of early critical theory. We may read in Habermas's development of communicative reason and his dispute with mimesis the best contemporary effort to revitalize a passion for theorizing the strongest possible link (which is still justifiably weak) between public reasoning and its relation to the production of moral ends. This effort has only increased in intensity, and a recent countermovement has even sprung up, defending the mentor Adorno from Habermas's parricide, as it were.[47]

Much of the contemporary effort to rehabilitate the often hidden but surprisingly optimistic strain in Adorno's political philosophy rests on the explication of his late work on aesthetics wherein the notion of mimesis plays a central role in underwriting a moral sensibility. The leading American intellectual historian of the Frankfurt School, Martin Jay, has insisted (1997) on the significance of mimesis in Adorno's theory of aesthetics, and others too have sought to clarify the role of mimesis in Adorno's thought, and its relation to the aims of critical theory.[48]

My own position on the intense debate waged over reason and mimesis is synthetic. The contrasts, I believe, have been drawn too starkly one against the other, and a rapprochement is possible, although neither under the star of reason nor mimesis, but in a necessary tension between them, a tension kept open by an ineradicable *temporal* and *hermeneutic* dimension to the *experience* of communication, a tension that very occasionally finds its synthetic apotheosis, and in *those* cases, mythically, by the affective power of participation.[49]

Habermas's rhetorical excesses to the contrary, if we look for Habermas's *own* use of mimesis, we shall find it, and so the initial question, which still must be asked (namely, what is Habermas's defense of reason against mimesis?) quickly turns to a far more subtle, difficult, and penetrating question concerning the way that Habermas entwines together mimesis and reason *within* his own theory. I contend that Habermas builds into his theory of communicative action a theory of mimesis that, properly understood, complicates immensely Habermas's claim to defend the inheritance of Enlightenment.

One might expect that Habermas—known widely for his overt defense of the "project of Enlightenment" and the normative status of rationality[50]—would take a position, following Plato, that stands opposed to the aesthetic evaluation of political life and its central conceptual operator, mimesis. The separation of politics from aesthetics—of politics *against* aesthetics, and aesthetics as emancipatory, where truth grounds (political) order and art aims at chaos—is an asymmetrical conceptual opposition that *today* aligns our poets and postmoderns with a *Nietzschean* effort to explicitly aestheticize politics and human purpose. This effort remains in some quarters in disrepute.[51] Habermas has written, after all, that "[m]odern art can no longer be tapped as a source of the moral" (1993a, 47). This is not to say that Habermas would follow Plato on all counts, or even very many. They would diverge on many issues, including the character of truth as otherworldly, the valuation of democracy, the proper delimitation of the philosopher's role in political life, the censoring of art, etc Objections to Plato's antidemocratic bent notwithstanding, Habermas in his defense of Enlightenment over myth would seem to share in the same *spirit* of Plato's exoteric teaching. In what sense? Habermas situates his project *with* philosophy on the side of *truth*, and this alone would seem to pit him against advocates of aesthetic mimesis, at least insofar as they promote a fervent unsettling of political life, Adorno's negating, subversive mimesis. On the side of resistance against tyranny, Habermas places his bets with human *critical* faculties, and therefore political opposition should not require a surrender to what Max Weber would call irrational charismatic authority.

Perhaps further confirmation of Habermas's antipathy to mimesis and the aesthetic might be found by observing that Habermas, like Plato, has fought his own battles against the poets, or, if not poets exactly, Foucault, Derrida, and Gadamer who, each in his way, follow Nietzsche and/or Heidegger in decrying the virtue of rationality, holding out a special place for the relevance and priority of the aesthetic. As Habermas puts it in his own foray into literary criticism (1992c, an essay on a postmodern novel by Italo Calvino): Those convinced of reason's superiority to aesthetic play must stand opposed to the "liquidation of the distinction between genres" of philosophy and science on the one side, and literature on the other. If Plato has introduced a science of statecraft and separated politics from aesthetics, then Habermas here follows suit. Habermas wishes to *redeem* the force of the rational by associating it exclusively with a theory of communication that, in deliberative argument, bears witness to its own inherently moral structure.

The philosophical-political stakes over the status of aesthetic truth consist in the *moral* character of the polis as anchored in the nature of *truth*. If truth is a fiction, so Habermas's argument goes, and fiction can bind its audience in the same way truth can, then the mimetic power of art would undo the gains of the Enlightenment, and in its affirmation of nonidenticality, would call reason its proper name: domination, or worse, play. The charge of *domination* challenges the supposed righteousness of reason; the charge of *play* challenges reason's claim to objectivity, and indeed, the possibility of truth. A truth claim becomes a will to truth, a moment of power without ground. For Habermas, aspirations to the good life require of politics that it ideally answer to moral criteria. Ethics should answer to morality, even as morality by and large should keep its nose clean of ethics.[52] Prioritizing aesthetic mimesis over reason would unsettle the stability of moral criteria. Reason, which should ennoble politics, would instead fall into arbitrary decisionism on the one hand, or, on the other, in Foucault's depiction (1979), find itself dispersed into the depersonalized techniques of power that defuse the grounds for personal responsibility altogether. The truth-value of reason that should establish for Habermas the epistemic foundation for political consensus would instead evaporate, leaving reason under the sway of mimesis as simply another brand of the ungrounded play of force.

Today's postmodern aesthetic, so Habermas's claim might continue, is fueled by those Nietzsche-inspired thinkers who, wishing an exit from a subjectivity restrained by the domain of reason, would advocate *experience* [*Erlebnis*] in general to unburden, as it were, rationality of its heavy duty of thinking the possibility and responsibilities of a just polis.[60] As Habermas charges, the "limit experiences of an aesthetic and mystical kind have . . . been claimed for the purpose of a rapturous transcendence of the subject" (1987b, 309). Habermas's primary worry is that otherwise sincere modern citizens would be tempted by the allure of aesthetic power. One should not invent a model for life "by generalizing the subversive forces which Nietzsche, Bakunin or Baudelaire expressed in their own lives" (1997, 50). For these models do not, in Habermas's evaluation, subtend a moral autonomy.[54] The triumph of aestheticism would make nonsense of the classic philosophic and political demand to "know thyself." Under the star of aestheticism, self-knowledge falls before the dream of self-actualization, a doing without thinking. For Habermas, this figure of unreflective activity that presents itself as asocial, amoral, and ahistorical is, in truth, none of these things, but rather the false result of poor philosophy, an oppositional thinking that posits a totalistic reason opposite an unhinged subjectivity. What Habermas calls a "scurrilous game"—the philosopher's last resort when the time for thinking is over and done with—promises a wild and primitive freedom, but cannot redeem its chits.

These charges *against* aesthetics might convince us that Habermas views the promise of mimetic relations as merely an irrational bogeyman, dangerous and misguided. In Plato, poetic mimesis aims at civil war within the soul and within the polis; for Habermas, ditto. Right? For both Plato and Habermas, reason must stand above that heteronymous, mimetic aspect in the soul that answers to aesthetic experience.

Such conclusions would coincide with many of Habermas's explicit renderings of mimesis and the mimetic impulse. *And yet*, in Habermas's work the opposition between reason and mimesis is rather ambiguous. For all that mimesis is at times simply equated with the irrational or the nonidentical, Habermas *also* claims mimesis as his own. And his claim *for* mimesis extends *beyond the explication he gives* for how the aesthetic sphere fits into his depiction of modernity's internal differentiation.[55] Indeed, Habermas's theory of communicative action can be adequately illuminated only when it is properly understood as an attempt to recompose the opposition between rationality and mimesis. If I am correct, Habermas actually pursues a *sublation* of rationality and mimesis, where communicative rationality, rightly put, is a theory of *rational illumination* or, better, *articulate mimesis*.[56]

Martin Jay indicates in a footnote that when Habermas writes on mimesis, "it is usually *assimilated* into his communicative notion of intersubjective rationality" (1997, 30, nt. 11, emphasis added). And again, Jay writes of Habermas's "attempt . . . to *relocate* mimesis *within* an intersubjective, communicative sphere" (1997, 33, nt. 22, emphasis added). Jay is correct, and he draws this conclusion from Habermas's response to one of Jay's earlier essays (1985). Habermas says in his response:

> Art . . . belongs to everyday communicative practice. It then reaches into our cognitive interpretations and normative expectations and transforms the totality in which these moments are related to each another. In this respect, modern art harbors a utopia that becomes a reality to the degree that the mimetic powers sublimated in the work of art find resonance in the mimetic relations of a balanced and undistorted intersubjectivity of everyday life. (1985c, 202)

Notice here that Habermas allows that "mimetic powers" are "sublimated in the work of art." This part of his remark should come as no surprise given the discussion earlier of Plato's critique of the poets; of course art employs mimetic power. However, it should strike us as very surprising Habermas's claim that there are "mimetic relations" within "a balanced and undistorted intersubjectivity of everyday life." This should give us pause, for it admits irrationality, or at least, "mimetic relations" as an element of "undistorted intersubjectivity." Can there be undistorted mimesis? It would seem that mimesis, defined precisely as distortion, the opposite of clarity and distinctiveness, has here shifted to its opposite.

In case there is any doubt that Habermas writes what he does not intend to write, Habermas elsewhere reiterates this claim: "there is already a mimetic moment in everyday practices of communication, and not merely in art" (1985b, 81). Mimesis, in other words, according to Habermas, resides *within* communicative rationality. This would be unclear enough were it not for yet another ambiguity that points in the *opposite* direction. In his *Theory of Communication Action,* Habermas announces that his project aims, among other goals, to lay open "the rational core of mimetic achievements" (1984, 390).

There is a distinct difference between these two formulations: The first places mimesis *within* communicative rationality; the second, rationality *within* mimetic achievements. Does communicative rationality operate mimetically, or does mimesis operate rationally? Which is it? And if it is both, how can this be? This assimilation or relocation of mimesis *within* rationality, or, its apparent opposite, rationality within mimesis, should come as something of a surprise to students of Habermas's work, and particularly, to both supporters and critics of Habermas who consistently take for granted Habermas's own self-accounting as a rationalist and a proceduralist. How can a wild and inconsolable aesthetic force (mimesis) so opposed to rationality get assimilated to rationality? Is this merely another moment of reason's domination of its other? Does this merely confirm Adorno and Horkheimer's assessment of the dialectic of Enlightenment? Is this an example of the truth-value of science claiming for itself the power of, and over art? Or, shall we read the mimesis within rationality as a shift in our basic conception of the political: politics as an aesthetic activity? If the aestheticization of politics is Fascism's program, then how does Habermas steer around *that* consequence?

And, on the other hand, if "mimetic achievements" (and which kinds?) *already* contain a "rational core," what is the character of this rationality? How can we *think* through a rationality of mimesis, or, further, mimesis and rationality *at once*? Do we *feel* this confluence instead? As participants, or (dis)interested spectators? Which is figure and which is ground? If these can be variable, then how rational is rationality, and how can mimesis have within it a rational core? If Habermas maintains (as he does) that the postmodern promise of a transcendence of subjectivity is a dangerous lie, then in what sense can he advocate a mimesis in communication that avoids vulnerability to the same charge? And to take one further step, if we grant the argument that rationality has been conceptually built up against its other, mimesis, then in what sense does this rational mimesis demand a new other? (We also might inquire, with scholastic concerns in the foreground, how this essentially Hegelian way of thinking, toward a reconciliation of reason and unreason, squares with Habermas's reliance on a neo-Kantian, proceduralist theory of speech norms. Is it Habermas's unease with his earlier Hegelianism that forces him later to claim a Kantian proceduralism?)

Few commentators have paid much attention to this issue of mimesis within Habermas's work,[57] and to date no one has worked through the implications for this assimilation of the irrational and the rational in the figure of communicative rationality. Standard interpretations and applications of Habermas's work rely on his self-explication as a defender of Enlightenment and a deliberative, proceduralist democracy. It is my contention that a rigorous re-reading of Habermas attentive to the assimilation of mimesis to rationality (and rationality to mimesis) will lead to a reassessment of Habermas's program, and accordingly, a reassessment of the status of his discourse ethics within contemporary political thought.

V. Toward a Reconstruction of Communicative Action

To restate my major claims: Habermas's theory of communicative rationality is built up conceptually from both rational procedure and aesthetic experience, but is unfortunately elaborated by Habermas (and Habermasians) in a way that privileges the moral status of the former while eliding the unifying and creative power of the latter. Where Habermas exoterically relegates the legitimacy of aesthetic experience to its own functional sphere (that of artistic production and subjective reception), a proper emphasis on the interleaving of mimetic and rational elements within his figure of communicative action can help us to locate Habermas's larger target, namely, the way that communication might remedy the motivational deficit due to the loss of meaning in modernity.

This conclusion will emerge later from a close reading of Habermas on the issue of mimesis (Chapter 2), subjectivity (Chapter 3), and aesthetic experience (Chapter 4). A reformulation of Habermas's project on the basis of mimesis that emphasizes the aesthetic power of communicative rationality captures the unconcealed secret of Habermas's project, one that has remained hidden to many observers because of the apparently sharp break between Habermas and his Frankfurt intellectual forebears, and likewise, between Habermas and postmodernists. The promise of Habermas's work, lamented at one time by Leo Lowenthal (who co-wrote with Adorno and Horkheimer portions of the *Dialectic of Enlightenment*) as signaling the suspension of utopian energies in critical thought (Wolin 1992, 63), instead is, I would argue, ambitious and audacious, and even utopian. My hope is that when considered as a theory of rational illumination, or articulate mimesis, Habermas's discourse ethics will be reconsidered both by those who have dismissed it based on Habermas's overemphasis on a neo-Kantian moral universalism, as well as by those who have accepted it all too readily as a rationalist defense of the Enlightenment project.

Chapter 2

Mimesis in Communicative Action

Habermas and Plato

> And the public, when they see that we have described him truly, will be reconciled to the philosopher and no longer disbelieve our assertion that happiness can only come to a state when its lineaments are traced by an artist working after the divine pattern.
>
> —Plato (*Republic,* Book IV, 500d–e)

Chapter 1 set out a simple and schematic opposition between reason and mimesis, where mimesis is largely given over to Adorno's usage: a nondominative relation between humans and nature, and the subversive mimesis epitomized in the best modern art. In this chapter, we shall see that this schematic opposition does *not,* in fact, fully capture the scope of issues at hand. The stylization of mimesis as *the nondominative mode of engagement with the nonconceptualizable* aims to figure itself as resistant to the tendencies of Enlightenment's reason toward domination, but to think of reason and mimesis as bipolar opposites is to *remain within* the rhetorical field of argument set out by metaphysical thinking in general. Those like Adorno who advocate a mimesis in an aporetic sense, a mimesis as opposed to a reason that it is fated to resist, articulate a spirit of a self-annihilating modernity. This kind of Nietzschean poetics, indeed, this *tragic* structure, will be rhetorically compelling only within the terms of metaphysics. It gains its rhetorical strength from the doubling back and forth between the singular and the universal, and is symptomatic of modernity's philosophic contradictions rather than a genuine release from them.

To the extent, therefore, that Habermas can successfully construct a *post*metaphysical philosophy, he cannot in good faith from that position continue to link mimesis with the irrational (so as to banish it from the interiority of moral thinking). Habermas cannot continue to view mimesis as the root of an aporetic poetics. It operates this way within Adorno's framework, but to relinquish Adorno's framework requires putting the relation between reason and mimesis on a new footing. As with his reconstruction of reason, it makes good sense to evaluate and potentially reformulate a notion of mimesis apart from a subjectivistic account of consciousness and, instead, appropriate for postmetaphysical thinking. To maintain an appropriate standard of rigor, Habermas's critique of metaphysics must move past its own rhetorical polemic against mimesis cast as a mode of noncognitive engagement. This shift in approach will open up the possibility, indeed, it acknowledges the necessity for us to rethink mimesis under the paradigm of intersubjectivity.

In this chapter, I elaborate the foregoing argument by first, in Section I, rehearsing some of the issues surrounding the inadequacy of modernity's subjective thinking, particularly as an anti-mimetic mode of consciousness, in order to then, in Sections II to VII, introduce a range of mimetic thinking by investigating Habermas's unacknowledged appropriation of Platonic mimesis. I will show that Habermas, in fact, already deploys mimesis, but without acknowledging the full implications of such a move.

I. Modernity and Its Anti-Mimetic *Cogito*

Habermas's critique of Adorno expresses a dissatisfaction with a modernism that couches itself within metaphysical bounds. Adorno's knowingly paradoxical concept of the nonidentical, from Habermas's perspective, appears *complicitous* with subjective reason's identity-thinking insofar as a toggling from pole to pole within this asymmetrical opposition does nothing to remove the essential difficulty of being caught in a closed circuit. That is, despite Adorno's potent and apt critique of instrumental rationality, he can present no *alternative* to the structure of metaphysical thinking as a whole.[1] Adorno and Horkheimer render darkly an instrumental rationality gone wild, where a disciplinary reason aimed at a mastery over nature turns on the self and social relations, reducing questions of validity to differentials of power. An instrumentalized totality finds its natural and terrible counterpart in an impossible singularity of the other.[2] Habermas regards their "uninhibited skepticism regarding reason" as a digressive reversal of critical theory's commitment to historically based critique, rehearsing instead the sins of an abstract Platonism, a retreat to "theory, purified of all empirical connotations" (1987b, 129–30). From Habermas's perspective:

> [W]e [should] drop the somewhat sentimental presupposition of metaphysical homelessness, and if we understand the hectic to and fro between transcendental and empirical modes of dealing with issues, between radical self-reflection and an incomprehensible element that cannot be reflectively retrieved, between the productivity of self-generating species and a primordial element prior to all production—that is to say when we understand the puzzle of all these doublings for what it is: a symptom of exhaustion. The paradigm of the philosophy of consciousness is exhausted. (1987b, 296)

That we can see the rounding out of a metaphysical epoch, however, underlines certain similarities of attitude toward modern consciousness that Habermas *shares* with a postmodern sensibility.

Habermas cites Baudelaire's 1863 definition of "modernity" as providing a familiar aporetic encapsulation of modern consciousness: Modernity expresses that uncanny simultaneity of the fleeting and the eternal, an actuality that invokes and incants what is invariable and unchanging. The concept of eternal Beauty, for example, comes to be itself through its particularity in otherwise ephemeral, even trivial expressions (e.g., an etching of fashionable clothing).[3] Baudelaire's modernity resolves itself into neither particularities nor totalities, but rather, it produces aesthetic tremors in the experience of the simultaneity of both. A modernist aesthetic consciousness bears its confidence still in the shadow of a discredited religious faith perpetually anxious to resolve the heterology of experience and life-forms into a moral and redemptive unity (e.g., God), but barring a theological referent, a secular semblance of the sacred in the reception of aesthetic productions.

For Habermas, the modern attitude is marked by a particular time-consciousness, one that originated with a Left reading of Hegel. Unlike a normatively Christian worldview, where the here-and-now is essentially a sacrifice made for redemption in the afterlife, a modern orientation, secular through and through, displaces the demand for a heavenly future to the here-and-now. We are living the future every moment, and it resounds with the totality of history all primed for this moment.[4] And now this moment, the aesthetic tremor of Baudelaire's modernity. Where every meaningful moment is aesthetically charged from its own interior, what becomes of the normative order that had been metaphysically figured as prior to and external to the human world? Moderns view their own present as a time of "*continuous renewal*," which demands of modernity that it "can and will no longer borrow the criteria by which it takes its orientation from the models supplied by another epoch; *it has to create its normativity out of itself*" (1987b, 7).

To understand why modern thinking must uncouple itself from a *philosophy of consciousness paradigm*, we might briefly consider the *subject* of consciousness, for the concept of the self that animates Adorno's faith in a category of the nonidentical is already collapsed into reason's darling, the subject—even at its modern origin, in René Descartes's figuration of the *cogito*. Descartes's notion of the *cogito* occurs *outside of* and *prior* to any representation of itself. Michel Henry interprets the Cartesian *cogito* as a

> force [which] collapses in on itself in an immediation that is so radical, and in this immediation is submerged into itself in such a way that there is no room in it for any difference, no distanciation thanks to which it would be possible for it to perceive itself, to represent itself—*to be conscious in the mode of representation*. (1991, 165)

Following Henry: Descartes's advent of a modernist philosophy proposes, properly speaking, not a *subject* but an antisubject, fully dedifferentiated—a nonbeing that inaugurates representation but that is not itself subject to representation, is not simultaneously able to be experienced and to be thought of (because cognitive consciousness already would presuppose the distantiation on which reflection is predicated). In this sense, the *representation problem*—the notion of Truth as the *correspondence* between word and thing, appearance and reality, thought and the *cogito* that thinks it, on the model of mirroring, as Rorty has shown (1979)—appears as the antisubject's other, and as its subsequent working out of itself. In this way, the formulation of the Cartesian subject already entails its own critique, that it cannot but be inaccessible, and that its relation to what can be thought and known cannot be grounded in its self-certainty, in its self as the self-enclosedness of its subjecthood. The toggling between reason and the irrational *within* metaphysical thinking has at its core the impossible limit of the *cogito*'s perfect self-presence, and so at its far, political horizon, a perfect unity claimed ultimately by Hegelian Reason.

For Michel Henry, the irrational, unrepresentable "subject," although only "half-perceived" by Descartes, inaugurates the modern problem of representation: "the subject is nothing other than this: that which in making appearance appear, in this same gesture, makes be everything that is"

(1991, 164–65). And this is why, when we consider the appearance of "accident" and "biography" as troubling the *cogito*, as that which must be cleansed from a self in order to reach a purified state, Lyons will write: "Rhetorically the whole *Discours* is based on the movement away from the disappointments and the self-estrangement that come from *imitation*" (1982, 522, emphasis added). Mimesis threatens to infest the purity of the *cogito*. No trace of another can be found in the self which is nothing but what it is, and what it is is nothing that can be—it *is* antisubstance, if such a paradoxical formulation may be allowed. The *cogito* is dreamt of as inured from infection by any this-worldly effect. We may supplement Henry's account of the self as an undifferentiated unity with a remark by Lyons, who provides a *negative* depiction of Descartes's *cogito*:

> What vanishes in the *cogito* is the autobiographical "I" of the narrative of preparation. . . . The subject of the *Cogito* has no body, no past, no relationship to others, no project or method, no location in historical space. The *cogito* is a momentary and solitary act. . . . Thus the solitude of the metaphysical subject is characterized by an absence of any *similar* subject. (1982, 520, and nt. 15)

The *cogito* is fundamentally anti-mimetic, pure absence from any thing (or at least, any *this-worldly* thing). To be sure, in the *Third Meditation,* Descartes cannot resist imagining that God puts his *stamp* on the *cogito,* ensuring that the *cogito qua* pure absence is nevertheless marked by the only mimesis it *cannot* resist.

In this vein, Balibar (1991) argues that Descartes's *subjectus* is *not* equivalent to our modern, autonomous, self-incarnating individual that we associate with liberal modernity's myth of itself. Rather, for Descartes a human is *subject* to God's authority and authorship. The human exercises his or her will only because he or she (and the objects in the world) share in the substance that God has created. In many ways, the twists and turns in political philosophy—Habermas's no less than any other—turns on locating the point of *irresistible* mimesis. For Descartes, it is the stamp of God; for Habermas, as we shall see, it is the unforced force of understanding in communication.

So the Cartesian anti-mimetic *cogito* acts as a figure of a withdrawal from metaphysics, but, as a finite imprint of an infinite God's own stamp, one thereby drawn forward into metaphysics nonetheless. The Cartesian anti-mimetic nonsubject represents an anti-figure imagined as *prior* to the *experience* of participation. What links together all humans could be sought only prior to their mortality and historicity, behind their involvement with and despite any difference that sprouts merely from this world. That said, we may, like Descartes, posit an anti-mimetic *cogito* as a future anterior, as a forgotten atomistic origin brought back to mind, but in positing this figure, us moderns, in a self-reflexive attitude, cannot pretend to confirm *that* we share in it *in the moment* that we share in it. It is but (Cartesian) dogma to imagine the closure that reflection holds open despite itself.

In classical metaphysics there is a confidence in an *a priori* similarity of position and essence that stands behind all difference, a confidence we cannot share. It is then a short step to Immanuel Kant's categorical imperative, where an underlying *sameness* of all (rational) creatures is presupposed, which therefore drives the structure and necessity of moral duty. We respect others not in their otherness but for their moral similarity. As Ricoeur summarizes,

> In order [for Descartes] to avoid slipping into subjectivist idealism, the "I think" must be divested of any psychological resonance, all the more so of any autobiographical reference. It must become the Kantian "I think," which the transcendental deduction states must be able to accompany all my acts. The problematic of the self emerges magnified, in a sense, but at the price of the loss of its relation to the person who speaks, to the I–you of interlocution, to the identity of a historical person, to the self of responsibility. Must the exaltation of the *cogito* be paid at this price? (1992, 11)

Descartes's anxiety over self-certainty leads toward a (Kantian) moral law that must presuppose all subjects under the law to be, on all relevant indicators, the same, bearing nothing but the imprint of the stamp of God. We find in Descartes the evacuation of the subject as a historical being and therefore an inability to secularly ground moral insight.

It is the principle of nonidenticality that Descartes gives to the subject that Adorno will posit in *nature*, human nature no less than the natural environment. And yet, this is true for Adorno only given his acceptance of Rousseau's tragic narrative in his *Discourse on the Origin of Inequality*, that with the advent of civilization, human nature has gradually but definitively turned away from its natural, anti-mimetic state to become saturated by the artificiality of man. This presents for Adorno the perhaps hyperbolic proposition of a subjective mimesis-with-nature/art—a making of the self as nonidentical to itself through a nonintentional "procedure" of identifying with the nonidentical.[5] Habermas gladly follows the critique of Cartesian metaphysics insofar as he detects in Adorno that mimesis-as-solidarity-with-nonidentity is already driven toward a reason as "identity-thinking."

In this early light, we can see that Habermas's promotion of a paradigm shift from a *metaphysics of the subject* to *communicative rationality* must coincide with a renewed attempt at configuring reason's relation to mimesis, where mimesis takes place *within* and not insulated from history. A paradigm shift to communicative consciousness must prefigure mimesis. *After metaphysics, mimesis and anti-mimesis alike cannot operate simply in the opaque register of the nonidentical,* and furthermore, concepts of self and self-becoming must have within them the resources to resist spiraling backward to, on the one hand, a Cartesian subjectivity that, as pure negation, is fully anti-mimetic, nor, on the other hand, to the extreme of a Hegelian Reason as a saturated mimetic totality.

II. Divine Mimesis

For us to examine how subjectivity and morality might evade the modernist toggling between mimesis and anti-mimesis, a fuller examination, indeed, a *genealogy* of mimesis is required. The remained of this chapter will put Habermas and Plato into conversation on the central and ambivalent concept of mimesis. Mimesis figures in both authors as the pivot that links together politics and morality in a theory of identity-formation. I will show here that mimesis operates in a different register than that which operates from Descartes through Adorno, that is, neither as an antipolitical concept nor as a nonidentical notion, but as one that is thoroughly political in its effects, and operates as a socialization process in the sense that *mimesis* as a keyword frames how to figure the proper mode of participation in political life.

Through a close reading of several of Plato's dialogues, we will see that the key aspect of Platonic mimesis is its affectual quality that orients the identities of political subjects. This will suggest that affectual identification forms the core process in dialogue insofar as communication links together socialization, self-realization, and communal identification. Against this backdrop it will become evident that insofar as Habermas *relies* on a theory of mimesis for his theory of communicative rationality, he must in some way take into account this *affective* dimension of dialogue, or explain why an affective dimension of communication can be distinguished *in practice* from, and then subordinated to, or extracted from, the *moral* character of communicative action.

Habermas's implausible (because one-sided) approach to the affective dimension of communication indicates that a rethinking of Habermasian communicative action is necessary in order for it to adequately figure the link he wishes to make between moral communication and the distinctively modern problem of a deficit of meaning in the world. Additionally, with respect to the *opposition* between reason and mimesis, in investigating Plato's usage we will find that mimesis acts as a power that *aids* reason and does not simply oppose it, although it can. Similarly, reason itself does not abstain from employing mimetic power for its own purposes (e.g., in Plato's myths).

What I will emphasize in this comparative examination of mimesis is that the *exuberant* and *ecstatic character* of mimetic experience is, in Plato's dialogues, *shared* by reason, but absent in Habermas's explication of communicative reason. We would expect reason to have an *affective* quality because of its *transformative* power. Indeed, Habermas uses precisely *explosive* imagery to rhetorically depict the *power* of reason, in communicative action's critical power to "burst open" (1984, 120) everyday dogma and habituated understandings. Reason is not simply a matter of calculative capacity, but rather a participation in truth, the kind which changes people's lives, orients their self-images, grounds their moral relations. In Chapter 1, we saw that Habermas refuses to endorse the (false) promise of a subject-transcendent experience. Nonetheless, some version of *affectivity* belongs at the center of communicative action. Habermas cannot simply wish it away, and the secular differentiation of knowledge-spheres[6] does nothing to diminish or dilute its potency. After arguing this point in the present chapter and in the next on Habermas's theory of the self, I will in Chapter 4 begin to reconstruct Habermas's theory of communicative rationality on the basis of mimesis with reference to Walter Benjamin's account of modern experience.

A reconstruction of communicative action along the lines of affectivity in the experience of communication is vital given Habermas's diagnosis of the pathologies of modern society. The cost of increasing rationalization and the disenchantment of the world shows up as a deficit of motivation and meaning, which Habermas's theory of communicative rationality, as it is currently framed, does not redress, nor, I argue, can it do so as it stands without fuller attention to the mimetic aspect of intersubjective communication. In Plato's dialogues, mimesis gains its full scope of ambivalent meanings in that Plato polemicizes against mimesis while at the same advocating it and employing it for his own purposes. This analysis will enable us to view Habermas's own ambivalent relation to mimetic power.

Habermas himself has commented on Plato's use of mimesis, thus providing an opening to bring classical and contemporary political philosophy together on this issue. Habermas uses the figure of mimesis to set off his brand of *critical* theory from *traditional* theory. I will emplot mimesis in the same way, but emphasize not only the differences between traditional theory and critical theory but also the *continuities* that are due to this core concept. Because contemporary issues and not simply antiquarian interests motivate this aspect of my study, I will make an effort to keep Habermas's project always in the foreground, although it will take the entire chapter to clearly articulate its scope.

Habermas has gone to some length to position himself at opposite ends of the political and philosophical spectrum from Plato. Already in his 1965 inaugural address at Frankfurt, Habermas (1971, appendix) attacks what he calls "pure theory," and its palpable lodestar, the philosopher. Habermas renounces metaphysical truth together with its progenitors, asserting that we need to study language, the nature of which is the only thing we can ever hope to really understand. He accuses those who rely on metaphysical truth as engaging in scandalous activity, where the scandal arises from classical philosophy's other-worldly orientation: Why should truth reside *outside* of history, *outside* the scope of interests *within* the world?[7] Habermas's criticism of "pure theory" also is motivated by epistemological skepticism: How does a saint or prophet or poet or philosopher come to know a metaphysical truth? To discount metaphysics here is to invalidate the way Plato's philosopher-king comes to experience truth. In Habermas's account, pure theory on the Platonic model strips itself of empirical dross and temporal flux; the mystic philosopher's epistemological method amounts to myth, one that demands a cosmic inspiration:

> When the philosopher views the immortal order, he cannot help bringing himself into accord with the proportions of the cosmos and reproducing them internally. He manifests these proportions, which he sees in the motions of nature and the harmonic series of music, within himself; *he forms himself through mimesis*. Through the soul's likening itself to the ordered motion of the cosmos, theory enters the conduct of life.[8] (1971, 302, emphasis added)

This interpretation that Habermas provides of divine mimesis captures an important aspect of Plato's philosophical-political agenda, namely, to deliver a myth that can justify the rule of philosophers. The philosopher's self-knowledge arrives as a mimesis of the cosmos. In the cosmic ordering of the philosopher's soul, worldly attributes are without independent significance or special authenticity, and therefore dissolve before other-worldly perfection. This mimetic assimilation to the divine underwrites the *political* authority of philosophy and philosophers, and already by way of critique, we can see that for Habermas a capitulation to this divinity would signal a surrender of critical capacities. Any divine legislator (as in Rousseau's model[9] based cynically on the same procedure,) is overripe for the modern age.

At this stage in my analysis, it is imperative to underline the fact that *divine* mimesis does not exhaust the ways Plato uses mimesis. Habermas's thin account of Platonic mimesis bypasses the *range* of meanings of mimesis, and ignores the fact that Plato does not merely valorize mimesis; elsewhere, he explicitly condemns it. Mimesis takes many forms in Plato and singularly does the work of many different concepts.[10] I will work this out in the following analysis, for if a differentiation of concepts—here, mimesis—provides one of the historical markers of progress in intellectual history, this differentiation should not blind us to the condensation of issues bound together which does not dissolve simply because reason can map its disaggregation.

To show this, I will discuss here more fully the mode of mimesis already introduced, mimesis as divine possession, to emphasize a key aspect of mimesis generally, the experience of ecstatic self-loss. After that and by way of contrast, I will introduce a more prosaic and, for Plato, a more insidious mimesis, one which bears a close resemblance to Habermas's own project(!). We will see that whereas Habermas expels divine mimesis by the front door, it returns in other guise through the back.

Plato writes that a republic's citizens would hardly be willing to accept a philosopher as their king, at least not "until a god inspires the present rulers and kings or their offspring with a true erotic love for true philosophy" (1997c, 499b). Although this statement carries some sarcasm—because citizens do need, but should not need the myth of divine inspiration—note that, analytically speaking, divine inspiration links philosophy to erotic love. *Philosophy* is the love for wisdom, but how is the love of wisdom associated with erotic love? We see here that Eros and philosophy both share in the God's divine inspiration. The God must inspire rulers with erotic love for philosophy; only then will citizens embrace a philosopher as their own ruler. Plato's account gives philosophy an *ecstatic* character, where reason does not merely oppose desire but requires it and is made potent by it.

In *Phaedrus,* Plato classifies together erotic love and philosophy as two (of four) types of divine madness. Here we find confirmation of Habermas's interpretation of Plato that we saw above: "The philosopher alone," Plato writes, "applies himself to the divine, he is reproached by most men for being out of his wits; they do not realize that *he is in fact possessed by a god*" (1973, 249d, emphasis added). As the philosopher is possessed, likewise the lover, and in both cases, the possessed person is drawn away from this-worldly concerns and toward a conformity with the divine:

> every man desired to find in his favorite [beloved] a nature comparable to his own particular divinity, and when he lights upon such a one he devotes himself to personal *imitation of his*

> *god* and at the same time attempts to persuade and train his beloved to the best of his power to walk in the ways of that god and to mould himself upon him. . . . His whole effort is concentrated upon leading the object of his love into the *closest possible conformity with himself and with the god he worships*. (1973, 253, emphasis added)

For the lover, the madness of Eros inspires him to a self-forgetfulness in a complete mimetic conformity, he and his beloved together, to the image of the God. Mimetic communion under Eros, through the procedures of "persuasion and training," produces a possession where all distinctions are leveled as lover, beloved and the God become a singular body, divine and whole.[11]

As in erotic mimesis, the mimesis of philosophers also is characterized by powerful affect. Plato dramatizes this affectual experience as *anamnesis*, the awakening of a primordial remembrance of the soul's journeying in the company of a God. This mythic journey (1973, 247) entails a look at the plane of pure Forms. All humans take this primordial journey, but it is remembered, although sporadically and with great effort, only by philosophers. To look on pure truth, pure self-control, pure beauty, and the rest of the Forms without doxic mediation is an awe-filled experience, and remembering such an event requires a special disposition. In pursuing their respective arts, both the philosopher and the lover ideally experience the extraordinary, where their very being undergoes, not transformation per se, but a sloughing off of this-worldly appearances so as to better realize in remembrance their truly divine aspect. To re-experience the divine is to find unconcealed one's half-forgotten soul, and to transcend one's corporeal self.

One commentator remarks on a moral *openness* that characterizes this experience. It is open because a soul " 'sees' but does not possess" the Forms, which suggests that any so-called knowledge of the Forms is actually merely provisional: "our knowledge of a Form, if not the Form itself, can always become other than it is" (McCumber 1989, 200).[12] What this contemporary analysis ignores to its detriment is the *interpenetration* of the knowledge-seeker *by* the Forms, the lovers *by* the God. The ecstasy experienced by the philosopher may be figured strictly as a matter of the positive attainment of knowledge only from a perspective external to the action. As immediate experience, it is not so much that the philosopher witnesses the Forms, but rather, that the Forms have inhabited him, have inhabited his mind, have ordered his soul. McCumber (203) confuses the issue by arguing that "lovers . . . fashion and adorn images as do sculptors (*Phaedrus*, 252d), [and that] the images in question are each other, and—far from being twice removed from reality—are themselves the most beautiful human reality possible." McCumber is correct that the depiction here of sculpture as a true image argues against the typical reading of Plato's *Republic* Book 10, where Plato castigates as false appearance artistic representations. To my mind, however, erotic love is not *redeemed* on the basis of the lovers acting like sculptors who sculpt one another. To the contrary, in Plato love is experienced *as if* it were conferred from another source, the God. What redeems the lovers is what McCumber's nonmystical reading leaves out of the analysis, the imitation *not* of the lovers of one another, but of the *God*. McCumber inexplicably leaves out this third term. Plato signals this necessity when he writes that lovers "find in themselves traces by which they can detect the nature of the god to whom they belong, and . . . by the aid of memory they lay hold on him and are possessed by him, so that they take from him their character and their way of life, in so far as it is possible for a man to partake of divinity" (1973, 253). One lover does not worship his beloved as himself, nor as a mere projection sculpted of his own desire. Rather, love and worship focus on and intensify those aspects of the beloved that resemble the God, and it is for this reason that the lover makes his beloved "in closest conformity with himself *and with the god he worships*" (253). It is the communion with God that ennobles and sanctifies the lovers—in love a divine possession takes hold. The divinity possesses *them*, and in the process shakes, interpenetrates and de-individuates the respective identities of the lovers. This elevated state is marked by purification and self-loss for the sake of powerful affect: Love is a sacred event of mutual belonging.

We can here rely on Gadamer who uses the Heideggerian language of *being-with* to characterize the philosopher's journey as similar to the lover's mimesis, as an experience of communion in ecstatic self-forgetting/being-with-another:

> In the *Phaedrus* Plato [describes] the ecstatic condition of being outside oneself. . . . [It is not] a mere negation of being composed within oneself. . . . In fact, being outside oneself is the positive possibility of being wholly with something else. (1989, 125–26)

In this light, consider Plato's admonition that the task of the mortal philosopher "is always [to] dwell in memory as best it may on those things which a god owes his divinity to dwelling upon" (Plato 1973, 249). Plato exploits the philosopher's privilege of "dwelling in memory" as entitling him to rule.[13]

The philosopher's deliberate turning toward[14] the purity of the Forms is rewarded by the recollection of his own partial divinity. The apparent contradiction of "being wholly with something else" and "dwelling in memory" is reconciled by mimesis—this being-with that is a recognition of sameness—because of Plato's ontological myth: Memory of the Forms *always already* inhabits the Soul. Knowledge and love are together a remembering. The self-loss experienced in philosophic thought is equivalent to a being-with one's true self, a looking backward and inward that brings one back outward in a primordial soul-communion with divinity. What you are truly is that which in you is divine. Therefore, in *this* world, the classical formulation of philosophic experience demands a self-recovery and a self-reconstitution, which confirms the philosopher's continuity with the divine and so justifies his rule over the republic.

In an intricate and fascinating passage in *Republic,* philosophy and Eros combine:

> it is the nature of the real lover of learning to struggle toward what is, not to remain with any of the many things that are believed to be, that, as he moves on, he neither loses nor lessens his erotic love until he grasps the being of each nature itself with the part of his soul that is fitted to grasp it, because of its kinship with it, and that, once getting near what really is and having intercourse with it and having begotten understanding and truth, he knows, truly lives, is nourished—at that point, and not before—is relieved from the pains of giving birth. (1997c, 490a–b)

The reasoning part of the soul is driven by erotic desire to realize a prior "kinship" between soul and reality. This mimesis *produces* understanding as its effect, as its child, with all the pains of childbirth, but in the end, as an overcoming of bodily suffering. It is a delirious, procreative and entirely joyful event of one's inner divinity realized. The concept of affective desire links the philosopher and the lover together, and the sensuous, bodily experience of mimesis effects desire's satisfaction. The classicist Dodds usefully notes that

> Eros has a special importance in Plato's thought as being the one mode of experience which brings together the two natures of man, the divine self and the tethered beast. For Eros is frankly rooted in what man shares with the animals, the physiological impulse of sex (a fact which is unfortunately obscured

> by the persistent modern misuse of the term 'Platonic love'); yet Eros also supplies the dynamic impulse which drives the soul forward in its quest of a satisfaction transcending earthly experience. (1951, 218)

It is true that for Plato, it is to the philosopher's shame that he or she must inhabit him or herself mortally, in "the pollution of the walking sepulchre which we call a body, to which we are bound like an oyster to its shell" (1973, 250).[15] Yet as we've just seen, this *interleaving* of philosophy and Eros shows that the dichotomy of reason–body is transcended in the Platonic, mimetic model of anamnestic experience, which is figured as *standing temporally prior* to the reason–body partitioning of soul. It is from the standpoint of the transcending of this partitioning, transcendence through cosmic remembrance, that subsequently we recognize divine reason as the highest calling. Such remembrance could only be disdained as self-loss by those blinded by the appearance of identities in this world.

Given the foregoing exegesis we can better understand why Habermas castigates Platonic divine mimesis as producing an "ontological illusion of pure theory" (1971, 314). Divine mimesis drives mad the would-be philosopher-king in an experience of self-loss and recovered memory. A philosophic life finds its redemption and just reward in such an experience, and this in turn serves to ground the legitimacy of Plato's appeal in *Republic* that his audience accept philosophers as political rulers. Divine inspiration delivers pure theory into everyday life, and ideal politics can be nothing but the cosmos revisited.

Habermas in his attempt to break with the authority of "pure theory," of metaphysical thinking, targets not merely the other-worldly orientation of Platonic philosophy, but also the *ecstatic* nature of the philosophic experience. For Habermas, the *validity* of philosophic insight must be wrenched free not merely of its anchoring in the divine, but also of its affective character. What I have tried to show so far is that for Plato, the *cause* of self-loss and the ecstatic character of philosophy does not belong to philosophy *as such*, but to mimetic experience as such. Habermas associates Platonic philosophy strictly with disembodied, pure theory, but this is not the full story.

As moderns, "we" cannot simply underscore with Habermas the false claims of pure theory to insist that modern political philosophy should drop the pretense of divinity. Rather, Plato's emphasis on the mimetic experience of the philosopher has a *this-worldly analog* for nonphilosophers. A more prosaic mimesis, like its divine counterpart, entails an ecstatic self-forgetting and a reconciliation of being-with. But this being-with is not divine. It is social, as in being-with-someone-else. Although Habermas may rightly wish to undercut the status of pure theory, it seems to me that sweeping aside pure theory does not thereby clean the slate with respect to producing a new model of thinking and acting for the purposes of social, communicative understanding. Habermas's political philosophy must, in one way or another, deal with Plato's characterization of the ecstatic character of the mimetic experience in prosaic social encounters.

This is made all the more evident when we notice that the achievement of self-realization in mimetic activity accrues not only to the philosopher and to the lover, but belongs to the constellation of issues surrounding mimetic power as such. When we consider later in Sections V and VI of this chapter how mimesis operates within Habermas's own theory of communication, the absence of a recognition of the necessity of affectivity will become glaring. We will be forced to question the plausibility of Habermas's formulation of an affectless argumentative procedure over and against a mimetic power which enacts affectual self-loss and reconstitution of interlocutors *as* participants in the joint activity of understanding.

III. Prosaic Mimesis

In the previous section I highlighted Habermas's disdain for "pure theory," and turned to describe Plato's mythic account of *divine* mimesis for philosophers and lovers in order to illuminate the character of mimesis in the process of identity-formation. As we saw, mimesis does not simply weigh in favor of a *disembodied* rationality, but to the contrary, can require the interaction of both mind and body, although to be sure, to the benefit of a transcendent anamnestic remembrance. The characteristics of mimesis we have so far uncovered emphasize that which depersonalizes and dislocates a person such that he or she is able to more fundamentally realize how or who they already are, and thus produce identity anew. Were we to limit our discussion of mimetic power to *divine* mimesis, as Habermas would wish us to, we might conclude that every mimesis perfects the soul. As an instance of pure theory, then, we could simply dismiss Platonic mimesis in the same way Habermas dismisses metaphysics in general (i.e., through the resources given by the pragmatic, linguistic turn in philosophy, as a fetishization of "pure theory"). But as it turns out, mimesis in Plato is not reserved solely to philosophers and lovers, but belongs to the experience of everyday life. Mimesis belongs to politics as language belongs to meaning.[16] Mimesis not only brings philosophers and lovers to self-realization, but it stands more generally as the key process of identity-formation (and dissolution) in the polis entire. Habermas does not address this "low" aspect of mimesis, conveniently raising his field of vision to the role of mimesis as divine inspiration. We are faced, however, with a broader perspective on mimesis, because in Plato precisely, mimesis operates at multiple levels, and as we shall see, Platonic *politics* rests on the *control* of mimetic power.

A nondivine mimesis, or what we might call *habituated* mimesis, is that process which, in Plato's design, fixes and also threatens the identities of the remaining two social classes of his polis, the guardians and the craftspeople. I have chosen the expression *habituated* because it implies a constitutive power to mold a person such that the imitation can be expressed bodily. Unlike the philosopher who relinquishes the body as he is mimetically possessed by a god, guardians and craftspeople must imitate other people as models, and they do so with voice and/or bodily movement. This imitation can be trivial or comic, as in mimicry, or it can be a mimesis that is formative, making or molding a personality. The crucial difference between extra-worldly and this-worldly models has important political consequences. Although the Forms cannot be imperfect (only our ability to imitate them can be imperfect), Plato worries over this-worldly models because the models themselves are suspect, and furthermore, people are seduced easily into imitating the wrong models, or, more confusedly, many models in turn. The just governance of the Republic turns out to require heightened vigilance over the dissemination of models, which amounts to the regulation of mimetic power. The Platonic state aims to integrate person and polis; mimesis is its integrating process. Plato is particularly wary of mimetic power in the hands of his rivals, the poets, themselves prolific disseminators of imitative models. Plato's elevation of the philosopher to the divine rests on denigrating the employ of mimesis by poets. The question then becomes: Who shall control the mimetic power that permeates the polis, philosophers, or the poets and sophists?

Plato tells us that mimesis is basic to human constitution. He explains that "imitations practiced from youth become part of nature and settle into habits of gesture, voice, and thought" (1997c, 395d).[17] Thus, as to the Republic's guardians, "[i]f they do imitate, they must imitate from childhood only what is appropriate for them, namely, people who are courageous, self-controlled, pious, and free, and their actions" (395c). Why is avoiding bad models so vital? "Lest from enjoying the imitation they should come to be what they imitate" (395d). It is the *pleasure* of imitation that seduces, that turns a temporary imitation into a permanent trait of character. As with the philosopher and lover, so too with Guardians: At stake in the struggle over mimesis is their very being. The affective power of mimesis is here constitutive, and therefore represents for Plato a power that demands control. Human spectacle provides models that can lure even the most disciplined soul from lofty virtue.

In case there is any doubt of the diremptions possible by wrong-headed mimesis, Plato provides a long list (395d–96b) of human models to avoid imitating: A guardian shouldn't imitate a young woman or an old woman, an abusive woman nor a quarreling woman, a bragging woman nor one possessed by sorrows and lamentations, nor a woman who is ill, in love, or in labor. A guardian must not imitate slaves doing slavish things. A guardian must not imitate bad men who are cowards, who are libelous, who use shameful language, who make themselves like madmen in word or deed. A guardian must not imitate metal workers or any craftsmen who are not guardians. A guardian mustn't imitate neighing horses, bellowing bulls, roaring rivers, the crashing sea, thunder, or anything of that sort.

We can, of course, find in this listing much to be offended by, much that rings false—why shouldn't a guardian imitate an old woman? What I wish to emphasize here is limited to the remark that Plato's mode of constituting citizens rests on the emulation of models. What lies behind Plato's proscriptions is the theory that a guardian would become *like* his models. To imitate a madman would make a madman of the imitator. To imitate a bellowing bull would make the imitator like a bellowing bull. Plato worries over the allure of these *deviant* models most of all for their affects on the guardians, that class entrusted with the security of the republic, and the class from which the ruling philosophers will be selected. A guardian must be wary, and because he cannot but imitate, he must imitate only a good man, and indeed, imitate him "as if he were that man himself" (396c). To do otherwise is to irrationally seek one's own unhappiness in the dissolution of one's character.

Not only should a person avoid imitation of bad models, he or she also should avoid imitating *many* models. Each person's well-ordered soul depends on each imitating a single model: "a single individual can't imitate many things as well as he can imitate one. . . . [Thus] he'll hardly be able to pursue any worthwhile way of life while at the same time imitating many things." (394e). This rule of course holds for guardians, the city's protectorate, but applies with no less force to craftspeople who, with an even weaker grip on their desires, are far more prone to imitate many things or imitate the wrong models.

Such proscriptions of *bad* mimesis shore up Plato's elusive definition of justice: "the principle that it is right for someone who is by nature a cobbler to practice cobblery and nothing else, for the carpenter to practice carpentry, and the same for all the others." (443c). In other words, to every person, a single techne, a single art. Why is this justice? Because control of prosaic mimesis allows divine mimesis to order the polis. Where each person works on his or her single craft, his or her ability to aim for the

Real (i.e., the other-worldly) increases, whereas turning away from the distractions in the world of (mere) appearance.

Therefore, we must complicate Habermas's depiction of mimesis in Plato: Plato does not simply advocate mimesis; he advocates the strict ordering of mimesis, and this demands the policing of prosaic mimesis. Where Habermas wishes to open up a definition of justice that respects the principle of democracy, Plato's antidemocratic position restricts his definition of justice such that each citizen pursues, in body and mind, the imitation of a single, appropriate model.

Plato's moral warning with respect to everyday mimetic power is clear: People become what they imitate, so justice demands that each person imitate the one good model appropriate to his or her occupation. Where the philosopher assimilates himself to a god, guardians and craftspeople must assimilate themselves to the models that govern their respective activities. Imitate the other you would be, and you have a good shot at becoming that other. Plato will "admit [into his Republic] only the pure imitator of a decent person" (397d). "Pure imitators" do not emulate models that emerge from the Real so much as singular models of other humans who display virtue in their craft.

With respect to those wrong-headed fools who follow many models, Plato depicts a mimesis gone wild—a scene of ecstatic self-loss, notoriously achieved in a crowd:

> When many of them [slanderers of Sophists (!)] are sitting together in assemblies, courts, theaters, army camps, or in some other public gathering of the crowd, they object very loudly and excessively to some of the things that are said or done and approve others in the same way, shouting and clapping, so that the very rocks and surroundings echo the din of their praise or blame and *double* it. In circumstances like that, what is the effect, as they say, on a young person's heart? What private training can hold out and not be swept away by that kind of praise or blame and be carried by the flood wherever it goes, so that he'll say that the same things are beautiful or ugly as the crowd does, follow the same way of life as they do, and be the same sort of person as they are? (492c, emphasis added)

The crowd employs a mimetic power over the city's callow youth, swaying them to the crowd's judgment. The crowd is like a flood, a force of nature, noisy, excessive, and irresistible—and even nature gives up its independence, the "very rocks and surroundings" obeying and "doubling" the mimetic power of the crowd. Divine possession and the prosaic imitation of good models can redeem; the crowd possesses its members and renders their souls corrupt in its shifting image.[18]

IV. Poetic Mimesis

The image of the crowd raises the issue of thinking the polis as theater, as a forum within which virtuous souls should be enstaged, enstaged within the narratives of philosophers, as models for others to emulate. To safeguard the polis from a proliferation of bad actors via bad models, Plato insists on expunging from the polis their main disseminators, namely, those poets who employ their art mimetically. It is a distinction easily and often missed, but only *mimetic* poets are excommunicated. Poets who orate without mimesis, which is to say, those who practice their art in the proper manner (explained later) are free to stay in the city. I won't detail here Plato's extensive program to purify the *substance* of myths from contradictory and violent lessons—suffice it to say that while it is perfectly clear *for us* that preemptive, content-based censorship is chilling, it is less certain that the *manner* or *style* of delivery of speech should be a cause of political or moral concern.[19] Attention to the *manner* of enunciation provides an important point of contact with the Habermasian program. Habermas shows a keen interest in restricting proper enunciation to sincere illocution within the procedural context of free participation. Habermas and Plato are quite in agreement that politics must attend to the *manner* of speech. It is with respect to the *procedure* of speech where sharp differences between these two emerge. However, this Platonic and Habermasian dichotomy between manner and procedure is too simple, for as I shall now show, the mimetic *manner* of speech is proscribed because it relies on *affect* to seduce its audience. Mimesis trumps procedural differentiation; it moves to close the gap between speaker and listener. When we see below that Habermas's procedure of dialogue relies on mimetic role-switching, we shall understand that the affectivity of speech that Plato and Habermas both condemn as immoral (Habermas's *perlocution*) crowds back into the space from which it was exorcized via Habermas's procedure of speech.

Plato (1997c, 392c–94c) explains that there are three manners or styles of poetic diction: simple narrative, mimesis, and a combination of the two. The *first* manner of speech, simple narrative, is delivered in second-person prose, as in a calm utterance: "He said, 'I will fight you to the death.'" In the *second* manner of speech, unlike in simple narrative, the mimetic actor will yell, "I will fight you to the death!" in an angry tone, waving his arms menacingly. Mimetic narrative requires a poet-actor who speaks using the voice and bodily gestures of another person. He will mime the role of another and speak in the first person, hiding himself and becoming another, reveling in the appearance of another, and making that appearance seem presently real. The *third* manner of poetic diction, the mixed style, posits a speaker who will alternate consecutively between the first two manners of speech.[20]

Plato proscribes the mimetic delivery of poetry ultimately for the same reasons that he insists that every person imitate a single model: The justice of the city and, correspondingly, of each person's soul depends on it. A mimetic poet cannot follow the one man/one techne/one model rule for the simple fact that actors trade on their ability to violate the one man/one techne/one model rule. Poet-actors by occupation take on many roles, but by virtue of that fact, do none of them well. If an actor were to portray, say, a sea captain, he would not thereby be able to steer a ship; playing a military leader does not authorize him to lead armies. The poet can only take on the appearance of these activities, for he "has no worthwhile knowledge of the things he imitates" (1997c, 602b). He is thrice removed from knowledge, aiming to make appear an image of an image of truth. What makes this effort so disreputable for Plato is that the poet-actor has no wish to become like that which he imitates. He mimes the motions of a warrior without any real courage to engage in battle. He toys with the structure of truth and virtue, trading on the mimetic power invoked in his speeches and actions while insulating himself from its consequences, and indeed, showing that mimesis itself can be toyed with. The lesson poets teach—scurrilous from Plato's position—is that one can play at emotion without being affected. Indeed, success for the poet does not hinge on whether he employs *knowledge* or *is* virtuous, but rather on whether through making the semblance of truth and virtue appear, he can stimulate his audience into feeling what they would feel were they to encounter truth or virtue in reality. Thus he encourages audience members to play at mimesis, at false feeling which they can take to be true, deliberately bracketing the falsity in their enjoyment of the true remembrance of the emotion brought to immediate presence.

Of course, a poet's affective power to stimulate his audience has nothing to do with whether the poet can successfully steer a ship or lead men to war. Indeed, poets don't aim to steer ships; the semblance of knowledge or courage will suffice. What then is to be gained by Plato's judgment against them, that they would make poor pilots and poor generals? Well, one may ask of the poets: What is the utility of presenting imitations beyond the bounds of knowledge? What is the purpose of artistic presentation, and to what end should mimetic power be put?

In Plato's judgment, the mimetic poet is guilty of pure simulation, a mimesis with disintegrative effects. The poet calls out the appearance, but evades the reality, of all that he imitates. The poet's soul as a consequence becomes thinned out, disordered, scattered, fully corrupted.[21] The poet's mimetic power is a non-self-identical *pantomimesis*, the imitation of the mere appearance of many things, a resounding chamber, a cacophony. The poet holds out the promise that one's soul can be stimulated but unaffected constitutively by art—a disinterested spectator, a temporary drunk without a hangover. Plato's thesis is that the poets are wrong; mimetic power makes or breaks the inner harmony of the soul. (Simulation becomes assimilation, which is why Plato recommends his own mimesis claimed to aid the constitution of a single and self-identical soul resonating anamnestically with the Real.) Poets, then, either underemphasize their power or they are reckless in not reining it in.

The damage, however, is not limited to the poet's own soul, for the poet does his work on stage, and embodies a model for the audience, a model to be communicated, to be imitated. The better he is, the worse he is, for he corrupts the audience. The disorder of the poet through public performance spreads disorder resounding through the polis. In Plato's account,

> [e]ven the best of us hear Homer or some other tragedian imitating one of the heroes sorrowing and making a long lamenting speech or singing and beating his breast, you know that we enjoy it, give ourselves up to following it, sympathize with the hero, take his suffering seriously, and praise as a good poet the one who affects us most in this way. (1997c, 605c–d)

Mimetic poets have a special talent to affect their audience, and so they pose a special threat within Plato's system where justice depends on the right imitation of the right models. The successful pantomime aims at an affectual cathexis between the images he embodies and the audience. The audience identifies and sympathizes with the poet's roles on stage and gets caught up in the action.[22] The mimetic poet has the power to *possess* his audience, and, given the content of most plays, Plato insists, such imitations bring out the worst in the viewers:

> in the case of sex, anger, and all the desires, pleasures, and pains that we say accompany all our actions, poetic imitation has the very same effect on us. It nurtures and waters them and establishes them as rulers in us when they ought to wither and be ruled, for that way we'll become better and happier rather than worse and more wretched. (1997c, 606d)

As Athens condemned Socrates for corrupting the youth, so too Plato in his fictional Republic charges the mimetic poets for corrupting citizens:

"an imitative poet puts a bad constitution in the soul of each individual by making images that are far removed from the truth and by gratifying the irrational part" (606d). Indeed, "with a few rare exceptions [mimesis] is able to corrupt even decent people" (605c). Affect operates like a contagion, spreading from stage to household; distinctions between fiction and fact, appearance and Reality give way to passions' discord (436–47): "if we let our pity for the misfortunes of [the characters on stage] grow too strong it will be difficult to restrain our feelings in our own" private affairs. The mimetic power of the actor is not limited to the theater, but resonates through the polis entire.

V. The Manner of Mimesis

The foregoing analysis has shown that Plato's prohibition of the dissemination of bad models and pantomimesis shores up his general mimetic theory forming an internally harmonious psyche and state, that each person "becomes who he is" by imitating a single (good) model. By imitating many models, a person becomes a chaotic force, dangerous to him or herself and the polis. At stake lies the soul of both citizen and polis, mimetically doubled in one another, anchored by the mimetic relationship of the philosopher to the divine. Against Habermas, mimesis in Plato is not merely a myth of divinity made incarnate by the work of philosophy. For Plato, prosaic mimesis is about connection, infection, repetition, performance, formation, and the risk for deformation. It can integrate; it can disintegrate. The experience of mimesis brings to presence the truth of the other in the imitation, but such mimesis can be engaged in for prurient ends, and this Plato finds dangerous. The battle over the control of mimetic powers—what Plato (1997c, 607b) calls already the "old quarrel between poetry and philosophy"—is political in the most genuine sense, for it effects the character of belonging.

With this analysis established, we now can turn squarely to Habermas's theory of communicative action. The remainder of this chapter will set up Habermas's general program, detail communicative action as a modern rendering of mimesis on a rational basis, and begin to probe the consequences. My major interpretive claim will be that Habermas champions what Plato denigrates—an everyday pantomimesis. The question to pose, then, is: Can communicative action perform the political work of Platonic mimesis without the antidemocratic politics of the *Republic*? Can Habermasian mimesis produce both truth and political solidarity without throwing mimetic subjects into the soul-chaos Plato fears? In other words, can Habermasian mimesis ground a genuinely democratic politics, or does he vindicate Plato's antidemocratic politics? Can Habermas's discourse ethics meet the Platonic objection that pantomimesis writ large leads to relativism and political chaos?

Jürgen Habermas remains one of the few political philosophers who stalwartly claims the defense of the best intentions of the Enlightenment. As I indicated in the introduction, the modern age's release from a binding faith in an extra-worldly, singular guarantor of ethics (God) and rightness (Truth) presents at once the impetus and most serious of obstacles to Habermas's efforts. Habermas resolutely shares with postmodern philosophy the conviction that the philosophical environment in which "us" moderns make and keep our commitments—political alliances, heartfelt beliefs, moral obligations—stands or falls without the benefit of an everlasting, true, extra-worldly source of value and Good. A Platonic myth of the Forms inspires no one. If philosophy is to have any role at present, it cannot pretend to divine wisdom, nor refer knowledge to a dogma of faith. Reason is not God-given, and yet reason *in* language marks off for humans a *postmetaphysical* resource for coming to terms with perennial questions of the nature of morality, self, and political solidarity. Put somewhat more faithfully, Habermas is wedded to a modernization meta-narrative in intellectual history that begins with Plato but moves secularly through Kant and Hegel to a young Marx, and to the linguistic turn at the beginning of the twentieth century, coupled with the American pragmatism of George Herbert Mead. Habermas takes what Hannah Arendt called "the rise of the social" (Arendt 1958) and the decline of authority (1961) as the basic condition of current political philosophy. Although Habermas concurs with more aporetic philosophers that modern philosophy cannot lead humanity toward an already existing Truth, he nevertheless postulates that *reason*, reconsidered as located *in* the world, *in* human history, remains as a necessary resource for normative guidance in social and political relations.

Habermas's response to our modern condition relies on a positive normative program based on a new conception of rationality in speech-acts. In an attempt to outmaneuver moral and cognitive relativism, he argues that *intersubjective* understanding harbors its own foundation for moral life, a foundation located *in the grammar and manner of argumentation itself*. It is his emphasis on the *manner* of argumentation in which we can locate the trace of Plato's restrictions on pantomimetic poets. As we shall see, where Plato delimits the style of poetic delivery to simple narrative, excommunicating mimetic poets, so too Habermas delimits the manner of speech for the purposes of coming to understanding. The difference between the two models—and it is an intriguing one—is that where Plato orients each soul to mime one model, and ideally the cosmos, Habermas has each soul mime every other soul, but *through argument*, and therefore according to ideal rules of speech endemic to a process of reaching understanding. This difference proves decisive for evaluating the consequences of communicative action carried out mimetically.

Habermas argues that the possibility for modern morality in political life is located at the smallest unit of human interaction, in conversation. It is via language that ethical and moral priorities are determined, and people become who they are. Language has its own intrinsic norms which emerge whenever people speak with one another for the purposes of understanding, and it is on the basis of meeting the demands of speech norms that, procedurally speaking, the justice of speech encounters can be assured.[23] Anderson (1983, 63) notes that for Habermas, "[l]anguage . . . becomes, not merely the hallmark of humanity as such, but the promissory note of democracy—itself conceived as essentially the communication necessary to arrive at a consensual truth." Where in Plato, justice took the form of the mimetic reduplication of models and man, a turning from the many to the one, as it were, justice in Habermas requires democratic participation, where consensus implies an agreement that does not eliminate but rather preserves the existential differences between speakers, for "only with a consciousness of their absolute differences and irreplaceability can the one recognize himself in the other" (Habermas 1992d, 48).

Habermas's analysis of communication begins with the observation that human activity can be divided into two types. The first implies technical mastery, and the second an open-ended, nondominative interaction.[24] We should locate the normative resources for the soul-producing aspect of communication (comparable to the role of divine imitation on the Platonic model) in the latter and not the former. Aiming at technical mastery implies the instrumental use of others for the purposes of achieving a predetermined goal. In the second mode of activity, by way of contrast, interlocutors treat one another as partners in a common, open-ended project, as friends or peers.[25] We should recognize in this distinction a Kantian imperative to treat people as ends and not means. This distinction also carries a Marxian objection to reification. Habermas in fact would reformulate the concept of reification such that it arises as an aspect of *distorted* communication. Undistorted communication turns on the character of the relation between speakers. Good communication allows a person to be *motivated* by reasons rather than *influenced* by the persuasive rhetoric of the speaker. As Habermas puts it:

> Whereas in strategic action one actor seeks to *influence* the behavior of another by means of the threat of sanctions or the prospect of gratification in order to *cause* the interaction to continue as the first actor desires, in communicative action

> one actor seeks to rationally *motivate* another by relying on the illocutionary binding/bonding effect (*Bindungseffekt*) of the offer contained in his speech act. (1990, 58)

In this distinction between *causation* and *motivation*, Habermas provides his own Platonic demarcation of rhetoric from rational speech. Habermas wishes to delimit the normative standard for those soul-producing communicative moments to simple narrative, to the expression of reasons and the sincere recounting of whatever tacit knowledge seems necessary to shore up grounds for mutual understanding. To *this* extent, Habermas is an anti-mimetic thinker: He fears what he calls (after John Austin and John Searle) the *perlocutive* or manipulative element in speech, from which distorted truths, social relations and self-perceptions emerge.[26] However, as we shall see in Section VI of this chapter, and in Chapter 3, Habermas postulates a theory of *mimetic role-switching* as *the* process of coming to understanding. It is a question as to whether he can have this cake and eat it (too), whether he can endorse imitation writ large and avoid resuscitating Plato's fearful account of the consequences.

Notice in the passage just cited that *motivation* relies on what Habermas calls a binding/bonding effect, the *Bindungseffekt*.[27] This effect is crucial in underscoring the *continuity* between mimetic power in Plato and mimetic power in Habermas. This concept is the fundamental metaphor that denotes the mystery whereby rational arguments contain any force at all. Where Plato worried over the poet's power to entrance his audience, Habermas must show that the everyday mimesis in communication can carry the power of entrancement *without* the trance. Habermas explains his hypothesis, that

> [t]he disenchantment and disempowering of the domain of the sacred takes place by way of a linguistification of the ritually secured, basic normative agreement; going along with this is a release of the rationality potential in communicative action. The aura of rapture and terror that emanates from the sacred, the *spellbinding* power of the holy, is sublimated into the *binding/bonding* force of criticizable validity claims and at the same time turned into an everyday occurrence. (1987a, 77)

What should be questioned here is the character of this "sublimation." The word religion, after all, derives etymologically from the Latin *ligāre*, which means to tie or bind, as in a ligament: Religion means to bind once again. The *power* of the modern *Bindungseffekt* is drawn from the dispersal of religious power made defunct by reflection. Rationality has killed God, but has stolen some sacred fire for itself. The *Bindungseffekt* is the modern form of ritualized, sacred, mythic aura[28] turned into rather trivial, everyday, and ubiquitous interaction.[29] The achievement of understanding does not take its binding power from God, and yet the affectual *experience* of participating in communicative action derives from sacred origins. The spellbinding power of rational discussion—we've all felt it, no?—can be no less overwhelming, but its *force*, Habermas insists, must arrive via *rational procedure, via intersubjective agreement.* This is not the cosmos revisited; it is democratic experience imprinted—in the activity of argument and understanding. At the level of the experiencing subject, individuals participate in communicative action, such that they "*bind their wills* and are thus able to enter into obligations" (1998d, 324). This self-binding self is Habermas's analog to Kant's moral actor, who freely chooses to act according to good will alone.[30] It is a genuine question, however, whether or not Habermas's explicit account of the subject of discourse can bear unrevised Kantian autonomy.[31]

VI. The Grammar of Mimesis

The refining of mimesis then—the elimination of its entrancing powers—depends on rational procedure and intersubjective agreement. But the procedure, it turns out, is nothing less than pantomimesis, and a pantomimesis that is an *unavoidable* and *necessary* feature of ideal discussion, for the illocutionary *Bindungseffekt*, Habermas says, "is rooted in the *mimetic act of role-taking*—that is, in ego's making his own the expectations that alter directs to him" (1984, 390, emphasis added). The onus, then, is on Habermas to provide arguments that defend against the Platonic charge that democratic pantomimesis would fragment the polis and the soul into incoherency, civil war.

To address this issue, it is important to notice with some precision how Habermas characterizes the activity of communication, this "mimetic role-taking." Habermas tells us:

> The telos of reaching understanding, inherent in linguistic structures, compels the communicative actors to alter their perspective; this finds expression in the necessity of going from the objectivating attitude of success-oriented action, which seeks to *effect* something in the world, over to the performative attitude of a speaker who seeks to *reach an understanding* with a second person about something. (1992d, 81)

The open-ended, nondominative form of communicative interaction—of presenting in simple narrative the arguments as well as the tacit foreknowledge necessary to ensure one's interlocutor's uptake—therefore, demands also a "performative attitude." Mimetic role-taking is *the* process that enables a competent speaker—indeed, it in part *defines* competency—to disassociate oneself from one's own quasi-natural contextualized identifications such that one can understand another's expectations of oneself. This mimetic process endemic to discourse constitutes the self-same condition necessary for humans to understand a "*pluralism of ultimate value orientations*" (1990, 76). This pluralist, democratic vision is intended to infect the soul, to produce democratic souls via pantomimesis. Habermas has done nothing but put a positive evaluation on the practice of pantomimesis. Of course, Plato fears the resultant chaos; Habermas believes the potential chaos of pantomimesis can be risked, because it may be reined in by the adherence to the norms of speech themselves.

We should notice here that although the *Bindungseffekt* is supposed to carry the weight formerly assigned to the power of religious, sacred aura, in Habermas's account none of the *affect* is borne by the *effect*. What deracinates this effect? Habermas's theory posits a decentered subjectivity as the result of pantomimetic, norm-governed speech-acts, but where is the talk of the ecstasy of insight so prevalent in Plato's mimetic myth, for philosophers and lovers no less than for poets and cobblers? The parallels between Plato and Habermas end at this point. We would like for Habermas to provide a discussion of the *internal character* of a modern pantomimesis. What is it like to *experience* the multiple role-switching? What is it like to overcome one's quasi-natural socialization and move to a higher or wider plane of identity and identification, of individuation? If the vital power of communicative action is transformative and productive, as "the medium for the reproduction of lifeworlds" (Habermas 1984, 353), then it seems unavoidable to address how speech participants are affected in their performative and thus creative attitudes. I would cite Habermas's language on the issue, but unfortunately none exists, as he studiously avoids an aesthetic description of the process of coming to postconventional, pantomimetic consciousness. Habermas needs an aesthetic vocabulary in order to capture the experience of communicative action insofar as ideal speech depends on the "orientation" of speakers toward understanding, that is, on a "dispositional" rather than a "non-dispositional account of reason."[32] Habermas delivers only the thinnest account of the *experience* of pantomimetic role-taking, an account that draws our attention to just two formal features: the grammar of the speech situation, and the norm that governs the giving and acceptance of reasons.[33]

The grammar of understanding involves the three pronouns necessary: I, you, and he or she or they; or alternatively, ego, alter, and the generalized other. These are three irreducible speaking positions implied in all speech, and they are the three perspectives that a speaker must be able to figuratively occupy in order to successfully engage in communicative action. This tripartite model is strictly a formal accounting mechanism. As Bowie writes:

> grammatical structures can only be said to direct activity, not to constitute the activity itself: the refusal [of Habermas] to acknowledge this threatens to lead to a reified linguistic idealism, in which the transcendentalised structures of language are themselves the determining factor, rather than one aspect of a more complex process of world-constitution. (1999, 381)

What it may mean for me to take the position of another, what it might mean to *understand* in the way another does—Habermas does not say. What could it mean, for example, to "make another's expectations my own"? How do we characterize this mimetic shifting of perspective *for* communicative action?

The grammar of pronouns does aim to achieve for Habermas one defense against polymimeticism's power to dissolve selves into their identifications. Recall (in Section II) that for Plato the philosopher and lover participated in the God. This kind of archaic narrative aims at communion and being-with. Grammar for Habermas indicates an irreducibility of linguistic subject-positions, such that even when a person takes the attitude of another, his or her own self does not disappear: "The grammatical role of the personal pronouns forces the speaker and the hearer to adopt a performative attitude in which the one confronts the other as *alter ego*" (1992d, 48). The different speaking/hearing positions are irreducible, and are structurally preserved. Habermas does not address the fact that for "strong agreement" (1998d, 320 ff.),[34] the fact that different subject positions are preserved formally hardly matters—which of course is the point. Grammatical differentiation is not precisely suspended, but, perhaps, as Gadamer (1989, 125–26) characterizes experience, speakers achieve not a "mere negation" but a "positive . . . self-forgetfulness" for the purpose of understanding. It is quite strange and misleading, in fact, that Habermas should insist on just this point, of grammar over experience, for he has argued strenuously that the presumed objectivity of a neutral observer *must* give way to the *performative* position of a participant; and yet only from a nonparticipant's view will the grammatical distantiation prove decisive. It must be said that from the internal, esoteric perspective of agreement, grammatical distinction loses its purchase. The attention to grammar requires a concomitant intersubjectivist phenomenology to explain how understanding might be brought into being.

Habermas's second characterization of speech involves the normative principle that governs the morality of linguistic interchange. For this,

Habermas offers up a signal improvement over Kant's categorical imperative, namely, principle (U) defined this way: "For a norm to be valid, the consequences and side effects that its *general* observance can be expected to have for the satisfaction of the particular interests of *each* person affected must be such that *all* affected can accept them freely" (1990, 120).[35] (U) is "intended to compel the *universal exchange of roles*" (1990, 65), and to govern the grammar of the interchange. Improving on Kant's categorical imperative, this universalization principle is to operate not simply as a monological *projection* of one subject's views onto others, but rather takes place within *actual* conversation, for "only through the communicative structure of a moral argumentation involving *all* those affected is the *exchange of roles* of each with every other forced upon us" (1982, 257). For my purposes, however, what I wish to emphasize, on the one hand, is that communicative action under (U) *requires* the exchange of subject positions (i.e., pantomimesis). On the other hand, Habermas's discussion is strictly formal, speaking to the structure of communication and saying nothing of the experience of communication. Habermas depicts the event of communication as procedural; mimetic role-taking amounts to stimulating a mere "yes" or "no" response to whatever is being discussed. This yes/no position shows up repeatedly in Habermas's writing as the gut response in the uptake of reasons.[36] There is a banality of affect to which Habermas aspires when depicting the creation of meaning in communicative action:

> every factually raised claim to validity that transcends the limits of a given lifeworld generates a new fact with the "yes" and "no" responses to its addressees. Mediated by this cognitive-linguistic infrastructure of society, the results of the interplay between inner-worldly learning processes and world-disclosing innovations become sedimented [in social reality]. (1993a, 165)

What is covered over in this depiction of creation—"world-disclosing innovation"—without affect? What is involved in the "sedimentation" of world-disclosing innovation? And, what are the consequences for casting the aims of communicative action not as critically active understanding but rather as sedimentation, that is, as forgetting, a settling into the terrain of, shall we call it, common sense?

VII. Toward the Affective Bond of Understanding

Plato defines (a nondivine) mimesis as acting like another, either in gesture or voice. His politics centers on regulating mimesis to ensure that citizens follow the right models and are protected from exposure to the wrong ones. Mimesis directs souls outward, toward others, toward models. Should a citizen imitate many models, the soul turns chaotic Plato fears pantomimesis writ large and therefore expels its practitioners from the Republic. Each citizen needs the model appropriate for him or her. Plato accepts and is not threatened by the experience of ecstatic self-loss as long as each citizen's rapture is stimulated in the right way by the right model. One man, one techne, one model. Justice.

Habermas's universal role-taking is nothing but Plato's horror and scourge, pantomimesis writ large. Habermas shifts the ground of justice toward a pantomimic model of interaction. Decentering, so long as (U) applies, reaches toward a democratic model of justice, because every person potentially affected by the discussion will have a say. Habermas tries to *save* his version of mimesis not through *external* (social) control (as in Plato's control over myths and poets) but *immanently* by way of a pragmatics of communication, by arguing that the mimetic contact is in fact a mimetic contract, mediated through and governed by language that itself warrants the promise of order and structurally preserves different subject-positions. What Habermas fears in the Platonic cultic scene of exuberance is, in his own mimetic model, sublated into sociation and rational language use. Interlocutors achieve mutual recognition in submission to the light of norms applied. Where Plato could indulge in a mythic scene of possession, Habermas resorts to a ubiquitous role-playing under the formal principle (U). Habermas raises the Platonic vice of pantomimesis into a modern, democratic virtue, a modern definition of political legitimacy.

Plato wrote that mimesis writ large would devolve into rule by the shifting crowd. A civil war of the soul would find its counterpart in bloody civil war and the rule of tyrants. Habermas hopes to evade this damning verdict on pantomimesis because he has introduced into language itself validity claims, and into the soul an openness suitable to and characteristic of modernity. Certainly civil war is a possible outcome of democratic public deliberation conducted by democratic souls, but only when (U) is violated. Habermas's hope is that validity claims will be redeemed. The role-taking game of democratic speech need not result in chaos; it also aims at a kind of universal community resulting in more and not less social justice.

If the pantomimetic procedure is necessary for Habermas's communicative action, then in what sense do speech norms *govern* pantomimesis? I have suggested that the speech norms are *not* immanent to the experience of communication for they operate at a purely formal, abstract level. Communicative action claims not only to constrain identity-forming power, but also to subtend an ability to preserve *critical* distance, such that speech participants are not seduced by speech, but rather adopt another's reasons as their own *without force*, or rather, with the unforced force of the better argument. Plato's habituated mimesis is closer to a trance-like hypnotic suggestion in that no critical consciousness exists *within* the mimetic relation. Consider, for example, the parting words in *Crito* (1997, 54d) where Socrates gladly accedes to his death sentence because the Law's whisperings ring "as the Corybants seem to hear the music of their flutes, and the echo of these words resounds in [him], and makes it impossible for [him] to hear anything else."[37] The trance of the Laws prevents Socrates from living the examined life; indeed, the State's mimetic snare ensures his death.[38]

It seems to me that Habermas implicitly distinguishes the mimetic *procedure* of the speech-act (role-playing) from the mimetic power (*Bindungseffekt*) inside of it, and withholds an account of what occurs within the event of understanding. It is my contention, and my main contribution, if I have one to offer in this text to this point, that principle (U) can govern *how* humans come together in language, but it does not penetrate the *how* of understanding. What occurs within the event of understanding? Principle (U) may obliquely govern an abstract model where *I* takes the position of *alter* and vice versa, but it cannot govern in any sense the transformation of speech-participants that ensues. Once speech-participants stand at ease within the space of coming to understanding, the action of communication takes place anew, as it were. Habermas has advanced a postmetaphysical position. His model does not permit speech norms to exist *a priori*; rather, they emerge each time anew from any given pantomimetic encounter. We therefore reach an extraordinary conclusion: the mimesis of understanding takes place in a different register of experience than the rules that govern the joining to conversation.

To be sure, Habermas is correct when he says "existential self-understanding is evaluative in its core" and depends on "two components":

> the descriptive component of the ontogenesis of the ego and the normative component of the ego-ideal. Hence, the clarification of one's self-understanding or the clinical reassurance of one's identity calls for an *appropriative* form of understanding—the appropriation of one's own life history and the traditions and circumstances of life that have shaped one's process of development. (1993a, 5)

To the extent that a transformation of speaking subjects happens *in* language, speech norms must be permanently *external* to understanding, whereas the mode of "appropriation" of one's own life history occurs quite differently. Is this mode of appropriation rather like the Hobbesian covenant, the "let us make man" fiat echoing the procreative power of God? Or, is it like the Kantian mode of moral respect where Will posits a moral law that it then obeys *as if* the law preexisted one's own utterance of it? We may usefully think of Habermas's model of communication as producing a post hoc fence *around* the mimetic moment, and on this account, the mimetic moment—which in Plato characterized that divine madness out of which insight arose—remains intractable to governance, because we are establishing an affectual bond. That it occurs in the medium of language does not mean that it is induced by the satisfaction of speech norms, nor confirmed in its validity in any but a post hoc, critical exercise. Habermas's explication of his normative model doesn't incorporate the affectivity that it presumes to regulate, and does not link affectivity to the production of the normative fence that surrounds it. This is a mistake.[39] If communicative action is supposed to bear the brunt of the work for the replenishing of meaning in the world, it seems ripe for exuberance and creative power. If we wish to reconstruct Habermas's model of the event of creative transformation in understanding, then more work needs to be done to show how the articulation of the form of communication meshes *with* and does not simply stand apart from meaningful action. In short, communicative action needs a better account than Habermas provides of the nonsubjectivist, mimetic-appropriative, world-disclosing power of language, one that can accommodate an affective power that is not viewed reductively as private and privative, but as genuinely intersubjective.

Dews wonders, "whether it can be anything but political caution which prevents Habermas from admitting that philosophy, too, [as with religion] may have a certain autonomous contact with the 'extraordinary,' and tap into the ultimate sources of meaning" (1995b, 210). Gadamer notes: "If revelation allows itself to be completely encompassed by thinking reason, then it forfeits its religious binding force" (1992, 160). Of what gluten is the binding force in communicative action?

In 1972, Habermas suggested an intention to "enlist the services of Benjamin's theory of experience" (1988, 120). That theory of experience, he argued, was not involved in ideology critique (a view Adorno wrongfully projected onto Benjamin) but instead held that primary experience lived out its memory in *language*, and that via a "mimetic faculty" even suffering moderns could "tap into" this raw experience of language.[40] Both Habermas and Benjamin worry over the depletion of meaning in the modern world. Habermas's explicit formalism and self-explication as standing against the irrational exuberance of archaic mimetic theories should not, I think, blind us to the mimetic structure that, as I have attempted to show in this chapter, and will articulate further in the next, belongs *as such* to communicative action. The principle *value* of communicative action is that it allows for the *production* of new meaning over and against strategic action that merely rearranges resources on the basis of preexisting "interests." Communicative action is formulated to *replenish* and nurture the stock of meaning. In this capacity, the *experience* of mimesis takes its modern form in the linguistification of the sacred. Habermas's theory of communication holds out hope in a *rationally* mimetic procedure for the production of social bonds; for his theory to be convincing, an account of affect, of which Habermas is largely silent, must be elaborated. The aesthetic aspect of communication has been omitted to the benefit of describing its formal, cognitive element, and Habermas's theory, I'd argue, requires a rethinking of the affective element of mimesis. For communicative rationality to prove effective as an account of ideal speech, we must think through how to draw within it a nonsubjectivistic theory of the affective bond.

The mimetic character of communicative rationality can be clarified if we ask: *Who* is the subject of discourse, and how is the *who* put into effect by the process of role-switching in communicative action? This investigation will be made possible by tracing Habermas's concept of the self to its source in the social interactionist theory of the American pragmatist, George Herbert Mead. In the next chapter, we shall see that Mead, too, struggles with and against mimesis, and is troubled by the *affective power* of communicative rationality.

Chapter 3

The Subject in Communicative Action

Habermas and George Herbert Mead

> The author, the artist, must have his audience; it may be an audience that belongs to posterity, but there must be an audience.
>
> —George Herbert Mead (1934, 324)

As we saw in Chapters 1 and 2, Habermas posits communicative rationality as a moral alternative to *mimetic power*. These two modes of interaction are asymmetrically opposed in Habermas's account because communicative rationality requires that speech participants retain a decisive autonomy to make reflectively conscious, moral decisions, to participate in communicative action on the basis of principle (U). Habermas follows Kant's definition of autonomy: the subjective freedom to willfully bind oneself morally.[1] Mimesis, to the contrary, would seem to describe a state of possession, the substitution of conscious autonomy for the authority of another, an unconscious submission, or, in an active sense, to act as another, to speak in another's voice, to imitate body and gesture, such that this masquerade could, in time, become one's own gesture, one's own voice. We saw that for Plato, mimesis cannot be done away with. It is endemic to education for children, but also throughout the course of a human life:

There is no replacing mimesis by self-sufficiency,[2] for the proper care of the soul by the philosopher, the lover, the citizen comes through dialectic that demands an affective submission before a model. It is a directed and disciplined mimesis that Plato advocates. Plato demands that political institutions and authority limit and focus mimesis, not excommunicate it. Plato expels mimetic poets so as to reserve the control of mimesis for philosophers.

Although Plato's mythic formulation of mimesis in *Phaedrus* links erotic love, philosophy, and recovered memory of perfect Forms, Habermas's mimesis, as I construe communicative action, does not seek to recover nor reproduce a mimetic unity in Forms, but rather, it works through language to pragmatically bring about shared understanding. Habermas wishes to grant the status of rationality to the process of coming to understanding. As I have stated, it is my intention to challenge Habermas's self-understanding, not to dismiss communicative action's rational aspect, but to put into question Habermas's rhetorical move of strictly opposing communicative rationality to mimesis, and thereby to question the nature of rationality anew.

Rationality and mimesis stand opposed only from the vantage of the philosophy of the subject. Habermas's paradigm shift (from subjective reason to communicative reason), which takes as its object of analysis the intersubjective, pragmatic use of language, actually works to overcome the opposition between rationality and mimesis, such that self-consciousness admits mimetism as its mode of becoming. Habermas's philosophical apparatus points in this direction, yet he remains stubbornly insistent in wishing to disarticulate reason from mimetic power.

The question we must pose to Habermas is whether the paradigm shift from the philosophy of consciousness to intersubjectivity can, as he wishes it might, stave off the sacrifice of submission and self-loss characteristic of the mimesis he condemns. Habermas insists that it must, for he puts great emphasis on the autonomy of will in the application of moral insight. Identity-formation through self-loss characterizes traditional views of mimetic power. These characteristics pose problems for the demands of Habermas's critical theory: of vigilance and resistance to the claims of dogmatic authority, of reasoned argument against a mimesis conceived of as submission to aesthetic spectacle. Divine and aesthetic mimesis swamps autonomy and yields a concept of reason akin to myth, a surrender to other-worldly authority.

Divine mimesis to the side, it is a *prosaic* pantomimesis that Plato condemns and Habermas endorses. As we saw in Chapter 2, for Plato, pantomimesis is the mode of being of the protean soul. Does Habermas's turn away from divine mimesis run him into the arms of Proteus? If, as

I argued above, principle (U) stands in an *external* relation to the event of understanding in communicative action, then what happens within the actual process of taking the attitude of the other—within the fence (U) provides, but uninflected content-wise by its conceptual clarity and moral rectitude? Is Plato's worry indeed justified, or is there something that is neither metaphysical like the Forms, nor quasi-metaphysical like (U), which nonetheless prevents selves in communication from unraveling in pantomimetic distraction?

I argued in Chapter 2 that for pantomime to produce understanding, the formal modeling of grammatical jump-shifting that Habermas develops is necessary but insufficient. More must be added to make the case that participation can produce understanding, and in particular, participation via the procedure of "taking the attitude of the other," to use Mead's felicitous phrase that Habermas adopts. For a normative projection implicit in every actual, lived conversation to yield agreement on validity claims—whether this agreement is strong or mere understanding[3]—the procedural rules of argument would not only have to be followed in an abstract way, but also *experienced* by speaking subjects. In this chapter, the guiding impulse is to show how Habermas arrives at his notion of role-switching as the process of interlocution, and to press a bit on what it would mean to take up a second-person perspective, and similarly, to take the position of the "generalized other," that third-person perspective whose interests represent so-called universalizable interests.[4]

To investigate Habermas's theory of the self and the practice of role-switching, we must turn to his source, Mead. I will show that the trouble with mimesis and aesthetic experience is already present in Mead's work and thus troubles Habermas's appropriation of Mead's thought. Mead himself desperately wishes to avoid attributing a theory of imitation to rational conduct, but in the end, I will argue, cannot, and neither can Habermas. Sections I to III present Mead's general program; Sections IV to VI present an immanent critique of Mead, with my own agenda gradually coming to the fore; Section VII elaborates Habermas's appropriation of Mead. As we shall see, Habermas ultimately rejects the signal way that Mead tries to preserve the distance between a self and his social identifications, and consequently is forced to think within a field of mimesis rather than over and against it.

I. Two Phases of the Self: I and Me

Writing and lecturing at the University of Chicago for thirty-five years until shortly before his death in 1931, George Herbert Mead pioneered philosophical investigations into social psychology and what came to be known as the field of symbolic interactionism.[5] He is best known for his theory that the self is irredeemably social. Habermas throughout his work is quite explicit in drawing on Mead. He points to Mead as the first to establish linguistically mediated interaction as the basis for social analysis (1987a, 5)—indeed, he flatly states:

> The only promising attempt to grasp the entire significance of social individualization in concepts is, I believe, initiated in the social psychology of George Herbert Mead. (1992a, 151)[6]

Mead formulates his concept of the self against three currents of thought: scientific positivism's reductionism of self to an atomistic subjectivity (at the time represented by behavioralist psychology), the theory of hypnotic-suggestive mimetism (which during the late nineteenth and early twentieth centuries was propagated by one the founders of sociology in France, Gabriel Tarde, in *Laws of Imitation*, which found its parallel in appropriations of Adam Smith's still influential *Theory of Moral Sentiments*),[7] and German Idealism's figure of the Absolute.[8] Against these currents, the Meadian *self* is posited as emerging as a performative effect of generalized role-playing. In light of the previous discussion of Adorno and Plato, we may provisionally view Mead's concept of generalized role-playing as manifestly a social and democratic pantomimesis, against Platonic divine mimesis but also Adorno and Horkheimer's archaic animistic/naturalistic pantomimesis.

For Mead,[9] to say that the self is an effect of social interaction is to assert that the self as such does not appear prior to its socialization, and that the self arises to become itself only by internalizing the attitudes of others toward it. Consciousness is not "a precondition of the social act. The social act is the precondition of it" (1934, 18). Similarly, he writes: "Mind is then a field that is not confined to the individual, much less is [it] located in a brain. Significance belongs to things in their relations to individuals. It does not lie in mental processes which are enclosed within individuals" (1964, 247). Mead defines the self as having two parts, what he calls the "I" and the "me." Mead's *me* is the repository of the social, whereas his *I*, although arising as an effect of social interaction, stands permanently outside the social. The *me* is that part of oneself that comes to formation through the eyes of others.[10] In Mead's words, a person

> enters his own experience as a self or individual, not directly or immediately, not by becoming a subject to himself, but only in so far as he first becomes an object to himself just as other individuals are objects to him or in his experience; and he

> becomes an object to himself only by taking the attitudes of other individuals toward himself within a social environment or context of experience and behavior in which both he and they are involved. (1934, 138)[11]

In this process of self-objectification, that is, of an original and originating decentering in social interaction, a person prior to gaining self-consciousness *first* sees only how others perceive him or her. Only following this initial identification—which is no identification at all, for there is no subject who does the identifying, there is simply the plurality of identifications that come to form a composite syndrome as a view of oneself from others' eyes—does a person develop his or her own objectivating view of him or herself.

To illustrate: One can hear multiple and even conflicting accounts of a person's exploits, but only with another step, that of appropriative recognition, does one realize that yes, that is *me* they are talking about! This second moment, the taking up of a view of oneself as one's *own* view of oneself *is* self-consciousness (and this is the case, however one's own view may, in fact, misrepresent another's view of oneself). One knows how one will act only after one has internalized others' views of oneself; thereafter, and on that basis, one may gauge and avow one's own response. More: for Mead, self-consciousness becomes *rational activity* when one *deliberately* adopts the attitude of others so as to provoke in oneself one's own responsiveness, one's own attitude.

Mead's rendition of rational subjectivity links up with Habermas's postmetaphysics insofar as it breaks with the Hegelian assumptions of an I that splits itself off from itself to then recognize itself in the other.[12] In Mead, the otherwise Hegelian circuit of recognition is held open temporally, and is thereby transformed, for self-consciousness is neither the beginning nor the end of the process. A social interactionist view of the self does not release the self back into itself: It requires the continuous circuiting of interaction, for the social is the medium of the self's appearance. Mead argues explicitly against those who understand Mind as original and so seek the origin or end of Mind. Better for Mead is to perceive the *social process* as the unavoidable medium in which selves take place. From this perspective, a person must simply give up as bad theory the telos of making oneself identical to oneself, and this is so because, for Mead, the self's *me* stands as an object to be encountered in an ongoing social process. Such a self-encounter can take place only with oneself figured as other to oneself in temporal motion, as continually emerging.

Once a person witnesses his or her own self as an object, he or she may indeed take up this object as his or her own, which prompts the question: In taking up *me* as an object, *who* takes it up? The answer to this question supposes a who that does the taking up of one's self-conceptions but that is not itself already subject to those conceptions. This *who* is Mead's *I*. In taking up one's view of oneself from having occupied the position of others, a person becomes cognizant of one's own internally divided self, which is to say, a person knows that his or her whole self cannot one-sidedly be reduced to his or her social identifications. *I* is the other to the socialized *me*.

Having divided the self into two, and further, acknowledging that the socialization process can produce not only a single *me* but multiple *me's—one's self as a plurality, responsive to multiple sets of respondents*—Mead then takes on the burden of explaining how an internally and externally divided self can nonetheless become and remain integrated in its own bearing. When a self is confronted by multiple dissonant interpretations of itself, or conflicting role-expectations, he or she may consciously adopt a self-interpretation, and in so proceeding, author a composite *me* from the position of the *I*. In such circumstances, the *I* does the work of *reconstructing* a sense of *me* as *me* from the material at hand, material produced via the taking up of others' objectifications, anticipating how others might respond to the composite that I creates. The self as split in this way is entirely cognizant that the *me* is fundamentally conventional, not an essence but a product both of circumstance and of one's own reconstructive labor on oneself. The *I*'s reconstructive work is vital ethically insofar as it wins freedom from the social for the *me*, but a me that remains oriented to the fact of social perception or social recognition.

Self-conscious reconstruction, by anticipating the attitude of the other, *is*, for Mead, the essence of rational conduct: "Rational conduct always involves a reflexive reference to self, that is, an indication to the individual of the significances which his actions or gestures have for other individuals" (1934, 122, nt. 29). Whenever a person is thrown into relief as a person and must adopt a conscious attitude toward him or herself, he or she does so by taking up the attitude of others toward him or herself from the vantage of an *I* not exhausted by such identifications. Of course, not all conduct is rational. A person may act automatically (1934, 195), as in taking a leaflet handed to him on the street. Automatic behavior does not force self-consciousness on an activity. Rather, "it is when we take the attitude of the other in making an offer to us that we can express ourselves in accepting or declining such an offer, . . . then the individual appears in his own experience as a self; and until this happens he does not appear as a self" (1934, 194–95). Only when we accept or reject another's gesture with due consideration does the situation shock one's conscious thought to self-awareness. This also means that humans do not simply have selves, like we might have a watch or a grape. A self is an emergent property of self-consciousness that itself is a product of reflective interaction. It arises when worked on, and otherwise, it is not. Like Nietzsche's doer behind the deed, Mead's doer arises when one begins to seek a cause behind an effect. And, it is no less *there* for being posited. Mead, in fact, is trying to reverse our intuitive grasp of these two modes of response: an unthinking response (e.g., taking a leaflet) that we might call a "natural response" Mead will call "automatic": For Mead the gesture is inauthentic (i.e., not natural) insofar as it is the social process working itself out without an actor's self-conscious intervention. In contrast, autonomous behavior is rational, which means for Mead it is authentically generated: A person has staked out a position of individuated freedom vis-à-vis an otherwise socially determined response.

In contrast to the *appearance* of the self, Mead's *I*—that position from which one perceives and claims one's own *me*—is not determinable. When an *I* reaches toward self-determination, it cannot help but posit a *me*, leaving its own ineffability untouched. Thus, the *I* and *me* are not simply two parts of the self. They are different in kind, where the I represents the point of free indeterminacy from which one recognizes and shapes how one may become determined socially.[13] Self-recognition occurs always as a retroactive exercise, the *I* locating its trace in its socially determined *me*. Not unlike Dasein in Heidegger, Mead's *I* is thrown outward, and stands always looking back, even as the entire complex of the self moves forward temporally.[14]

The *I–me* distinction marks the difference between the signature on your passport and the ineffable you who signs it and witnesses retrospectively the ink dry on the paper. If based on your biographical past you have become a scholar or a dancer, your identity emerges from social performance, from learned skills, from habituated conduct that you repeatedly confirm and extend through social interaction. You also may, of course, have your confidence shaken by receiving a bad review, or tripping unintentionally on stage. What concerns Mead is that the person we all know as a dancer ultimately has the freedom, tomorrow, to quit dancing and take up script-writing, or, within the field of dance, to break with convention and create new forms of movement. The creative, unbounded potential in humans resides in the fleeting, fugitive, figureless *I*, not in the socially overdetermined me. Mead has no difficulty associating the *I* with such epoch-changing individuals as "Einstein," but he insists that "[g]reat figures in history . . . are only the extreme expression of the sort of changes that take place steadily through reactions which are not simply those of a 'me' but of an 'I' " (1934, 202).

It is essential to Mead's notion of *me* that society can hold individuals responsible for public activity, as in legal disputes, but that a person's whole self is not *determined* by society's judgment, nor even one's own. Why does Mead postulate these two phases of the self? He is quite explicit: "If [the self] did not have these two phases there could not be conscious responsibility, and there would be nothing novel in experience" (1934, 178). The ephemeral nature of the *I* promises that one is never all that one appears to be. Others can know only the *me*. Furthermore, you too can only know yourself as an object, as others know you. You are blind to your own *I*. The Delphic command to "Know thyself!" will in this sense always remain an open question. Self-knowledge comes against its permanent limit in the *I*. To this extent, one remains mysterious to oneself, and the capacity for creative innovation, that which will pro-duce from the unknown into being, belongs to every human.

II. The Individuated Self

As just explained, Mead divides the self into two inseparable but qualitatively different parts, one noumenal, the other phenomenal, one mysterious, the other overdetermined by the social, one free, the other constrained, one a fount of creativity, the other a nexus of social control—a self both free and socialized. This formulation allows Mead to avoid the one-sided errors of German idealism—of abducting the self into the noumenal—and of behavorialism, which attributes too much freedom of choice to atomistic subjects unresponsive constitutively to their humanity. Mead's formulation of the two parts of the self describes *self*-recognition, and attributes the *genesis* of determinable identity to the *social*.

I shall return to the theme of the *genesis* of social identity in Sections III and IV of this chapter. Here, I wish to pursue a preliminary issue: How, given the power of the social, can the figure of the *I* remain insulated from overexposure to the social? For Mead, a self becomes individuated and socialized at once, and that is because self-consciousness develops in a medium of meaning, and meaning is animated relationally:

> [m]eaning as such . . . arises in experience through the individual stimulating himself to take the attitude of the other in his reaction toward [an] object. Meaning is that which can be indicated to others while it is by the same process indicated to the indicating individual. . . . When we find that we have adjusted ourselves to a comprehensive set of reactions toward an object we feel that the meaning of the object is ours. . . . We must indicate to ourselves not only the object but also the readiness to respond in certain ways to the object, and this indication

> must be made in the attitude or role of the other individual to whom it is pointed out or to whom it may be pointed out. If this is not the case it has not that common property which is involved in significance. It is through the ability to be the other at the same time that he is himself that the symbol becomes significant. (1934, 89; 1964, 244)

For Mead, meaning is an aspect of "experience," and this "experience" is the activity of "being the other at the same time that [one] is [one]self." Meaning is composed of language, what Mead refers to as "significant symbols." As such, meaning has an "objective" existence in the sense that it is neither a "state of consciousness" nor a feature of "mental" life. Rather meaning makes its appearance

> entirely within this field . . . of [social] experience, [a field within which l]anguage does not simply symbolize a situation or object which is already there in advance; it makes possible the existence or the appearance of that situation or object, for it is a part of the mechanism whereby that situation or object is created. (1934, 78)

Objects appear as such in their linguistic materiality produced in the activity of common understanding; social experience is constituted by significant symbols. The activity of role-switching, to "be the other at the same time that he is himself," allows meaning to arise which posits the reality as such to which the meaning refers: "The significant symbol is nothing but that part of the act which serves as a gesture to call out the other part of the process, the response of the other, in the experience of the form [i.e., the person] that makes the gesture" (1934, 268). Meaningful gesture acts as a stimulus on both speaker and listener. Because meaning arises as one takes the other's attitude, a person thereby enables him or herself *as* this other to call out his or her own response as such.

To be clear, and Mead often is less than clear: I do not take another's attitude as my own. Rather, I take another's attitude so that my own response can arise. I have to be another in order to be myself, and this being another involves anticipating the other's response. As Mead understands it, such anticipation is possible because the other's response is intelligible, it arrives in the form of a significant gesture or symbol that, by definition, belongs to the common stock of the social as meaning. Even thinking, which we perhaps assume to be a private matter, is for Mead nothing but an inner conversation,[15] that process which handles intersubjective meaning in language by having internalized multiple perspectives so as to call out one's own response. I will return below in Section IV to question the plausibility of Mead's notion of a "response" that preexists its calling but that appears only as an answer to a calling. At this point, however, we can say that Mead introduces an active intersubjectivity as an alternative to a theory of unconscious imitation (Tarde) and consciousness as a self-projection and re-appropriation (Hegel).

Of course, humans have "whole bundles of such habits which do not enter into a conscious self, but which help to make up what is termed the unconscious self" (1934, 163).[16] For Mead, the unconscious is merely unreflected activity—action's own activity, which can be read as unmindful habit, but also impulses that await their stimuli. Animals, for example, perform unreflected gestures. Although a dog will respond to another dog, it does not reflect on its own response as such. Humans, when acting habitually, without thought, behave as animals, which is to say, unconsciously, unmindfully or automatically. In such cases they allow through inattention a stimulus to determine their response rather than determining their response for themselves. What distinguishes humans from animals, for Mead, is the *breaking of habit,* and self-determination of response. It is *meaning* that interrupts the flow of habit as in "an awakening" (1934, 163).[17] Meaning breaks habit by shocking into articulate relief otherwise unreflected gesture, thereby occasioning a response that is *conditional and contingent, rather than necessary and automatic.*

Now, what is it that occasions this awakening? Mead argues that when confronted by an ambiguity of circumstance, humans must problem-solve, and thus human *attention* may rise to the level of rational action.[18] For example, if the weather is not quite rainy and not quite clear, should I bother to bring along an umbrella? (It is this kind of mundane example that Mead tends to use, but such processes are not fundamentally different for more momentous occasions.) Ambiguity in the nature of the *stimulus* implies that any number of responses could be called up. Without a ready response, I am forced to think about it, to nail down the (true) nature of the stimulus (rainy or clear), and I must judge and then act because of the ambiguity. In this way, I endow the stimulus with meaning, all the while conscious of the interpretive contingency of my response. My response is not habituated but chosen, and I know it. In this choice lies not only the contingency of meaning imparted to the stimulus, but my self-awareness in the process of rational choosing. For Mead, *a self-consciously rational response determines the nature of the stimulus as such, not vice versa.*

If this is so, how in the first place can the stimulus (given only retroactively its specific significance) prompt a self into self-conscious activity? The answer lies in the nature of experience. When weather as stimulus shocks a human into awareness, the human is not a blank slate, looking confusedly at the storm clouds raging above, but a person already intimately, however incompletely, attuned to weather, its demands, and our array of anticipatory responses. Rational choice here refers to the hermeneutic-reconstructive act of identifying the nature of the stimulus given one's past experience (with unreliable weather) as based on the pragmatic decision oriented to the present and future (to bring or not bring the umbrella, to yield to an aversion to being wet, to pay the cost of being needlessly burdened by an umbrella should the clouds hold their water, etc.) and clarified with the interpretive tools (e.g., significant symbols) given by one's immersion in social experience.

Of course, as Mead (1934, 131) well knows, using weather as an example isn't entirely suitable for his ultimate aims of clarifying the relation between rational action and consciousness: Thinking a rainy day won't stop the rain, significant symbols do not wholly constitute their objects that after all have a natural, extra-linguistic life of their own. Social life, however, is different. In a social situation, one's response may determine the nature of the stimuli, provided we grant that in the *conversation* of *significant symbols,* the determination of meaning emerges from the to-and-fro of question and answer, query and response: "The consciousness of meaning . . . is a consciousness of one's own attitudes of response as they answer to, control, and interpret the gestures of others" (1934, 132–33).[19]

Shared meaning, then, arises in a series of hypothetical triangulations where speech participants take the role or attitude of the other, and thereby come to understand the meaning of some thing or event by occupying all of the subject positions concerned with that thing or event. Meaning takes shape over the course of conversation. In participation, one becomes self-aware. As he says: "One senses the self only in so far as the self assumes the rôle of another so that it becomes both subject and object in the same experience" (1936, 63). To say that a speaking subject is both subject and object of his own experience is a conceptual strategy designed to resist those who argue that a social self, conceived of as without a permanent essence, would be dispersed and permanently fragmented, identical with its many identifications but never with itself. Mead's *I* as *subject* remains pure of the intersubjective character of its *me* and the intersubjective meaning that it employs to rationally reconstruct a situation. For Mead, rationality requires reflective distance from the meaningful world even as the *I* is nothing but its work on the meaningful world, a world that includes its self as an object under construction. In short, for Mead taking the attitude of the other does not disperse or shatter a preexisting self into its many identifications; rather, such a process posits the ineradicability of one's self in the first place. It makes room for one's self to emerge in shared-meaning formation.

The very structure of modern society, too, resists the collapsing of the self into its social identifications is. Mead, in fact, employs an Adam Smithian model of exchange when detailing the process of taking another's attitude, for the *me* exists in a division of labor. In economic exchange, a person trades an object for that which he or she deems more valuable. In doing so, he or she must put a value on the object to be traded, but of course, from the seller's perspective, this object is expendable. Its value is expressed in its exchange value, its price, and this value gives the "universal" character to the value of the object. To plumb what universal values others will put on an object, the seller must call out

> in himself the attitude of the other in offering something in return for what he offers; and although the object has for the individual [seller] no direct value, it becomes valuable from the point of view of the other individual into whose place the first individual is able to put himself. (1934, 301)

Within this exchange relation, each participant has his or her own "unique standpoint" within the network of expectations:

> each individual self within [the exchange] process, while it reflects in its organized structure the behavior pattern of that process as a whole, does so from its own particular and unique standpoint within that process, and thus reflects in its organized structure a different aspect or perspective of this whole social behavior pattern from that which is reflected in the organized structure of any other individual self within that process (just as every monad in the Leibnizian universe mirrors that universe from a different point of view, and thus mirrors a different aspect or perspective of that universe). (1934, 201)

Mead argues here that the functional differentiation and complexity of modern exchange relations runs counter to the potentially fragmenting force of society on the self as interdependence increases. Necessitated by the diversity and complexity of social relations, individuation and socialization are of a piece, and thus the modern self produced as an effect of social relations retains an autonomy of a kind—not necessarily a moral autonomy, but minimally, an existential autonomy. Humans become more individuated, that is, more themselves, more irreplaceable in unique biographies, as they find their place in the world through increasingly more complex social relations. As Habermas puts it, lauding Mead's efforts:

> There is a difference between a self which is alone, isolated, atomized as a result of overwhelming societal pressures which dislocate and fragment human existence, processes which "singularize" us, as opposed to processes which "individuate" us in a rich and "emphatic sense." . . . The "I" is at once the motor force and the placeholder of an individuation that can be attained only through socialization. (1987a, 41, 1992a, 196–97)

III. From Play to Game

I have been explaining how Mead attempts to fashion the self as both an effect of the social process *and* as a free spirit. Individuals are driven to think when confronted by the uncertainty of new experience. Although thinking operates with the tools of sociality (and therefore does not on its face leave room for freedom), it is, on the psychical side, the *I*, and on the social side, the division of labor, with which Mead hopes to preserve for each person a unique, emphatically individuated time and place resistant to saturation by the social. Strictly speaking, the "I" is universal in its emptiness (and therefore not individuated in any identifiable manner); the "me" is subject to individuation, attached firmly to the social as its medium of appearance while distinguishing itself in time and space given complex, modern society. Despite the communal building up of a common world, it is "continually breaking down" because "problems arise in it and demand solution. . . . The experience of the individual is precious because it preserves these exceptions," even as the individual in a state of exception interprets his or her experience with the objective tools of meaning, such "that they [e.g., these initially exceptional experiences,] become common experience" (1964, 341). Each person's work on meaning contributes to the working up of common experience. It is the *I*'s function to continually re-establish the binding character of common experience as meaning.

In this section and the next, I will examine Mead's theory of self-development, for as we saw in the previous section stressing individuation, Mead's theory of self-development, too, is primed to resist fragmentation as well as saturation by the social, that is, to preserve the self against the risks associated with mimesis.

Mead's theory of self-development couches the process of consciousness (as "taking another's attitude" or "role-playing") within a developmental stage-theory of human socialization: from bodily gesture to vocal gesture, to role-imitation, to the ability to employ signs and significant symbols in language, and then to a form of role-playing that involves taking the attitude of the "generalized other." It is this last feature, the emphasis on a language-theoretical adoption of a whole society's standpoint that makes Mead's theory particularly attractive to Habermas. Habermas's importation of the linguistic turn into the philosophical underpinnings of Marxism finds in Mead a compatible theorist of the historical, sociogenesis of human identity because for Mead, it is *linguistic interaction* that, in giving rise to an identification with the whole of society, effectuates a human consciousness given over to the moral promise implicit in social order: a cosmopolitan self suitable for a cosmopolitan society. Together with a *concrete* generalized other—understood as one's specific, ethical community—lies the *abstract idea* of the generalized other, its own *I*, as it were, that normatively sets the table for a self's ability to judge one's attitudes and society's norms, to reform them and perhaps to perfect them.

In positing the existential, epistemic, and normative individuation of selves, Mead pays close attention to *three* moments in self-development: play (as the mindful adoption of roles), game (as educated play under rules), and the extrication from the rules of the game (the reflexive capacity to think and judge beyond a given set of rules).

During *play*,

> a child is continually acting as a parent, a teacher, a preacher, a grocery man, a policeman, a pirate, or an Indian. It is the period of childish existence which Wordsworth has described as that of 'endless imitation' [citing Wordsworth's "Ode: Intimations of Immortality," 1807]. . . . This takes place because the child is continually exciting in himself the responses to his own social acts. . . . Having in his own nature the beginning of the parental response, he calls it out by his own appeals. The doll is the universal type of this, but before he plays with a doll, he responds in tone of voice and in attitude as his parents respond to his own cries and chortles. This has been denominated imitation, but the psychologist now recognizes that one imitates only insofar as the so-called imitated act can be called out in the individual by his appropriate stimulation. That is, one calls or tends to call out in himself the same response that he calls out in the other. (1964, 284–85)

Notice here that child's *play* for Mead is an imitation of adult life; it is to "play at" (1934, 150)—a pantomimetic exercise where the one part of the self imitates roles in the social world and in so doing brings to presence the latent[20] response already "in his own nature."[21] A child acts as a parent, so that he or she can bring to light and develop his or her parenting impulses; he plays a pirate so that, presumably, he can bring to light and develop his pirating impulses, and so on. Mead, to describe this role-playing, in fact uses without acknowledgment Plato's definition of mimesis, but a mimesis that has migrated inward, as it were, as an internalized *image*: a person plays another's role in his imagination "with his intonations and gestures and even perhaps with his facial expression" (1964, 146). For Mead, such images retain their status as appearance, as object, even as they are imported into consciousness. That is, the appearance of the other as an objective image is not assimilated to the self. It remains an object, "the impersonal" (1934, 321) aspect within, and the whole self—the *I–me* dialectic—is thereby alienated internally from its identifications even as these constitute the material for its self-identity. Mead calls this a "personality structure." Mead: "Indeed, it is only as he has in some sense amalgamated the attitudes of the different roles in which he has addressed himself that he acquires the unity of personality" (1964, 245).

Mead, however, resists calling children's pantomimesis "imitation" because he has by fiat narrowed the definition of imitation to automatic, mindless copying.[22] For Mead, the child's imitation is not automatic but self-directed: Role-playing activity functions like a calling or a cipher that gives a positive form to impulses preexisting within the child. That mimetic play is an inadequate, callow mode of interaction for Mead, however, is plain:

> I can only refer to the bearing of this childish play attitude upon so-called sympathetic magic. Primitive men call out in their own activity some simulacrum of the response which they are seeking from the world about. They are children crying in the night. (1964, 285)

Chapter 1 discussed this phenomenon of primitive, tribal sympathetic magic partially defended by Adorno as cultic mimesis, a mimesis that invokes the nonidentical. For Mead, sympathetic magic is to be condemned because it operates by the conscious polyadoption of roles without the telos of transcending role-play.[23] Sympathetic magic imitates roles that it grasps in an *immediate* way, but not in an immediate *and* abstract way. Why is Mead so undeniably anxious about imitation? Unconscious mimetic action is coercive, implanting a "simulacra" of responses; conscious play is the unforced stimulation of latent responses. Imitation cannot provide the resources by which human animals can become self-conscious selves.

For Mead, child's play must graduate to the rational conduct in *games* wherein the taking of another's attitude calls up a genuine response in light of the perception of the rules of the game, as opposed to its dramatic action alone. Simply put, *games* are rule-governed, collective play. In games,

> the child must not only take the role of the other, as he does in the play, but he must assume the various roles of all the participants in the game, and govern his action accordingly. [To employ the example of baseball, i]f he plays first base, it is as the one to whom the ball will be thrown from the field or from the catcher. Their organized reactions to him he has embedded in his own playing of the different positions, and this organized reaction becomes what I have called the "generalized other" that accompanies and controls his conduct. And it is this generalized other in his experience which provides him with a self. (1964, 285)

In the developmental shift from playing to gaming, what arises is rational conduct itself. In a child's development, the uninhibited pleasure taken in the pantomimesis gets lifted to a collective endeavor, where a team is constituted as such by its being circumscribed by the rules of the game, and thereby is infused with a certain pleasure at a higher level, a theoretical pleasure, as it were, and no less real for being nonsensuous. Mead writes: "In the play period, . . . before the child has reached that of competitive games . . . the child is as varied as his varying moods; but in the game he sees himself in terms of the group or the gang and speaks with a passion for rules and standards" (1964, 246). A disciplined role-playing is transformed into gaming, and gaming is nothing but a coordinated and disciplined mimesis. Instead of playing many roles sequentially in real-time, a player does so only virtually: I am not the batter and the pitcher at once, but rather as a pitcher, I pitch well only if I can virtually take up the attitude of the batter, the catcher, the ball, the outfield, the wind, the umpires, the fans, and so on.

Rationality means simply that a person *actively* takes the attitude of others, in light of the rules that govern the meaning of their collective conduct, in order to arouse his or her own latent response. The difference between play and game is that in the latter, the conscious imitation of others takes account not merely of others' activities, of their roles, but of the rules that affectively bond such rule followers as sharing a community in common. Mead writes:

> What I have attempted to do is bring rationality back to a certain type of conduct . . . in which the individual puts himself in the attitude of the whole group to which he belongs. This implies that the whole group is involved in some organized activity and that in this organized activity the action of one calls for the

> action of all the others. What we term "reason" arises when one of the organisms takes into its own response the attitude of the other organisms involved. (1934, 334)

Role-playing bequeaths reason to the players insofar as to play properly requires a playing off of others, to anticipate one's own response in anticipating others' responses. This is nothing less than to understand and to play by the rules of the game.[24]

Although to his discredit Mead does little to substantiate the imputed analogy between games like baseball and social relations more generally, he takes up the suggestiveness of the concept "generalized other" to indicate that society at large, in order not to performatively contradict itself, must have implicit rules that permit the unconstrained taking up of others' attitudes. At the limit of such role-switching, one takes the attitude of the whole community of addressees. Democracy represents this ideal insofar as within democracy, "the individual can be as highly developed as lies within the possibilities of his own inheritance, and still can enter into the attitudes of the others whom he affects" (1934, 326). As Richard Bernstein writes,

> Like Dewey, Mead was, of course, aware that there are nondemocratic communities. But if we follow the logic of the development of the idea of community, if we realize that selfhood depends upon the capacity of the individual to assume the attitudes and the role of others, then we can detect an inner dynamic in the development of community life. This is a tendency, which may, of course, be frustrated and distorted, but it is a dynamic toward the achievement of *mutual recognition*. Implicit in the very idea of community is the regulative ideal of a universal democratic community. (1998, 150)

Mead praises a "journalism that is insatiably curious" and the "modern realistic novel," for aiding the project of "overcoming the distances in space and time, and the barriers of language and convention and social status, [such] that we can converse with ourselves in the roles of those who are involved with us in the common undertaking of life. . . . We must be others if we are to be ourselves" (1964, 292). Modern techniques of communication and reportage create a larger and larger audience, and therefore an ever increasingly universal public whose attitude one must adopt to become a fully cosmopolitan self. (Mead did not consider that the inner coherence of that universality might, in its expansiveness, suffer or become so abstract as to be without traction.)

Freedom of self, however, is not unconstrained liberty, for the *I* cannot be divorced from a *me*, and this *me* always answers to effective history, that is, a history performed in public, an ever-expanding public And yet, for Mead this idea of public is not beholden to any existing public; it is rather an imaginary which stands behind any existing public. Even the rebel who snubs his or her contemporaries must construct in language an audience past or future, so that he or she may hear his or her own voice of reason speak. The indeterminability of the *I* ensures that a self is ultimately free to turn against the judgment of all contemporaries:

> A person may reach a point of going against the whole world about him; he may stand out by himself over against it. But to do that he has to speak with the voice of reason to himself. He has to comprehend the voices of the past and of the future. That is the only way in which the self can get a voice which is more than the voice of the community. . . . We are not simply bound by the community. We are engaged in a conversation in which what we say is listened to by the community and its response is one which is affected by what we have to say. . . . We can reform the order of things; we can insist on making the community standards better standards. . . . The process of conversation is one in which the individual has not only the right but the duty of talking to the community of which he is a part, and bringing about those changes which take place through the interaction of individuals. (1934, 168)

Reason requires as its sounding board and its vehicle a virtual public, if no actual public will suffice, to pursue its ethical duty, to improve the rules of the game that govern the manner of role-switching in society. After all, a person "can not hear himself speak without assuming in a measure the attitude which he would have assumed if he has been addressed in the same words by others" (1964, 145–46).

IV. From Image to Symbol

I wish here to take a second, critical sweep through Mead's theory of role-switching that informs the passage in child development from play to game. The stage of children's *play* as thus described is useful within Mead's framework only to the extent that play is *on the way* to game, which is to say, on the way to the rational use of language in the practice of role-taking that at its limit authorizes a critical stance toward one's own community.

If play were strictly imitative it would, within Mead's framework, foreclose the conscious development of self as the art of one's *I*. What play does then, in Mead's account, is produce[25] the latent—that is, it calls the latent into being, making it operative, as in, say, a child's copying of parents' talk might stimulate the hitherto latent parenting impulse of the child. Such a gesture does not yet rise to the level of rational conduct (i.e., a *controlled* calling out of one's own response), but it is a necessary precursor to the activity of adults who, unchained from playing at role-play, in their maturity, can deliberately adopt their roles as their respective *me's* with reference to authentic impulses.

Of course, this formulation of a "true role" or "authentic role deliberately adopted" raises the epistemic question: How can a person or an observer reliably distinguish play imitation from true-imitation? What can it mean to have a true copy, and what standard of authenticity can a self hold up, against which it might know its faithfulness to the roles it adopts? The answer, perhaps unsurprisingly, follows in spirit Plato's theory of anamnesis. In Plato, as we saw in Chapter 2, a true mimesis—divine mimesis—produces the cosmos revisited in the harmony of soul; a prosaic mimesis, in contrast, brings a soul into conformity with an ideal, this-worldly model, more or less unhinged from the Forms. Where the *recovered memory* of Forms warrants the philosopher's self-rule and political authority, a prosaic mimesis requires rule by a higher authority, backed by anamnesis. In making room for the validation of social pantomimesis, Mead, too, looks to memory.

One cannot understand what it means to "take the attitude of the other" as an act of self-positing in, and of, a field of social emergence if we do not take into account Mead's notion of the memory-image. Mead defines "imagery" or "image" as the "sensuous contents" (1934, 340) of mind. Such images are *sensuous contents* insofar as they can give rise to a response, even though the objects to which they refer are not present. Just as "perceptual sensuous experience" arises from a person's encounter with a thing, a memory-image is how people perceive "objects which have been present but are now spatially and temporally absent" (340). Images play a necessary role in raising a self to self-consciousness because in the process of role-switching,

> [i]t is not until an image arises of the response, which the gesture of one form will bring out in another, that a consciousness of meaning can attach to his own gesture. The meaning can appear only in imaging the consequence of the gesture. (1964, 111)

In other words, a self becomes aware of the meaning of his or her *own* response only in imaging the other's anticipated response. Meaning arises from role-switching, depending on the anticipatory image that precedes taking the other's attitude.

How does one know what to anticipate as the other's response, that is, what determines the "sensuous content" of the image? The image of the anticipated response is essentially the memory stuff of past instances of like situations forcing their way into the present. Such images appear at the behest of a self attempting to recognize and properly interpret the meaning of his or her own gesture virtually right before his/her eyes or ears. Indeed, such memory-images "may merge into immediate perceptions, giving the organism that benefit of past experience in filling out the object of perception" (1934, 340) In this mental process, such, memory-images are not private. A memory-image construed as subjectively private "fails to function as the direct stimulus for the setting-free of the impulse" (338). Memory-images are not memory in the sense of being authentically retrievable by one and only one person. They are rather images *of* that which is in principle accessible by one's entire linguistic community.

Mead argues, for example, that the task of artists is to elicit an emotional response from an audience, and they do so on the basis of rationally reconstructing affective imagery. The method of audience arousal is precisely that of taking the attitude of others imaginatively:

> It is the task not only of the actor but of the artist as well to find the sort of expression that will arouse in others what is going on in himself. The lyric poet has an experience of beauty with an emotional thrill to it, and as an artist using words he is seeking for those words which will answer to his emotional attitude, and which will call out in others the attitude he himself has. (1934, 147–48)

Wordsworth, Mead reports, sometimes allowed ten years to pass before a poem would find its final form. Why the hiatus between the initial inspiration and the poem's final form? As Mead explains it:

> [the] process of finding the expression in language which will call out the emotion once had is more easily accomplished when one is dealing with the memory of it than when one is in the midst of the trance-like experiences through which Wordsworth passed in his contact with nature. (1934, 148)

The "trance-like experience" with nature is too immediate. Indeed, this is Mead's criticism of felt experience in general. Lived experience is not known experience. The memory-image must emerge, and, in Wordsworth, is only amenable to lyric form as memory recalled. The lyric calls back to presence an emotion that predicates the re-presentation.

We should notice two aspects in Mead's positing of the artist's trance-like immediacy that later finds articulate form in the lyric. First, this general structure of a passage from fully felt experience to that "same" experience recalled in articulate form through memory follows precisely Mead's discussion of the so-called evolutionary movement in child development from child's play to games. Second, although the original trance-like experience, or child's play, *warrants* the poet's effectiveness, it is only in imagery recalled to mind in which art both finds its public and redeems its origin in experience as such. The origin is endowed with affective power in retrospect. The entire chain, from origin to affective power, finds completion only as a whole—the end retroactively identifies its origin, and only through psychosocial reconstruction can such a chain be analytically disclosed.

As we saw in Chapter 2, Plato denounces mimetic poets for their soul-destroying potential. Where Plato's mimetic poets are unhinged from the Forms that lie in back of virtuous action, Mead's mimetic poets—indeed, the mimetic selves that we all are—participate by virtue of communicating within the common stock of memory-images in taking one another's attitudes. In art as in science, such reconstructed significant symbols do not ever shed their worldliness in "the shadowless landscapes of that Platonic heaven" (1964, 329). Instead, accrued and composite experience (*Erfahrung*) marks the effective image. As with his concept of meaning, Mead treats memory-images as "objective" material, which is to say, their existence depends on the *I's* activity of post hoc reconstruction with the tools of shared, linguistic understanding.

As we saw above, *impulse* is educated instinct, those "congenital tendencies"[26] that through life experience develop and adapt in the form of responses that a person calls up by taking the attitude of another. It is such impulses—one's own response—that memory-images stimulate when taking another's attitude. In other words, memory-image "enables" a person to recognize an object before hm or her as a stimulus to be responded to, and to recognize one's own response. Above all, it is the image of others' responses that allows a self to take another's attitude in the first place. This is because

> in responding to ourselves we are in the nature of the case taking the attitude of another than the self that is directly acting, and into this reaction there naturally flows the memory images of the responses of those about us, the memory images of those responses of others which were in answer to like actions. (1964, 146)

Although Mead does not expressly draw the analogy between memory-images and significant symbols, he makes this provocative and elusive remark: "Since the symbols with which we think are largely recognized as word images, ideas and images have a very close consanguinity" (1932, 75). Consanguinity! It seems clear that in his stage-theory of human development, symbols take over from imagery their function of calling out one's own response in anticipating the other's. Symbols, like images, "stand for . . . portions of experience which point to, indicate, or represent other portions of experience not directly present" (1934, 122, nt. 29). The referent of such symbols is not the *Real* in any objective sense, but rather intersubjective images. The historical existence of memory-images and of word-images lies within the social medium of meaning. This linguistic reference tableau is *not* Saussure's system of arbitrary signifiers, nor is it a Cartesian identity between word and thing; it is a framework that steers between and beyond objectivism and relativism. In this sense, although Mead never says so directly, we have a shift from the "sensuous contents" of memory-image to the *nonsensuous* contents of word-image, idea and "concept" (1964, 246). During the maturation process from child to adult, from play to game to abstract thought, "the features and intonations of the *dramatis personae* [e.g., one's pantomimetic models, here, one's parents] fade out and the emphasis falls upon the meaning of the inner speech, the imagery becomes merely the barely necessary cues" (1964, 147). The sensuous imagery in one's mind of one's parents fades, and what subsequently is called to mind is the nonsensuous meaning that takes place as significant symbols, as language.

V. I the Artist

As we have seen, in Mead, word-meaning images as significant symbols are essentially the nonsensuous archive of educated impulse that one stimulates by taking the attitude of the other in thought and speech so that one can call up one's response in a given situation. Play is simply the engine of proto-reasoning, and reason reconstructs the objective, nonsensuous content of meaning-images. Thinking, too, partakes of this social world, for "[w]e do our thinking in the form of conversation, and depend upon the imagery of words for our meanings" (1964, 302). Self-consciousness for Mead arises in a recursive structure: a person takes the attitude of the other *so that* his or her own meaningful response can arise. The imagery of roles fades before the abstract meaning that is rather like the husk of the mold from which the roles have been cast. It would be fair to say, if we were talking about the ontogenesis of humans as such, that the mold is cast from the inside out, except that the modern humans Mead speaks of are born into a world of meaning already constituted in the form of a nonsensuous archive of significant symbols. Like Bakhtin (1986, 69), who reminds us that one never speaks the first word into the void, Mead knows perfectly well that language preexists us. We might say that babies born into modernity reproduce as they develop the whole course of human development, but this teleological sentiment could only become true if the express labor of adults on children were to take place, for the meaningful roles that children imitate are nothing but those roles already effective at particular times and places.

Where in our earlier study of Plato we saw him arguing that formless pantomimesis threatened the dissolution of psyche, Mead counters that word-images may provide the forms for meaning that arises in role-switching in a historicized pantomimesis. We could not have the quasi-metaphysical rules of Habermasian speech-acts except by virtue of a *political* gambit in their favor, but even without them we are not therefore left unbound. By allowing that the normative structure of a game and its functional division of labor provides the enabling context in which players become rational selves, Mead believes he is able to salvage the social from pure mimeticism. Pantomimesis in Horkheimer and Adorno hearkened back wistfully, although obscurely, to a self who by mimesis drew close to nature. Mead's pantomimesis, in contrast, is social and lends itself to rational judgment, self-development, and *social* participation. In role-switching, an individual is never merely self-identical, but is rather, always and at the same time, oneself, one's others and an *I* capable of transcending the social act in order to recognize its *me*. Horkheimer and Adorno diagnosed modernity with the sickness of calculative rationality writ large, imprisoning people in mechanized, instrumental, and profoundly despiritualized relations to one another. Mead, too, saw modern life as posing this threat: "The isolated man is the one who belongs to a whole that he yet fails to realize. We have become bound up in a vast society, all of which is essential to the existence of each one, but we are without the shared experience which this should entail" (1964, 301). Nevertheless, in contrast to Adorno and Horkheimer's pessimism, Mead characterizes the promise of democratic pantomimesis, our willful inhabiting of the roles of one another, as not only more benign, but as productive of the me *and* the I, which is to say, of a socialized being *and* a free spirit.

Rationality in Mead's account does not enchain us so much as it responds reconstructively to meaning that is shocked into appearance by the ruptures in habitual experience which allow the self to emerge at all. What this suggests is that the "rich" and "emphatic" sense of the irreplaceability of each self, which Habermas lauds in Mead, takes, ultimately, a *negative* character. It denotes not the ability to take up and internalize meaning, but the ability to operate *beyond* the nonsensuous content of significant symbols in order to refashion it: "In our reflective conduct we are always reconstructing the immediate society to which we belong. . . . We are continually reconstructing" (Mead 1934, 386). In this sense, the Meadian self must not merely recognize its intersubjective content, but rather act aesthetically, as an artist of one's self and society. Reconstruction is a productive, creative, aesthetic act.

Mead's *I*, then, is nothing other than a play on Kant's theory of genius: "*Genius* is the innate mental predisposition [*Gemütsanlage*] (*ingenium*) *through which* nature gives the rule to art" (Kant 1951, 46). Kant's genius does not follow rules, and cannot derive [*ausdenken*] the rule that he is to follow in creating art objects, but rather by a gift of nature produces beautiful objects that other lesser artists may imitate in their quest, doubtless futile, to produce art by imitative means. After all, says Kant, "Everyone is agreed that genius is entirely opposed to the *spirit of imitation*" (47).[27]

Where Kant says that genius is a gift granted by *nature* to only certain individuals to produce exemplary art objects, Mead makes three shifts: The first, is that Mead's notion of genius characterizes *every* self's *I*, not merely those talented few, and thus he democratizes the distribution of genius. Second, the *aesthetic reproduction* of *me and its immediate society* is every *I*'s principal art. The *I*'s activity is a form of praxis that builds up the *me*, but leaves the genial *I* unfazed. The *I* appears as enslaved by the *me* insofar as its action is *for* the *me*. In this way, Mead tames the Hegelian Master—it is the Master who labors on the slave who is the Master's own nature, the stuff of sociality. It is also a way for Mead to account for the movement from *poiesis* to *praxis*: The *I* is merely a function of the self's self-making, and so the internal estrangement between *I* and *me* is preserved.[28]

Furthermore, the primacy and unavoidability of the social process makes the production of *me* amount to a contribution to the social process—a restamping. The stamp that in Descartes was God's own impression on humanity has become in Mead the articulation of the reciprocal stamping of self and society:

> Human society, we have insisted, does not merely stamp the pattern of its organized social behavior upon any one of its individual members, so that this pattern becomes likewise the pattern of the individual's self; it also, at the same time, gives him a mind, as the means or ability of consciously conversing with himself in terms of the social attitudes which constitute the structure of his self and which embody the pattern of human society's organized behavior as reflected in that structure. And

> his mind enables him in turn to stamp the pattern of his further developing self . . . upon the structure or organization of human society, and thus in a degree to reconstruct and modify in terms of his self the general pattern of social group behavior in terms of which his self was originally constituted. (1934, 263, nt. 10)

Following modernity's self-conception, not only shall the self as a whole find its nature only in the social, but there too the origin and anchor for moral conduct. Opposing the Cartesian "stamp" of God, and underscoring his own postmetaphysical proclivities, Mead finds "moral endeavor" arising from social interaction:

> evolution in moral conduct can appeal to no environment without to stamp itself upon the individual; nor to him to adapt himself to a fixed order of the universe, but environment as well as individual appears in immediate experience; the one coterminous with the other, and moral endeavor appears in the mutual determination of one by the other. (1964, 88)

Mead is well aware that people most of the time operate by habit and automatic behavior, and he downgrades such activity as unbecoming of a self. Therefore, it is the aesthetic work of the genius *I* that attends to the shift in the ground of experience—meaning that constitutes the *me*—by which individuals may redeem morally one's self and society.

That said, the third and no less significant shift from Kant's genius to Mead's is to displace the *origin* of genius from nature to the social process. The *I–me* pair arrives together via socialization, and Mead's attempt to break with metaphysical thought—which I will call into question in the next section—depends on the temporality of the social as the unavoidable condition of the emergence of genius.

Memory-image in Mead operates like anamnesis in Plato. It is the memory-image that authenticates the experience of role-taking dialectically with the response that actually does emerge. A child is a person still coming into that common stock of memory via play. An adult, to the contrary, inhabits the field of memory-images such that the *re-cognition* of an object or event can strike him or her as true, every reimaging an involuntary memory already present.[29] A competent speaker mimetically role-switches on the basis of an image, and given the anticipated response, performs his or her own gesture, which serves as a candidate to be added to the collective stock of memory-images. Mead's nonsensuous, linguistified "memory-images" are decisively *not* eternal and unchanging like Platonic Forms. Where in Plato, pure Form trumps the worldly significance of manifestations modeled on it, in Mead, each living encounter of conversation, while raising images from the common stock to authenticate the use of meaning, produces in the same stroke, from the rational reconstructive power of *I*, a *new set of memory-images* that "merge" with those of the past. In this way, social forms, gestures and responses emerge always to be reconstructed. *The temporality of experience is constitutive of the being of images*, and our use of those images in provoking a self into appearance marks the rational process of self-making and world-making.

VI. Mead's Anti-Mimesis

I have been explaining how Mead, in his elaboration of the genesis of the self and the operation of social pantomimesis, tries to avoid the assumptions of German Idealism and a positivistic behaviorism, positing the self as an effect of social interaction rather than as an *a priori* existent. As we have seen, Mead also explicitly constructs his theory of the self to counter theories of imitation. He does not wish to conceive of the self as *wholly* saturated by the social, nor would he accept that a strict causal connection could exist between one person's activity and another's. A purely imitative self, in Mead's account, could not also be creative and free. How would intelligence be conceived? What would distinguish humans from animals? How would one escape the hermeticism of one's contemporaries' views? Nothing could justify pinning moral responsibility on a self who is nothing but a mere imitator of others, for to condemn one would be to condemn the whole.[30] A social self identified completely with his or her interlocutors, without remainder, would be no self at all; this "self" would identify with all and have no identity exclusively its own. It would forget the presence of others as other, but nonetheless live always outside itself. Indeed, it is the stubborn clinging to a *subjectivistic* theory motivating Mead, against his stated intentions, that forestalls his thinking about a self-critical *me*[31]—for Mead, the standpoint of criticism and creativity stands beyond the socialized *me*. Mead employs his notion of the *I* to allow the self free will that could resist total alienation and internal fragmentation, and thereby assure in this negating posture an ineluctability of the self.

In Leys's (1994) perceptive critique of Mead's anti-mimeticism, she takes up his example of voice. Above and beyond bodily imitation, action in the form of *voice* proves to be, for Mead, the one form of action to which a person can respond in *exactly* the same way as his or her interlocutors:

> In the case of vocal gesture the form [i.e., the human] hears its own stimulus just as when this is used by other forms [i.e.,

> humans], so it tends to respond also to its own stimulus as it responds to the stimulus of other forms. That is, birds tend to sing to themselves, babies to talk to themselves. (1934, 65)[32]

Voice is impersonal in this sense, because although it belongs to the speaker it is already potentially universal—where "universal" represents all "those rational beings with whom we are in contact" (1934, 269)—and this is so because meaningless vocal gesture adumbrates for humans meaningful speech that is hardly a mental or subjective matter:

> What language seems to carry is a set of symbols answering to certain content which is measurably identical in the experience of the different individuals. If there is to be communication as such the symbol has to mean the same thing to all individuals involved. (1934, 54)

Mead hopes with this argument to preserve the nature of selves from atomistic theories in that the "objective" meaning borne by symbols enables the taking of one another's attitudes, and therewith the formation of the *me*. Whereas the self-conscious taking up of meaning is rational, that is, dependent on the deliberate action-potential of each self's unique *I*, the stuff of meaning—made articulate as significant symbols—has a thoroughly social, that is, intersubjective character. The *me*, whose content is objective meaning, is partnered with the genius *I*, and in so arguing, Mead attempts to circumscribe both a thick and a thin character of a self, a relational but still relatively autonomous self.

On the other hand, the notion that selves speak in a voice that carries publicly available symbols, understandable potentially by all hearers in the same way, puts the self at a distance from itself. Voice is the principal mechanism that suspends the distance between separate subject positions because the self can hear its voice as others do. As Leys concludes, for Mead "the voice so conceived represents *specularity itself*" (1994, 235). Listening to oneself speak is a specular relation because Mead emphasizes the impersonal occupancy of the other's position: We join our audience when we hear ourselves talk.

Mead makes the specular analogy himself: An actor practices his gesture before a mirror, and by this method makes his bodily gesture present to himself in the way vocal gesture is always present to speakers. Looking at his own image in a mirror, the actor

> registers anger, he registers love, he registers this, that or the other attitude. . . . When he later makes use of the gesture it

> is present as a mental image. He realizes that that particular expression does call out fright. If we exclude vocal gestures, it is only by the use of the mirror that one could reach the position where he responds to his own gestures as other people respond. But the vocal gesture is one which does give one this capacity for answering to one's own stimulus as another would answer. (1934, 65–66)

For Mead, the vocal gesture is the mirror perfectly reflecting back one's outer image so as to call up one's inner response. Of course, if voice is impersonal or objective in the way that meaning and images *cum* symbols are objective, and Mead believes they are, the question arises as to the *origin* of voice itself.

When detailing the origin of meaningless gestural voice, he tells us that, for instance, birds learn their song not by imitating other birds. Rather, in hearing a second bird sing, a bird is stimulated to sing that same song which by instinct was already present in a latent form, merely awaiting its call. But where, Leys asks, does this song originate? With birds we may wish to rely on a theory of hard-wired instinct, but for humans and their employment of significant symbols, not to mention the faculty of taking the attitude of another, Mead steadfastly resists positing a presocial *self*, that is, a *self* already capable of meaning-making and taking. The mechanism of voice presents a problem for Mead because voice—the mirror of impulse—is in Mead the common instrument of intersubjective, impersonal, sociality. Voice is always already one's self in the attitude of the other.

Leys comments: "Mead's whole project would be undermined if imitation-suggestion proved to be internal to the production of the subject rather than an auxiliary process" (1994, 217–18). We already have seen how Mead's anxiety over imitation appears in the two central motifs of human development, from play to game and from image to symbol. Automatic behavior and play grate against the rationality that defines a self; symbols take on a mimetic form—the same meaning for all users—but without, Mead insists, compromising the autonomous *use* of those symbols. As in play and image, the difficulty arrives concerning the mimetic instrument voice when Mead tries to account for its origin, for those original impulses that predate their determinate form.

We know that Mead turns away from questions of origins to consider sociality as the irremediable, temporally flowing medium of self. Yet, his argument against imitation is rooted in the metaphysical conundrum of origins! It is one thing to argue, as Mead does, that rationality reconstructs—but what is the nature of the material it reconstructs? Because Mead cannot account for the genetic development from instinct to impulse to gesture to symbol—he can provide only a schematic *reconstruction* of the action at each stage—he disentitles himself to speculatively posit instinctual origins to explain subsequent human conduct. Indeed, it appears that Mead's "congenital tendencies" arise only post hoc, as reconstructions, posited *as if* they were original. If in a postmetaphysical mode we relieve ourselves of the metaleptic fantasy, the nature of the matter that reason partakes of is not "congenital tendencies," but is, instead, meaning itself, that which emerges in the process of our pantomimetic reconstruction of pantomimesis.

It is clear that Mead simply posits not only preconceptual instincts but also the *I*—for and aft, as it were—*as if* they were clean of the effects of *me*. This metalepsis parallels Kant's move of positing the moral law *as if* it were in effect prior to its positing, so that a self in obeying its own voice can consider itself to have obeyed another's, that of the moral law itself.[33] This "origin trick" pretends to validate the *I* as the site of reason—as the self's vocational workhorse—but it is a fiction of an outmoded style of thinking. Indeed, absent a blind faith in it, Mead must confront the fact that this empty *I* is thoroughly tainted by *me*—if not for any other reason, then because its very activity is not of freedom but of elaborating the *me*, and its mode of discerning itself as well as elaborating itself is the social mechanism of voice. At minimum, the *I* contains the linguistic resources (the nonsensuous archive of social meaning) that it cannot but use to effect its me. (Note that this is the same argument that damns Descartes's attempt to ground a consciousness beyond its humanity. The ego *cogito* must, after all, speak to us in a voice we recognize.)

A self as an effect of pantomimesis cannot *at the same time* possess an *I* that stands empty, isolated from taking the attitudes of others. An *I* that emerges, as Mead argues, *with* the development of the *me* can *never* be an empty limit concept. (The metaphysicians had it right, at least in form: Whether of the Forms, God, or nature, blank it is not.) What we might call the *I trick* only can provide the resources to combat immersion in the *me* if it were posited as *prior* to the social self, but of course this is the very transcendental move Mead's project (and Habermas's) of social interactionism intends to supplant.

To put this in slightly other terms, Mead is very happy with *conscious imitation* and very distressed by *mimesis that suspends the autonomy of the self, which replaces a conscious I with the introjected suggestions of others*. To admit that mimesis might characterize not only the origin of the authentic self but also, part and parcel, learning processes, would deeply unsettle Mead's conviction that the self develops *rationally* through taking the attitude of others. It would hinge rationality onto the experience of self-othering such that rational reconstruction would have no contentless point from which to operate. Mimesis as the mode of reason would signal, as it were, a *return* to experience, experience endemic to each pantomimetic role-taking act, to those instances in which the self emerges as such, as other to itself. Likewise, a self that takes into itself the attitudes of the entire community, the "generalized other," would embody this experience of self-othering, a feeling perhaps not unlike Freud's derisive reference to an oceanic feeling—Freud (1961, 20–21) puts in the same camp trance, ecstasies, and infantile helplessness—but one that finds determinate expression in the assumption of social roles.

Mead, however, figures communal religious experience as "complete identification of the self with the other" (1934, 276) that, in dismay, he calls "a sort of suicide of the self" (1934, 214).[34] In religious rapture, rational control is lost in "the fusion of the 'I' and the 'me' which leads to intense emotional experiences" (1934, 274). Such experience is pleasurable on Mead's model precisely because one leaves behind the controlling figure of one's own *I*:

> We get into an attitude in which everyone is at one with each other in so far as all belong to the same community. As long as we can retain that attitude we have for the time being freed ourselves of that sense of control which hangs over us all because of the responsibilities we have to meet in difficult and trying social conditions. (1934, 274)

But as Mead himself says, "data are not in the world out of which the problem has arisen, but belong to the statement of the problem" (1964, 328). If Mead has misstated the problem, and we drop the fiction of the *I* to the benefit of the *me* complex, then Mead cannot, or at least, does not account for the terms and conditions that mediate rational reconstruction in the process of taking the attitude of the other, and his depiction of a *me* without an *I* as "suicide of self" must be reevaluated.

Now, it may be that Mead's worry is groundless, that a self saturated by the social remains nonetheless in a situation of freedom, and this is because the social itself is not a seamless totality. Derrida, in a Levinasian mode, has argued that the saturation of the self by others, absent a metaphysical I, does not betray itself as a closed system. Why? Because the other that is *in* me does not act on me like a ventriloquist; rather

> The other who is in me is greater than I. I can only gain access to my selfhood (*ipséité*), my egoity, etc., from this relation to the other in me, but the other in me can nevertheless not be incorporated or introjected—who is in me, greater than I. And [by

> analogy] this also happens through mourning, the experience of mourning from which I constitute myself. (Derrida 2000, 468)

Derrida argues that an *ethical* distance always defers the reconciliation of self into a unified *I–me*. Mead's *I* here would be replaced by the other that always exceeds the *me*, but that is nonetheless, a content-full non-*me*. Derrida's claim is not unlike Descartes's argument in the *Meditations*, where the finite self is always already in a state of belonging to the infinite, to God, that the finite self can never wholly grasp. Derrida's modern switch is to replace God with "others" and to translate awe before God into "infinite responsibility" toward others.

Another alternative to Mead's view suggests the following:

> [i]t is, in fact, the *non-coincidence* of the subject with the identity that language, culture and society offers it, which is the precondition for moral autonomy. For autonomy is first taken up as a concrete ideal only by a subject who perceives a dissonance between the linguistic and normative structures of his or her society and the experience of the world as it is disclosed to the preconceptual life of the body. (Bowring 1997, 113)

For Bowring, the "preconceptual life of the body" is a source of moral intuition from which one knows that one *is not* equivalent to one's subjection. Although I would modify Bowring's characterization—and say instead that "language, culture and society" are the *venues* for multiple layerings, sedimentations, retractions, and so on, *from which* bodily intuitive insights may arise, rather than granting preconceptual intuitions an authentic trumping power—my limited point here is that these two alternative accounts throw into relief the problem with Mead's solution. Both of these alternatives find freedom for the self in the deferral of self-reconciliation without going metaphysical. Mead is worried that a theory positing a world full up of meaning would be unable to account for innovation from within. It is the indeterminacy built into the hermeneutical aspect of role-playing that breaks us out of the straight-jacket of determinism vis-à-vis the social medium of articulate meaning.

Mead would like to posit for the self an internal structure, the *I–me,* which as self-alienated has a permanent resource to shock itself from imitation to reflection. However, as we have seen, Mead's account of the genesis of the self shows that his figure of the *I* is better viewed as a last gasp of the transcendental ego, held over and against the self's truly intersubjective core, rather than belonging *to* the intersubjective core. In an oversimplified but still revealing comment, Mead candidly writes: "The 'I' is the transcendental self of Kant" (1964, 141).[35] We must therefore reject Mead's *I* as a holdover; and as will be shown below, Habermas ultimately formulates a separate and new, post-Meadian answer to the question of how to figure a postmetaphysical concept of self without leaving the *me* overdetermined beyond the point of freedom.

Despite this fundamental defect—his inability to think through a postmetaphysical account of a social self capable of self-reflection—Mead's investigations do add something new and crucial in his emphasis on role-taking as endemic to the development of the self. Against his own intentions, there appears now a rationality at the heart of mimesis, a rationality that takes shape precisely via role-taking, as meaning arises reconstructively in the nonsensuous image-content of language.

VII. Habermas's Intersubjective Ego

We can now turn to Habermas's appropriation of Mead's theory of the subject and intersubjectivity. We have seen so far mimesis in three guises, divine and prosaic mimesis (in Plato), animistic natural pantomimesis (in Horkheimer and Adorno), and now in Mead an ultimately incompatible mix of social pantomimesis coupled with a resolutely anti-mimetic *I*, which as I argued, must be dismissed as an asocial *a priori* despite Mead's best intentions. The question then to pose to Habermas is the following: How does Habermas deploy Mead's theory of the self and pantomimetic intersubjectivity without reintroducing the problem of the *I*? Can he do this successfully, or is his theory of communicative action doomed by the same transcendental defect? If he can evade this defect, from what subject position is principle (U) to be deployed? In other words, how can Habermas assuage Plato and Mead's evident anxiety over the elimination of an extra-social standpoint? Can Habermas's theory of communicative action remain a *critical* theory if the subject of communicative action in the moment of communicative action takes the attitude of the other absent the critical resources that Plato had invested in the forms and Mead in the *I*?

The fact is, Habermas over the course of his writing shifts his position as to how Mead's insights might contribute to an adequate theory of communicative action. Despite an early reliance on Mead's concept of *I*, Habermas eventually drops it in favor of an expanded view of the *me*, a *me* that comes into self-knowledge precisely through the adoption of others' roles. Habermas adopts Mead's notion of the social self insofar as the self in communicative action is posited as having an *intersubjective core*. This observation will lead to the conclusion of this chapter, that communicative action is nothing other than rational mimesis, elaborated as the practice of pantomimetic role-playing. This will then raise the question of how Habermas can derive from such an event not the chaos predicted by Plato, but the individuation, solidarity, and normative image of the world hoped for by (Mead and) Habermas.

Over the course of his work, Habermas adopts *two* positions on identity that I will refer to as early and late formulations. The early formulation sustains Mead's *I–me* distinction, whereas the later view drops the *I*. Habermas's early formulation registers Mead's *I–me* bifurcation in his extended treatment of Lawrence Kohlberg's developmental stage-theory of the self. Mead's concept *me* corresponds to a person's *role-identity,* whereas the *I* is represented by *ego-identity*. As in Mead, Kohlberg's concept of role-identity as used by Habermas provides the *social* contextualization of interaction, whereas ego-identity describes a context-less aspect of our selves. Habermas writes that a person may

> retract his ego behind the line of all particular roles and norms and stabilize it only through the abstract ability to present himself [or herself] credibly in any situation as someone who can satisfy the requirements of consistency even in the face of incompatible role expectations and in the passage through a sequence of contradictory periods of life. Role identity is replaced by ego identity; actors meet as individuals across, so to speak, the objective contexts of their lives. (1979, 85–86)

This explication of a context-free ego-identity "leads to the forming of an ego-identity severed from all concrete roles and norms" (1974, 93, as quoted in Davis 1992, 154). The sense of a context-less, ethical self that stands apart from and beyond its role-identity carries over from these texts of 1974 into the second volume of *The Theory of Communicative Action* in 1981, where Habermas reiterates, using almost the exact same language, Mead's distinction between a context-bound and context-free division within the self:

> In the course of the process of individualization, the individual has to draw his identity behind the lines of the concrete lifeworld and of his character as attached to this background. The identity of the ego can then be stabilized only through the abstract ability to satisfy the requirements of consistency, and thereby the conditions of recognition, in the face of incompatible role expectations and in passing through a succession of contradictory role systems. The ego-identity of the adult proves

> its worth in the ability to build up new identities from shattered or superseded identities, and to integrate them with old identities in such a way that the fabric of one's interactions is organized into the unity of a life history that is both unmistakable and accountable. An ego-identity of this kind simultaneously makes possible self-determination *and* self-realization, two moments that are already at work in the tension between "I" and "me" at the stage where identity is tied to social roles. (1987a, 98–99)

We can see from these two passages that Habermas imports Mead's *I–me* distinction into his theory of a postconventional subject. The *I* here performs a hermeneutic-reconstructive function, to read one's own past and to supply an interpretation which answers to the values of "unity" and "consistency." The *I* as ego-identity produces a retroactive consistency across a person's lifetime in what amounts to identity-repair work *qua* an art of oneself.

Habermas fears for those who are unable to delineate and consolidate their identity into a coherence, unable to locate themselves in historical continuity with the past. Habermas calls "terrifying" the potential *inability* to construct anew through remembrance: "It is terrifying both for past suffering and past sacrifice, which, without the possibility of a reconciling rememoration, is as good as lost, and for the identity of those who come later, who, without an awareness of the heritage which they have entered into, can have no idea of who they are" (1996b, 140). In these sentiments we can locate the melancholy of Walter Benjamin's angel of history (1968d, 257)[36] (who flies backward into the unknowable future, all the while watching the travesties of the past pile up before him) situated in the context of Marx's ironic-tragic historical narrative in the *Manifesto* (that the bourgeois style of life constantly revolutionizes and makes ephemeral—all that is solid melts into air!—all that it comes into contact with, itself included). A historical self-consciousness requires memory of experience to solidify the continuity of one's position vis-à-vis those who have sacrificed for a future to come, and indeed, to justify one's own suffering for the sake of future remembrance—a form of glory, responsibility, and meaningful purpose. Kompridis puts this very well: "what is called for is a relation to the past that *uncloses* that which may be closed to us forever, not as something to be 'preserved' for posterity in a museum of culture, but that without which we may find ourselves hopelessly unintelligible to ourselves" (2006, 270). We can sense here Habermas's early position, taking up as his own Arendt' themes of heroic action in *The Human Condition*. As will be analyzed further in the next chapter with respect to Walter Benjamin, coping with the "terrifying" loss of historical memory is one of the defining characteristics of modernity, and Habermas's theory of communicative action is, in part, spurred by an intention to recuperate what would otherwise be lost.[37] That an adequate formulation of this recuperation requires more than a grammatical accounting of the practice of taking the attitude of others is part of my point.

The criterion of "self-consistency," particularly in the face of "contradictory role systems," shows Habermas's allegiance to what we saw in Plato as a fear of an unmastered heteronomy of models, an unmastered pantomimesis, but the analysis has shifted: Plato sought to contain and organize diversity in the polis and in the soul, the latter by the former, and the former by myth. Habermas acknowledges public pluralism, but retains the ethical criterion of self-consistency for the ego.

Habermas's early formulation, where he uncritically adopts Mead's *I*—a contextless ego drawing *behind* the lines of a concrete lifeworld—gives way to a later, more subtle formulation. Here, ego is still responsible for sustaining the integrity of a self. Freedom and reason are not construed as subjective faculties, but rather are active only as aspects of intersubjectivity. A postmetaphysics posits the nature of the ego as intersubjective to the core; and autonomy can arise only as a result of, and firmly within the horizon of communicative interaction.

Notice in the two passages I will now cite, from 1988 and 1991, Habermas has dropped the metaphysical traces from his earlier incorporation of Mead's *I*:

> Even the innermost essence of a person is internally connected with the outermost periphery of a far-flung network of communicative relations. Only in the aggregate of his communicative expressions does a person become identical with himself. (1993a, 131)

And most assuredly,

> The ego, which seems to me to be given in my self-consciousness as what is purely my own, cannot be maintained by me solely through my own power, as it were for me alone—it does not 'belong' to me. Rather, this ego *always retains an intersubjective core* because the process of individuation from which it emerges runs through the network of linguistically mediated interactions. (1992a, 170, emphasis added)[38]

In a discussion of this shift in Habermas's use of Mead's formulation of the self, Koczanowicz quite rightly notes:

> ultimately it turns out that *I* appears as a moment of *me* because every change in the self has a social character. How, then, can there be any validity to maintaining the division of the self between *I* and *me,* instead of claiming that the self has a completely social character? (1999, 60)[39]

Given the foregoing analysis, there is no alternative here: The self *does* have a completely social character, and Habermas comes to accept this point of view, against Mead.

To avoid succumbing to a theory of the imitative constitution of selves, Mead posits the rational control of imitation that incorporates into its practice *rules* on the far side, and *memory-images* on the rear. Who performs this task of rational control? *I* do. This evanescent *I* is required by Mead because, he believes, without this placeholder we have only a singularization of selves in the functionally differentiated, far-flung division of labor, not the emphatic individuation of selves where selves take up their own selves as such. Without the *I,* who performs the taking up of other's attitudes? *Who* is left, but those attitudes already taken up from the beginning, those original play imitations which preceded games: sympathetic magic? Game backslides into play.

What is at stake here is the proper acceptance of the force of modernity in the Weberian narrative of the progress from tradition to society, from *Gemeinschaft* to *Gesellschaft*. Habermas is wedded to this narrative, and yet, in an important sense, we move from play to game and then beyond the iron cage motif to a higher dimension of play (call it play_2) that is the realm of theory-building and world-making: communicative action proper. Individuals become *individuated* within the *play* of role exchange, and not at all with reference to a Kantian noumenal *I*. Habermas is left then (as are "us" late moderns) with a task more difficult than that of Kant or Mead, who could still postulate a content-less, ahistorical self that resided within all of us, that bit of Spirit bequeathed on the poetic model of religion, on the older narrative of a collective soul. Habermas looks to modernity as a force of at least potential progress in the sense that it can transcend the social conventions that mark the upper limit of social action within traditional societies. His concept of self cannot, however, plausibly conceive of itself with the anachronistic notion that he or she is a self capable of transcending its hermeneutic fabric.

This is the only defensible position arising from, but moving past Mead, and it is the one Habermas eventually adopts. An intersubjective core is vital in that it is precisely communicative action, the coming to understanding with another, that does the work of self-formation. The game of critical theory decisively shifts from defending a noumenal *I* from impurities to articulating the moral grammar of *all-too-humanly* saturated role-switching in a far-from-unified social medium of meaning. The self is always already other to itself (as is society or community), and the other that it is, too, is hardly a still point in the current of intersubjectivity. In this way, communicative action does *not* stand so much as an unrealizable ideal, nor even as a normative counterfactual, but as endemic to human selfhood. Habermas writes:

> With the validity claims raised in communicative action, an ideal tension is imported into social reality itself, which comes to conscious awareness in participating subjects as a force that explodes the limits of the given context and transcends all merely provincial standards. To put it paradoxically, the regulative idea of the validity of utterances is constitutive for the social facts produced through communicative action. To this extent I go beyond Kant's figures of thought, . . . though without embracing the totalizing viewpoint of Hegel. (1993a, 164)

Habermas "goes beyond" Kant but not yet to the mature Hegel because, like Adorno, he resists identity-thinking and totality both. Against Adorno, Habermas does not pursue this aim exoterically through a fundamental mimesis with nature, nor a mimesis with art—both art and nature appeal to Adorno as politically suggestive because they represent an other to the inauthentic social. Habermas pursues his mimesis in the social. It is second nature, to be sure, but a second nature that has ceased to mourn for a lost first nature. It is, bluntly, the next evolution in Romanticism. Pantomimetic play is the ground zero of the way humans realize the humanity within themselves. And this ground zero, of course, is full-up and complex, and our insertion into it takes place among others through speech. Therein and thereby do we come to see ourselves for the first time, and naturally through the eyes of others. Habermas describes the ideal-speech event:

> When ego carries out a speech act and alter takes up a position with regard to it, . . . [e]go stands within an interpersonal relationship that allows him to relate to himself as a participant in an interaction from the perspective of alter. [Ego], who turns back upon himself in a performative attitude from the angle of vision of [alter], can *recapitulate* [*nachvollziehen*] the acts it just carried out. (1987b, 296–97)

The self recapitulates his own activity and thereby achieves self-recognition only from the position of others, and he can successfully imagine the position of others because that is all he already is, or better, that is *how* he already is. The emphasis here is on the dynamic of coming to be, of becoming, and this is a becoming that does not cease; even in death a self *lives* on in others' mourning, in their remembrance, in the imperative of memory, in their recapitulation of a life stilled by death. Nietzsche writes: "Recapitulation: To impose upon becoming the character of being—that is the supreme will to power" (as quoted in Agamben 1999, 91). In pantomimesis, precisely the self is already given over to others; the self is produced as individuated within this dynamic web and not without it, and reflection, too, is only another moment in the passage of intersubjectivity. Within Habermas's frame-shift, recapitulation is not a *will* to power, but rather the way of content-full intersubjectivity. And even for a self's own thinking, "[r]eflection, too, is due to a prior dialogical relation and does not float in the vacuum of an inwardness constituted free from communication" (Habermas 1998d, 309).

Taking up Mead's notion of the "generalized other," Habermas argues that, "[o]nly when [person] *A* in his interaction with [person] *B* adopts the attitude of an impartial member of their social group toward them both can he become aware of the *interchangeability* of his and *B*'s positions" (1990,154). The hypothetical presence of the "impartial member" is crucial insofar as this neuter—not a "mere observer" but rather "a representative of universality" (1993a, 40)—relieves any ego of solely actor-relative interests and values, and thereby permits the adoption of actor-independent reasons.[40] This *interchangeability* of subject position in the context of communicative action is nothing other than a pantomimetic event, where unavoidable intersubjectivity is realized as such. *Intersubjectivity is the flow of being other to oneself in articulate form, and our realization of it in communicative action is the moment of lucid rationality.* In Habermas's rendition, Mead's *I* does not do the work of reconstruction; this task of recapitulation is assigned to a *me* who operates from and identifies with the position of the other, and ideally, all others. This polymimeticism, an apparent chaos of ungrounded, suspended and interchangeable no-longer-subjects is what constitutes the way of reason, and Habermas rightly underscores its communicative and performative aspects so as to specify how precisely the mimesis proceeds through language and roles in light of rules. The who that reflects is not an empty *I* nor a *me* without bearings because we arrive into an intersubjective world—the lifeworld, and its theoretical self-manifestations—which is already full up with meaning, roles, and rules. Ungrounded chaos is not an option within the social medium of selves that is significant symbols, Mead's nonsensuous archive of social meaning. The collapse or sliding into grammatical indistinction in the action of mutual understanding is not "suicide" (Mead), but rather the temporal experience of understanding—one that, of course, may (must?) reinstall subject positions after the fact. Reason can no longer be opposed to irrationality *qua* abyss because pantomimesis takes determinate articulation in communicative action. In this way we can better understand the intuition behind Habermas's early formulation, that "[t]he very medium of mutual understanding abides in a peculiar *half-transcendence*" (1987a, 125). The speech norms that provide the fence around the mimetic moment of understanding do not regulate what is understood, nor the manner of understanding. They express instead a post hoc confidence in the affective articulation of the noncognitive event of modern pantomimesis. Such norms can be employed to "test" validity, but only in a positivistic, instrumental, strategic sense, apart from the pantomimesis that instaurs communicative understanding. Understanding occurs as a function of mimesis, not validation.

To conclude here: For Habermas there is a difference between a self that is alone, isolated, atomized as a result of overwhelming societal pressures that dislocate and fragment human existence, processes that "singularize" us, and those processes that "individuate" us in a rich and "emphatic sense" (1992d, 196–97). Habermas very plainly adopts, up to a point, Mead's pantomimetic staging of self-constitution, for his social model holds the promise of disclosing "the rational core of mimetic achievements" (1984, 390). As I have argued in this chapter, Mead develops a theory of the self that preserves freedom in a transcendental *I*, while insisting that consciousness itself can only arrive as an effect of social interaction. There is then a contradiction that Mead does not resolve. He wishes to hold onto the *I* because, he believes, what is novel in the world must come from without. Additionally, Mead is concerned with preserving a standpoint for moral judgment apart from the crowd, apart from those social determinations of the *me*. Habermas takes up Mead's concept of the *me* but ultimately, and wisely from the standpoint of postmetaphysical thinking, jettisons the *I*. This leaves Habermas to think through the Meadian social process wherein selves with intersubjective cores come to provisional self-knowledge only within, and of, the second nature that they can know as participants in speech encounters through the medium of language in the activity of role-switching. Habermas's self has an intersubjective core, and this means that the creativity and moral autonomy of Mead's *I* must now be derived from processes of socialization themselves, and reside within the capabilities of the *me*, or rather, many selves, in the experience of intersubjectivity.

Mead's insistence that the *me* comes to know itself first through imitative play, but more properly through meaningful games, that is, through the medium of linguistically articulate, rule-governed activity premised on taking the attitude of the other, is the clue that Habermas pursues. Habermas is able to find a moral basis to socialization by positing the "generalized other" as that *third*, agent-neutral position that competent speakers can identify with even as they argue their own causes. Such a formulation fills in for the concept of noumenal autonomy by giving a delimited, but abstract *form* to moral calculation. What a discussion of the formal conditions of communicative action leaves out of its account, however, is any sense of how such speaking and role-switching, that is communicative rationality, is supposed to make up for the *deficit of meaning* plaguing the modern lifeworld. Mead hoped to defend the self against the singularizing effects of modernity's division of labor by an emphatic individuation demanded by the *I*. Without the *I*, how is Habermas to preserve the modern moral sense that every self is inscrutable and worthy of respect, dignity, and rights? What is required to shore up our understanding of pantomimetic role-switching is a fuller account of the *experience* of this communication, a task I will now take up.

Although, as we see in the next chapter, Habermas early on declares Walter Benjamin's concept of experience as potentially fruitful for the task of illuminating the mode of communicative action, rather than elaborate the *experience* of this *me*, he instead claims insight only into its procedure, and frames his own theory *against* those accounts that emphasize experience (Habermas 1987b, 309–10). With a fuller account of the experience of communicative action, we can present, through my reconstruction, what may be the best case Habermas can make to redeem and produce meaning in the world through his theory of communicative action as *articulate mimesis*.

Chapter 4

The Experience of Mimesis

Habermas and Walter Benjamin

Language may be seen as the highest level of mimetic behavior and the most complete archive of nonsensuous similarity: a medium into which the earlier powers of mimetic production and comprehension have passed without residue, to the point where they have liquidated those of magic.

—Walter Benjamin (1999e, 722)

Without the influx of those semantic energies with which Benjamin's rescuing critique was concerned, the structures of practical discourse . . . would necessarily become desolate.

—Jürgen Habermas (1988, 123)

A word is not just a sign. In a sense that is hard to grasp, it is also something like a copy or image. We need only think of the other extreme possibility—of a purely artificial language—to see the relative justification of such an archaic theory of language. A word has a mysterious connection with what it "images"; it belongs to its being. . . . Experience is not wordless to begin with, subsequently becoming an object of reflection by being named, by being subsumed under the universality of the word. Rather, experience of itself seeks and finds words that express it. We seek the right word—i.e. the word that really belongs to the thing—so that in it the thing comes into language.

—Hans-Georg Gadamer (1989, 416)

I stressed in Chapter 2 the one-sided nature of Habermas's depiction of communicative action. How is it that Habermas should isolate affect from understanding in working out of his new postmetaphysical categorical imperative if it depends precisely on pantomimetic role-playing, that, if the Platonic tradition continues to exert its force, works on the basis of affectual identification? What is at stake in Habermas's emphasis on an affectless cognition, a reason within language but without feeling? Can we adequately come to terms with the moral conditions for the process of coming to an understanding by relying chiefly on clarifying the *structure* of the speech situation? Would we do better to theorize instead a scene of speech that does not evade the nature of the binding force on which understanding depends? The notion that the switching of subject position can confirm its own ideal, moral organization—as the mold or husk in which the practice of speech is cast—remains an empty formalism unless we can combine this analysis of the *grammatical* shift of persons (i.e., from first to second person, to third person) with an adequate notion of the *experience* of understanding.

Although it may be acceptable to conceive of grammar as a formal accounting method, grammar appears as an adequate index of Meadian perspective shifting only from the position of an *observer*, not from the position of a *participant*. Participants need more than this. Of what should this *more* consist? Habermas is quite clear in his hermeneutic criticism of objective sociology, that

> [m]eanings—whether embodied in actions, institutions, products of labor, words, networks of cooperation, or documents—can be made accessible only *from the inside*. Symbolically prestructured reality forms a universe that is hermetically sealed to the view of observers incapable of communicating; that is, it would have to remain incomprehensible to them. The lifeworld is open only to subjects who make use of their competence to speak and act. They gain access to it by participating, at least virtually, in the communications of members and thus becoming at least potential members themselves. (1984, 112)

Understanding, then, requires the ability to actually communicate, and this depends on the political figure of *belonging*. A theory of grammatical role-switching itself is inadequate for an interpretation of the belonging that communication produces, and for which communicative action matters. What must be understood is how Meadian role-switching can be affectually experienced for meaningful understanding to take place. It is

Habermas's eagerness to avoid a relapse to an explicit psychologism, to a philosophy of consciousness, which prevents him from taking full account of the affectual basis of understanding, even while he insists that selves possess intersubjective cores. Habermas's tripartite view of human relations—subjective, intersubjective, objective—places a subject's own self-relation as one of authentic expression. Mead had already moved past this view. A discussion of subjective feeling need not be restricted to the site of monadic psyches. Given Habermas's theory of the self as *intersubjective*, a road lies open to him, which he unreasonably foreshortens, that affords an intersubjective account of the affective experience of communication.

In our discussion of Mead in the last chapter we learned that the order of abstract significant symbols arising in the practice of role-switching calls on, through the mechanism of voice as mirror, a set of memory-images that themselves are intersubjective and not private. Mead's notion of role-switching puts the aesthetic task of self-making and world-making on the *I*, his adaptation of the Kantian creative genius.[1] However, as Gary Cook notes in his intellectual biography of Mead: "Mead tells us nothing about the relation of attitude-taking to the affective dimensions of experience" (1993, 98). Cook's comment is correct insofar as Mead withholds a discussion of the affective dimension of *conscious* attitude-taking. Of course Mead did not hesitate to count as "rapture" or "suicide" those religious or patriotic experiences of attitude-taking that fuse the *I* and the *me*. If I am correct that Habermas rightfully sheds Mead's *I*, but pushes ahead with his theory on the basis of an intersubjective ego as a tension-filled self, a repository of *me's* with varied capacities—creative, critical, unthinking, and rational—as varied and variable as the plurality of social roles that occasion the positing of one's own *me(s)* in response, then a reconstruction of communicative action can no longer evade the task of articulating the aesthetic experience of this rational pantomimesis. An account of experience is particularly vital because the problem of modernity as Habermas sets it out, following Weber's disenchantment thesis, is precisely the paucity and depletion of meaning in the lifeworld that would sap the motivation for action.

Modernity, as Nietzsche spelled out philosophically and Weber socio-historically, is characterized by secularism and a scientific method that makes calculable the stuff of nature, our selves and our human institutions. We moderns then must come to grips with the *motivational deficit* implied by this revolution in thinking: Once we accept the death of god, what gives meaning to human action? What is the spur to moral action? Once capitalism is relieved of its extra-worldly validation, for what guiding purpose do we live and work? Deep skepticism over universal sources of legitimation presents moderns anew with the task of filling out a normative horizon. Modernity's own sense of critical rationality has little tolerance for unwarranted conviction. The question today is one of value within the scope of *value-pluralism*.

This chapter rejoins the discussion initiated in Chapter 1 concerning Habermas's contribution to the debate over the normative character of our age, and specifically to consider modernity's crisis of motivation. Habermas inherits the question of motivation from Max Weber's *disenchantment thesis*, as filtered through Walter Benjamin's account of the linguistification of the sacred. As we know, Habermas, particularly in his late work, characterizes his contribution as based in a sharp separation of substantive recommendations from procedural ones.[2] I will argue against Habermas's self-explication insofar as this supposed separation of *ethics* from *morality* (where "ethics" in Habermas's vocabulary entails substantive norms, as adapted from Hegel's notion of a concrete "form of life" [*Sittlichkeit*], and where "morals" entails discursive procedural norms neutral to the substance of that which is up for discussion) is blind to, or more likely, a rhetorical cover for, its own endorsement of a substantive ethos.[3] Readers of Habermas should not take the nominally strict separation of ethics from morals, of the good from the right, as a neutral prescription, but as a rhetorical contribution to an ethical debate.[4] Even in the context of what Dryzek, for one, has called Habermas's "unremitting proceduralism" (2001, 657),[5] I will herein maintain, as argued in Chapter 2, that the proceduralism of communicative action breaks down *at the moment of understanding*, and that sustaining this moment of moral and ethical *indeterminacy* is, in fact, vital to Habermas's overall agenda, that of furthering the political and cultural aims of Enlightenment.

I will begin framing the relevant issues in this debate—over the source of moral motivation in a theory of modernity—by examining in section I Max Weber's discussion of motivation in a disenchanted world. Sections II to V take up Benjamin's response to this modern condition, following Habermas's own clue that Benjamin's theory of *experience* can fruitfully be brought to bear on this question. Section VI shows how Habermas implicitly incorporates into communicative action Benjamin's theory of experience. My main contention will be that Habermas's own theory of communicative action incorporates within its rational mimetic mode a modern form of illumination, adapted in only slightly altered form from Benjamin. The mystical nature of understanding is the secret force that makes communicative action compelling, and to read Habermas as strictly a rationalist and proceduralist is to fundamentally misconstrue his contribution to a theory of the normative resources within and for modernity.

I. Weberian *Pneuma*

Weber addresses the theme of the deficit of meaning and motivation in terms of the vocation for science. Science, like art, he says, demands of its practitioners *inspiration*. Weber (1946, 136) draws specifically on Plato's idea that searchers for knowledge are possessed, and like artists work in a "mania." They must be "inspired," and they should remain firm in their vocational convictions even in the face of obvious scorn onlookers may heap on them. Weber's advocacy of "mania" follows Plato's formulation: "The philosopher alone," Plato writes, "applies himself to the divine, he is reproached by most men for being out of his wits; they do not realize that he is in fact possessed by a god" (1973, 249d).[6] Weber's inspired scientists, however, do not rely on revelation alone. Hard work counts for something too, although hard work on its own cannot guarantee results. The scientist must be *both* inspired and deliberate.

But whence comes the inspiration for hard work? As we know, Weber's *other* thesis concerning modernity holds out the iron cage of materialism that threatens to imprison us "specialists without spirit, sensualists without heart" (1958, 182). The cage of secular materialism saps the religious hope that the work ethic might in an obscure way signal God's grace and a place in heaven precisely because a focus on this-worldly success turns persons away from a life after death that might redeem their labors. In the face of this historical irony, Weber recommends a stiff upper lip and a "manly" coping—that, together with the surprising injunction to find the "demon who holds the fibers of [your] life" (1946, 156). Obey this inspiring demon, and your inspiration will not be sapped; the energy you bring to your science will prove its own justification.

Although Weber closes his "Science as a Vocation" with this invocation of the inspiring demon, he suggests earlier in his essay that the inspiration for science, as in art, although no longer given by heaven, *can* in modernity reside elsewhere. In other words, he does *not* offer solely a private and lonely stoicism in the face of the world's and our own disenchantment. Balking at a vision of *total* despiritualization, Weber declares:

> It is not accidental that our greatest art is intimate and not monumental, nor is it accidental that today only within the smallest and intimate circles, in personal human situations, in *pianissimo*, that something is pulsating that corresponds to the prophetic *pneuma*, which in former times swept through the great communities like a firebrand, welding them together. (1946, 155)

What is this intimate "firebrand," this bonding agent, this "*pianissimo*," this "pulsating" intensity? Is this sex? Friendship? And how does the "pulsating" intimacy "correspond" to the inspiration of the prophet? What is the meaning of this "correspondence," this transference from the spirit world to the all-too-human?

Weber is coy as to the exact nature of the human relation in question. Regarding its functional effect, however, he tells us that this intimacy enacts in its artistry a bonding experience, just as the *pneuma*—the breath or spirit of God—had inspired whole communities "like a firebrand, welding them together." The taking place of the communal bond has become private, but its force is no less powerful. Where the young Marx had lucidly diagnosed money as "the bond of all bonds," with the power to both "dissolve and bind all ties" (1988, 138), holding out, nonetheless, a hope on other grounds for human reconciliation in the future, Weber posits *within* modernity itself an unalienated mode of being-with-another that resists the forces of modern rationalization and alienation. This more optimistic, although opaque, view is too often missed by analysts, in preference for his more provocative, poetically tragic iron cage thesis. In Weber's formulation of modernity, *pneuma* retreats deeply, by way of an underarticulated "correspondence," to manifest itself in the close-knit bonds among intimates. This converted *pneuma* holds no less a power nor significance for being relegated to the private. The bonding power of intimacy inspires the heroic scientist to integrity in his art, his vocation, and thus it underwrites and provides the source of heat for the progress of modernity itself.

Habermas generally follows this disenchantment thesis, but where Weber is merely suggestive Habermas has been at his most original. The theory of communicative action, I would suggest, aims to put a rational stamp on the "pulsating" in human intimacy that Weber claims has inherited the remains of genuine religious fervor. Where Weber still holds to an *inchoate* power in intimacy, Habermas aims to disclose the rational character even of this intimate bond, to make intimacy communicative, articulate, and thereby to put this rationalized experience into play with the moral presuppositions he finds in communication. And furthermore, at the social level of analysis, by virtue of the hypothesis that this *pneuma* can in principle be made rational, Habermas attempts to outmaneuver Weber's thesis that the disenchantment of the world begets irremediably a world of "gods and demons," that the absence of a holistic religious binding power leaves rivalrous clans to compete for supremacy with nothing to mediate among them but sheer power and conviction.[7] By positing the event of understanding at the center of a pluralism of *pianissimos*, Habermas attempts to empower communication itself as the centering and decentering element among divergent forms of action, as well as competing notions of the good life.[8]

Habermas himself presents the rationality of communicative action as decisively the *inheritor* of religious energies in a secularized world.[9] He writes: "The aura of rapture and terror that emanates from the sacred, the *spellbinding* power of the holy, is [in modernity] sublimated into the *binding/bonding* force of criticizable validity claims and at the same time turned into an everyday occurrence" (1987a, 77). This devolution of auratic religious rapture and terror into a domesticated, everyday *Bindungseffekt*—not dissimilar, actually, from Nietzsche's account of the rise of self-regulating subjects in *Genealogy of Morals*—raises the question of what, without rapture, provides the *gluten*, the "binding/bonding" power of agreement. Surely there *is* something like rapture or desire, if not always fear,[10] prompting and securing the motivation for agreement. The nature of the affective bond is lacking in Habermas's *explication* of communication, but an account is required to theorize the actual experience of understanding—that will be my claim.

We know Habermas's paradoxical response (1990, 160) to this question of motivation, that the "unforced force of the better argument" prevails; good reasons *motivate* but they do not *coerce* nor do they *compel*. And yet the status of the "unforced force" begs the question of agreement's force, its "absence of a motivational base" (J. Bernstein 1997, 252). Much rests on this concept of binding/bonding because this modern inheritor of archaic religion, the public instantiation of understanding, aims to make articulate what Weber's modern scientist could grasp only as a vague pulsating of private intimacy. Ideally, what makes good the bonding/binding of understanding in privately shared feeling will underwrite solidarity at a social and political level, and provide motivation for human community. It is the *experience* of communicative action's role-switching wherein this binding/bonding effect can work its magic.

II. Experience

In 1972, Habermas indicated his intention to "enlist the services of [Walter] Benjamin's theory of experience" (1988, 120). In particular he wanted to reconsider Benjamin's notion that in language there exists a genuine moment of nonviolence in mutual understanding, and furthermore, that the experience of language carries with it a critical aspect, one that causes us to suspect that this very nonviolence in language might conceal the machinations of domination. It is instructive, I think, to revisit Benjamin's account of *experience* that Habermas intended to adapt to his own purposes. Benjamin's concept of experience, I argue, can help us in a reconstructive mode to think past the procedural account of communicative action and through to its power.

As in the work of Hans-Georg Gadamer, Walter Benjamin's concept of experience operates in dialogue with that of Wilhelm Dilthey's insofar as he works within the space of two distinct notions of experience, *Erlebnis* and *Erfahrung*.[11] *Erlebnis* is that experience that takes us out of historical time and space and connects us with *life*, with that basic pulsating feature of our existence that punctuates mere historical events, shaking temporal accident from their permanent essence.[12] In contrast, *Erfahrung* is that mode of experience that is deeply historical, imprinted with the crisscrossing, layered tracks of events both planned and unforeseen, a road of life on which we amble along, where wisdom builds up as the form of recognizing what Benjamin calls "lived similarities."[13] Experiences as "lived similarities" refer to those events that, as experience accretes, come to resemble one another in their similarities and variations over a long life. These two modes of rendering experience are not exactly opposites. *Erlebnis* animates and motivates—it is linked to the sudden inspiration by Spirit, and seeks to overcome the alienation and bring to closeness subject and object. *Erfahrung* represents collective wisdom—the historical life of Spirit. Where *Erlebnis* is ahistorical in its tremors, *Erfahrung* gathers and collects the sedimentation of historical consciousness.

Habermas directs his polemic (1987b) at postmodernism's sole reliance on *Erlebnis*, experience that, Habermas insists, falsely promises an explosion out of time, as in the ravings of a prophet or an insane priest. Habermas writes, echoing Weber:

> This scurrilous game with religiously and aesthetically toned ecstasy finds an audience especially in circles of intellectuals who are prepared to make their *sacrificium intellectus* on the altar of their needs for orientation. (1987b, 309–10)

Experience (*Erlebnis*) that preempts any critical purchase on itself is suspect. On the other hand, Habermas is much more amenable to Walter Benjamin's concept of experience insofar as Benjamin wishes to think through a way to conjoin the messianic shock of *Erlebnis with* the historical wisdom and power of tradition that inheres in *Erfahrung*: In Benjamin, the flash of knowledge arrives in a *necessarily cognitive* form. To be sure, Habermas argues that "Benjamin did not succeed in his intention of uniting enlightenment and mysticism because the theologian in him could not bring himself to make the messianic theory of experience serviceable for historical materialism" (1988, 114). Nevertheless, Benjamin's failure to employ historical materialism for purposes of redemption does not prevent Habermas from declaring Benjamin's concept of experience ripe for historical materialism in a secular orientation.

Despite Benjamin's many innovations in thinking about experience, his insights are generally couched within the common historical narrative of the disenchantment thesis and normative crisis as outlined in Weber. Modernity's increasing secularization and the gradual sociological shift from community to society presents us moderns, in this account, with the occasion of a deep sense of loss—indeed, a new awareness for that which marked the prior epoch—as well as a newfound sense of the possibilities in the developing history of our aesthetic reception. It is in this sense that Benjamin writes, "The past can be seized only as an image which flashes up at the instant when it can be recognized and is never seen again" (1968d, 255). The aesthetic perception of the past in the instant of its return and sudden passing comes with a moral prescription of responsibility, for in us is invested the hopes of the past, of past victims, whose sacrifice stains even the highest achievements of civilization with a complicity in barbarism (256).[14]

III. Lament for Experience (*Erfahrung*) Lost

The sense of a lost past, a lament for lost meaning, can be seen, for example, in Benjamin's essay (1968a) on the storyteller, Nikolai Leskov.[15] The telling of a story is a practice embedded in a historical context. Wisdom is passed on by travelers, by elders, by those wizened ones who have experienced life. Their stories are told over the rhythms of the loom, in the gathering places, listened to, repeated, and layered over in the retellings with new variation, new application, which confirm and extend the accretion of tradition. Stories are not repeated by rote, but rather made useful, as in advice to farmers. The story is mined as raw material in the sense that it can be mobilized for practice, without thereby depleting it.

The story may be "exemplified by the proverb if one thinks of it as an ideogram of a story. A proverb, one might say, is a ruin which stands on the site of an old story and which a moral twines about a happening like ivy around a wall" (108). This thought image of the story as *ruin* underscores the distinction between *story* and reportage. The ruin gathers a truth to itself, unconcealing, despite its decay an aura that it may lend to multiple and even contradictory interpretations. Stories revive the memory that is their source and mode of conduct. Ruin memory is far from clear and distinct, yet its power thereby is clarified, readied for new purposes, new storytellers, new audiences.[16] Historical continuity is taken up, embodied in a convivial sharing that the storyteller submits to in his or her role as its voice. As he says: "Storytelling is not just an art; it is a kind of dignity—if not, as in the East, an office. It culminates in wisdom, just as, for its part, wisdom often substantiates itself as story" (1999d, 658). The priority of tradition over the storyteller is apparent, for:

> The storyteller . . . is the man who could let the wick of his life be consumed completely by the gentle flame of his story. This is the basis of the incomparable aura about the storyteller, . . . (108–9)[17]

Reportage, to the contrary, provides endless detail without nourishing the connective tissue of collective life. It is history without historicality, living without spirit.

Benjamin is attuned also to the *reception* of storytelling, which requires on the part of the audience a mental and bodily mode of "relaxation," a transmission that involves "assimilation": "The more self-forgetful the listener is, the more deeply is what he listens to impressed upon his memory" (91). The community in this way is constituted and sustained by word of mouth, an ear as a portal to an ever-renewed tradition, and a spirit ready to receive and revivify the impression of a story's stamp.

In Benjamin's account, and as part of the disenchantment thesis of modernity, the power of communal storytelling has eroded, overtaken by advances in the material basis of the production and distribution of new kinds of stories, together with an alteration in the reception of art on the part of the public. Oral tradition is overtaken by the novel and literacy. Writers and readers alike now toil with their texts in isolation. This new situation of laboring on texts changes the nature of the relation between stories and their public. The written novel, unlike the oral story, does not link up organically with the life of the community. Each novel is its own world, and a reader leaps between "real life" and the novel's world, any natural continuity being broken. And so the reader encounters the novel as, effectively, a disinterested spectator. A reader of novels is disinterested not because he or she is not absorbed in the book—to the contrary, he or she is *exceedingly* absorbed, but at the same time, there is no real connection between the novel and experience (*Erfahrung*). It is a pure leisure, a pure narcissism. The *successful* novel provokes an experience (*Erlebnis*) of indulgence of the disabling kind, without a communicative passage back to the building up of a life. Benjamin (99) endorses Georg Lukács's interpretation, that enjoyment of the novel marks a metaphysical homesickness. It does not pull a reader into a community, but posits instead a singular experience that disappears when the book ends—*finis*. The historical autonomization of art and the production of the literate reader are won at the expense of communal solidarity and a self-centering in a tradition of storytelling.

More so than the novel, the newspaper (and then the photograph and the film [1986b]) provides further innovation in the nature of cultural transmission and reception. We consume *news* in perusing the daily paper rather than absorb wisdom through the useful stories of experienced storytellers. Actual events are distilled into an empty concept, *news*. Newspapers exhibit "information," each bit standing in a radical side-by-side discontinuity to the next. Excised in its presentation from any historical referent, news cannot provide meaningful cathexsis.[18] Where stories Benjamin likens to a clay pot marked by the hands of the potter; news items show nobody's hands. Information answers to the norms of anonymity, prompt verifiability, and each news item must be understandable in itself, shorn of the long experience that would motivate its significance and virtue. The glut of information threatens storytelling; the demise of the storyteller implies that "the communicability of experience [*Erfahrung*] is decreasing" (86). With this, communicativity itself, as a human way of belonging with others is decreasing.

In Benjamin's work, the concept of traditional experience (*Erfahrung*), therefore, is used to anchor a lament. Modern life, he claims, makes it difficult (for us moderns) to share experience, but also to experience (*erfahren*) it at all, for the world comes to us in a series of fragmented and isolated bits, pure shock. This kind of shock preempts transmissibility and comprehension within a cultural context. Shock cuts contextual cords. The fragmented temporality of modern experience not only negates the binding power of communal ties, but also stands in as the mode in which self-consciousness develops. Benjamin generalizes to depict a mode of punctuated experience (*Erlebnis*), bereft of continuity, intense but isolated, absorbing but discontinuous.

What is *lost*, that is, the basis of Benjamin's *lament*, in this process of modernization, is above all, *memory*—memory as a mode and expression of communal solidarity.[19] As in Mead, Benjamin does not speak of memory as a subjective faculty nor as a private repository of biographical passages, but rather memory that resides collectively and transgenerationally, as the "chain of tradition which passes a happening from generation to generation" (98). This is the memory that the storyteller embodies, memory eviscerated as narrative cedes its function to the implacable, discontinuous news item. In the discontinuity of modernism's technology of expression and reception, *Erlebnisse* no longer enters *Erfahrung* because all happening is shock.

The continuity of tradition is contrasted to the experience of rupture, of continual but disconnected eruptions. Where tradition connects souls to one another through narrative, modern experience alienates by making each individual's experience solely his or her own. The novel reader in his or her reading is taken from the world and from him or herself, but this experience stands like a hiatus in one's life. It is not an opening of new ground as in Heidegger's notion of disclosure, but rather a hyperlink to a disconnection. Thus, and here is Benjamin's hyperbolic[20] and perhaps counterfactual point: *All* modern experience becomes so punctuated, ripped from the continuity of time, disjointed, out-of-time with itself. Disappeared are genuine social relations couched within and nurtured by common narrative. This is the modern condition, on Benjamin's reading. What is to be done?

The problem with modern life is not the rise of *Erlebnis* alone, but the sacrifice of *Erfahrung* to *Erlebnis*, that the hyper-sensation that separates us from one another cannot on its own produce the communal life that would, in binding us together, redeem it. It is in this exact sense that Benjamin criticized the revelation produced under the influence of hashish: The problem with the Surrealists is that they aim for the "state of surprise" without accepting that for this state to be effective it must speak to thought, and not merely revel in its own explosion out of history. The Surrealists, he says, have "an inadequate, undialectical conception of the nature of intoxication" (1978, 189). And Benjamin gives us his own dialectical answer: Hashish trance tells us about *thinking*; thinking about the hashish trance tells us about thinking. Thinking and hashish may both lead to what he calls "profane illumination," but neither authentically operate on the obsolete model of aesthetic receptivity based on aura. In this sense, Habermas too argues against those who would aim, like the Surrealists, at *only* the punctuation through the hard fabric of historical movement and the "unbounding" of the subject.[21] Habermas and Benjamin, I would say, share a call to epiphanic *knowledge*, not merely epiphanic *negation*.[22] Experience under modernity is rationalized. This calls for a dialectical *concept,* one that accepts that knowledge both affirms *and* negates, holding within it a moment of indeterminability, but that itself is determinate. World-disclosure must be thought of in the sense of the semantics in which it arrives, and not merely as revelation without communicativity. It is *this* aspect in Benjamin's thought that Habermas is keen to enlist, a developmental narrative which underlines the "diminution of the communicability of experience" (read: colonization of the lifeworld) in order that he may clear the ground to articulate a new mode of experience, that which occurs in communication. But that move, to language if not yet to communication, is already taken by Benjamin (examined in Section V) in the sense that Benjamin too posits a *new* receptivity of experience in a new age of artistic production. The linguistified experience of the rationality in role-switching must hold the potential of producing the affective tie that motivates it in the first place. But we get ahead of ourselves.

IV. Shock and Wisdom in Postauratic Experience

I have shown thus far that Benjamin's disenchantment thesis traces the decline of experience (*Erfahrung*) to the benefit of shock (*Erlebnis*), where *Erlebnis* diminishes the communicability of experience. To heal modernity's self-inflicted wounds, Benjamin attempts to think through how *Erfahrung* might be rehabilitated in an era of shock. Benjamin turns in particular to two efforts (Baudelaire's[23] and then Proust's[24]) that try to couch *Erlebnis within Erfahrung*. Without explicating these two efforts, I will here simply indicate that they inform Benjamin's own attempt to capture *Erlebnis* and *Erfahrung* in what he calls the "thought-image" [*Denkbild*],[25] for this notion links up with what we saw earlier as Habermas's appropriation of Mead's concept of "memory-image."[26]

What distinguishes Benjamin's own attempt to conjoin *Erlebnis* and *Erfahrung*, to bring the past into a philosophy of the present, is that he situates the "thought-image" as an experience quite late historically in the *reception* of art. Benjamin's lament for the loss of the storyteller and oral tradition is not a reactionary plea for a return to the cultic transmission of art. To the contrary, he historicizes experience itself. The fact that us moderns cannot authentically experience the aura of art as those souls of the middle ages forces on us a demand for a new model of thinking through the reception and validity of our own experience. If the frenetic speed and fragmentation in the transmission of knowledge is unavoidable, we need not thereby succumb to general meaninglessness, nor to the false fascistic re-invigoration of aura for the masses. Hartman (1999, 345) writes of modern art, that "[i]ntimacy and distance are being replaced by shock and diversion; and Benjamin refuses to value them negatively." To be sure, authentic meaning cannot any longer take its centering from any organic connection to a sedimented community, but this does not indicate the end of meaning nor the end of authentic motivation as such. The task for us is to locate a mode of reception adequate to advances in artistic production, and the displacement of aesthetic experience from the restricted sphere of art—art as authorized institution, art as autonomous activity separate and separable from life—to a generalized aesthetic reception of the everyday. Only in this way can we make sense of the *hopeful* dimension in Benjamin's ambivalent claim that "the instant the criterion of authenticity ceases to be applicable to artistic production, the total function of art is reversed. Instead of being based on ritual, it begins to be based on another practice—politics" (1968b, 224).

Benjamin points to film as the relevant venue to understand the modern receptivity of art (although we should keep in mind that attention to film belongs still to a *restricted* field of vision insofar as Benjamin wants to open up the field of the aesthetic beyond those objects and practices that are registered conventionally as art. (His mammoth, appropriately unfinished *Arcades Project* presents city life and the citation as the true testing grounds of his hypothesis. City life may today be obvious as a venue for thinking through an aesthetics/politics of everyday life [Wilson 1992, which emphasizes the *flâneur*]; in emphasizing the "citation," Benjamin is working with mimesis: speaking in another's voice, but with scare quotes which hold off assimilation to the other's voice.[27]) "The film," Benjamin claims, "has enriched our field of perception" (1968b, 235). We analyze film both intimately and theoretically, like experts (234), bringing to light an "unconscious optics as does psychoanalysis to unconscious impulses" (237). Our powers of analysis are heightened; our attention to detail is sharpened, and as in psychoanalysis, a world with dynamics of its own heretofore unappreciated opens up to the viewer. Viewers do not identify with the character on the screen, but rather with the camera lens and its ability to stage the action, to focus the visual detail into a commentary. With our ability to isolate one experience from the next, to parse movement and gesture, to stop action, we are able to see the same film through many analytical eyes at once. Bug-eyed. Our multifaceted reception of film imitates the mode in which the images are delivered. What he calls the "shock effect of the film" (238) is not a matter of content, but of form, and it is the form that breaks open the cupola of traditional Aristotelian narrative that had woven together storytellers and their audience into a single fabric. It puts the narrative-making power at the command of the viewer, although of course with the raw material of the film. As experienced moviegoers, we are so inured to shock that we can witness it, even dwell there in the kaleidoscope of our multiperspectival response, without being debilitated by it, that is, without losing the modern character of recognition, our scientific, clinical apperception of reality, ready to break the images down and build them up again. Reception becomes a mode of production, of authorship.

Benjamin calls this "[r]eception in a state of distraction" (240), by which he means that, *contra* the claim that film is simply and always a mind-numbing, narcotic entrancement, viewers can be entranced and analytical at once. The viewer can be possessed and yet remain self-possessed; or rather, the viewing self he says, is "absent-minded": The self is made and re-made through a hardening against the continual shock of experience. And so the shock hardly registers; ideally, it flows into the multichanneled reception of the modern cinemagoer, who bears the sovereign power of making anew. Shock destabilizes only premoderns; for moderns, shock heightens procreative power. This is why Benjamin can announce "a new positive concept of barbarism" based on the poverty of experience (*Erfahrung*): "For what does poverty of experience do for the barbarian? It forces him to start from scratch. . . . Among the great creative spirits there have always been the inexorable ones who begin by clearing a tabula rasa" (1999g, 732).

Fascism's manipulation of modern art techniques is to be understood as a *diremption,* but not the sole and necessary outcome of mass art under conditions of mass reception. Benjamin imagines that the film-going audience possesses the cognition of an expert, and views the film as a "surgeon" (1968b, 233) approaches his patient, as one who can dissect the tissues of the patient without nausea, without coming apart at the seams for having violated the inviolable. An altogether different reality is opened up when the surgeon faces tissue and organs rather than a human being as such. Without aura, we can come into exceedingly close contact with things that before held their auratic distance. Benjamin: "To pry an object from its shell, to destroy its aura, is the mark of a perception whose 'sense of the universal equality of things' has increased to such a degree that it extracts it even from a unique object by means of reproduction" (233).

Benjamin's explicit point is that modern art has withdrawn from any model of original-copy, of representation. Art is no longer a reproduction, a simulacrum of the authentic (i.e., a copy at some removes from reality); it is instead a new object all to itself, and one that disseminates itself right from its origin. Its context of origin serves as its Muse, not its anchor, nor its arbiter of purity/betrayal. Every act is an original, as is each reception. Film is the exemplar, above all, because the original of the film corresponds to no original event,[28] and each viewing is a happening. Each repeated viewing is a study in the art of film-making and film reception.

The point of this discussion of the technical *production* and *reception* of art, which is to say in a Marxist vocabulary, the means of production and consumption of art, is that the *mode* of artistic production is changing: the *autonomy* of art, pressed beyond the shadow of its sacred origin, cannot but migrate, as it were, into a conversation with life as a whole, that is, within the quite conscious effort of postconventional selves going about the hard work of making tradition and meaning for themselves. They cannot authentically absorb tradition from art on the discredited model of sacred aura, and so the aesthetic field opens up as a potential in any and all activity. Politics is a function of the aesthetic. The idea of "art for art's sake" is rooted in the idea that after the decline of religion, religion's integrative and mystical energies would be taken up by and confined to a restricted sphere of action and reception called "art." The viability of art as an autonomous *institutional* sphere, doing the work formerly charged to religion, is cast in doubt by Benjamin's analysis of experience in modernity. Habermas exoterically sticks to the "autonomy of art" thesis because it helps him to insulate questions of morality from aesthetics, and thereby shield communicative action from questions of affective power. His categories deny affective force to reason except as rhetoric's illegitimate incursion. Such insulation, however, comes at the price of demotivation, for in Benjamin's theory, even the clinical reception of modern life, because it exists in *language* (as we shall see in the next section), bears within it the motivational impulse for human solidarity. It is for this reason that Habermas, very occasionally, will admit that:

> Art . . . belongs to everyday communicative practice. It then reaches into our cognitive interpretations and normative expectations and transforms the totality in which these moments are related to each another. In this respect, modern art harbors a utopia that becomes a reality to the degree that the mimetic powers sublimated in the work of art find resonance in the mimetic relations of a balanced and undistorted intersubjectivity of everyday life. (1985c, 202)

But even with this admission, that the "mimetic powers sublimated in art" can "find resonance" with the "mimetic relations of . . . undistorted intersubjectivity," Habermas refrains from the advanced Benjaminian line, that we ought not anymore to think of art as affecting life from the outside reaching in, but rather, that affective power has long left behind the restricted sphere of art, and that communication already bears the force of feeling in its intersubjective sharing. This, at any rate, is the notion Benjamin introduces. A new mode of reception for a new art, and for a new postauratic self. Under the pressure of deauraticization through rationalization and secularization, modernity forces a relocation of the aesthetic into everyday life. It is not through our reception of art alone that we kindle the deep mimetic connection with nature, things, or people. Rather, we still invest art with this property because, in line with Plato, Mead, Adorno, and Habermas's philosophic prejudices, we hesitate to locate affective power within a generalized mimesis in everyday interaction.

V. Postauratic Experience as Mimesis in Language

The final turn in Benjamin's argument grounds the *cognitive* aspect of postauratic experience in *language*, for the activity of language, even in its communicative function, instantiates by means of resemblance. Language exists as a mimesis, as articulate nonsensuous similarity.[29]

Language instantiates the unknown, giving articulate form to that which is mysterious but essentially tractable by language. This power of language to articulate the unknown, as Coole (1997, 223) argues, grounds Habermas's dismissal of postmodernism's affection for alterity as such, and thereby enables him to shift the debate from "reason and its other" to a conflict between two kinds of reason: communicative reason and instrumental reason. Language as a mimetic instrument, however, never *fully* comes to replace or supplant that mystery of nature which language can only signal *for us*. This thesis resembles Nietzsche's "On Truth and Lying in an Extra-Moral Sense" (1989) except that in Nietzsche, language cannot reach the nonidentical, and so the use of language often betrays the user who too easily forgets his or her own creative role in producing identity in the world. For Benjamin, to the contrary, language by way of mimesis *does* in fact carry (residually) within it that which it manifests, for he asks: "What does language communicate? It communicates the mental being [*geistige Wesen*] corresponding to it. It is fundamental that this mental being communicates itself *in* language and not *through* language. . . . What is communicable in a mental entity is its linguistic entity" (1996a, 63). This view is fully consistent with Gadamer's famous insight that "being that can be understood is language" (1989, 470). This linguistic manifestation of spirit is what is reinvigorated in communication for the purposes of understanding. Communicative understanding always hearkens back, or better, brings into the immediate present, the original of language, that realm of pure nonviolence that is also a pure mimesis, a manifestation that is no other to the essence that is already linguistic in nature.

As Gasché (1988, 93) writes, for Benjamin "[a] name is the proper name, so to speak, of things' intention, or mode of signification. In other words, in thus calling by their name the each-time-singular mode in which things yearn to speak, man completes language as communication *in actu*, by naming it." Benjamin speculates that the shape of our writing had, originally, a magical purpose, of putting down a nonsensuous similarity to what we saw in the world: "[s]cript has thus become, like language, an archive of nonsensuous similarities, of nonsensuous correspondences" (1999f, 697).

The human power of naming is at once to express and affirm the human power of designating another as what it is, but also of recognizing that the other *is other*, and therefore deserving of *its own* name. To have identity in language is not just to find oneself respected in one's specificity. To be named and to find oneself distinct is also lamentable, for it signals a fundamental detachment, a separation and isolation, a condition of suffering that bears mourning and loss in the context of the Fall.[30] Communication partakes of this edictal suffering and pleasure, this encounter with the other that is always more than what we can name, which is the basis for participating in the experiencing of mimetic knowledge. Language as naming, therefore, is about the preservation and affective actualization of identity and difference *in the same gesture*. Mimesis finds its rational articulation in language, but an articulation that amounts to a nonsensuous *manifestation* of the other's otherness rather than simply a transposition from living nature to dead script, or from a sacred origin into a profane copy. It is the creative nonviolence in understanding that is reinvigorated in each new flash of communicative action.[31] Such nonsensuous correspondences do not appear in writing alone, but also, especially, in speech. Benjamin writes that "[t]here is a sphere of human agreement that is nonviolent to the extent that it is wholly inaccessible to violence: the proper sphere of 'understanding,' language" (1996c, 243). A language that becomes pure convention, as in Saussure's structural model, is pure deception. Bringing this analysis together with what I argued in Chapter 2, we should read Habermas's emphasis on the norms of speech and principle (U) as a shell to protect this echo of aura resonate in the experience of the calling-to-presence that part of Being that is linguistic in its nature.

Benjamin argues for language as nonsensuous similarity by making a startling comparison between language and astrology. Benjamin speculates that the human mimetic faculty once perceived similarities between humans and the cosmos like a "flashing up. . . . It offers itself to the eye as fleetingly and transitorily as a constellation of stars. The perception of similarities thus seems to be bound to a moment in time" (1999f, 695–96). Why does Benjamin link language to the occult? The occult assumes a mystery, a cosmic intangible which is *out there*, and to humans belong a metaphysical desire, a wish or a primal need to bridge the distance between mystery and their own being; or, if not to bridge that distance (because it's impossible) than to *experience* sensuously what amounts to God, or Spirit, or Nature. It is the same move we saw Plato make in bringing together the lover, his beloved and God (see Chapter 2, Section II). This sudden perception of cosmic similarities, for Benjamin, signals an anthropological mode of interaction: to make oneself similar to another, and to make another similar to oneself. The perception and experiencing of similarity occurs via a "mimetic faculty"—readily apparent in children, but not only in them: The human "gift for seeing similarity is nothing but a rudiment of the once powerful compulsion to become similar and to behave mimetically. There is perhaps not a single one of [a human's] higher functions in which [the] mimetic faculty does not play a decisive role" (1999e, 720).

But mimesis is no static faculty. As in Benjamin's account of the history of reception of art discussed above, so too the mimetic faculty has a history, "in both the phylogenetic and the ontogenetic sense" (1999f, 694). The mimetic faculty changes as children become adults, and so too in the long history of humanity, Benjamin speculates, a "transformation" has taken place "within" (695) the mimetic faculty. The historical shift, as we saw in the discussion of the storyteller, moves from cultic similarity in tradition toward cognitive assimilation under the shock of sudden illumination. In other words, the late mimetic experience of language assimilates the shock of *Erlebnis* to the cognitive articulation in modern *Erfahrung*. Where in Adorno, the "concept" or theoretical language betrays always nonidentical nature, for Benjamin, the concept may be, in modernity, nature's most truthful manifestation.

To be sure, this shift was implicit already at the origin of language, for, he writes, "[e]verything mimetic in language is an intention which can appear at all only in connection with something alien as its basis: precisely the semiotic or communicative element of language" (1999f, 697). The semiotic/communicative element of language is ostensibly *other* to what language signifies, but where language is *true*, this *signification* is no betrayal, but simply partial and, as it were, under the shadow of the original: "The mimetic element in language can, like a flame, manifest itself only through a kind of bearer. This bearer is the semiotic element. Thus, the nexus of meaning of words or sentences is the bearer through which, like a flash, similarity appears." The mimetic element is the heat that could never make itself felt without wax, wick, and flame.

The parallels here to Mead's project, as worked out above, are undeniable, with the difference that in Mead, the *referent* of meaning is ultimately more meaning, and this emerges from within the occasions of communication, fundamentally a social pantomimesis. Benjamin does not deny the truth of this view so much as he is more aware than Mead that the model of meaning as a social medium makes no sense except as a mimesis of the older, magical model of language as fundamental naming. Benjamin not only wishes for moderns to break with the past—to make it useful for what is to come—but also wishes to redeem the sacrifices of the past, and so in his theory the past has a stronger, affective pull. The *tabula rasa*, he knows, can be a useful fantasy, so long as it is not symptomatic of an unthinking forgetfulness—out of the preexistent, regardless, will the new construct its future. In Benjamin, cognitive understanding depends on the magical resonance of language with articulate Being. Benjamin writes: "Even profane reading, if it is not to forsake understanding altogether, shares this with magical reading: that it is subject to a necessary tempo, or rather a critical moment, which the reader must not forget at any cost lest he go away empty-handed" (1999f, 698). By this *tempo*, he means "swiftness" in the uptake, the participation in the temporality of the flash of understanding, or better, in the series of flashes: one cognitive recognition to the next of utterances which are nothing but flashes of similitude that join one's own perception to the truth of the nonrepresentable manifested in language. The critical bearing that, as we saw with respect to the reception of film, is a dialectical intoxication, a fulfilling trance in articulate form, ensuring that meaning for us is not simply lost in modernity's drift to nonsensuous language as its mode of interaction. In a hopeful, forward-looking vein, he writes: "It is the inherent tendency of dialectical experience to dissipate the semblance of eternal sameness, and even of repetition, in history. Authentic political experience is absolutely free of this semblance" (1999i, 473). In the long history of the demise of aura, the mimetic faculty has become bound up wholly in its semiotic bearer, in communicative language, which is why Benjamin can write that

> language is the highest application of the mimetic faculty—a medium into which the earlier perceptual capacity for recognizing the similar had, without residue, entered to such an extent that language now represents the medium in which objects encounter and come into relation with one another. (1999f, 697)

In this sense, together with what we saw above concerning Mead, we should read Habermas's intention, in *The Theory of Communicative Action*, to lay open "the rational core of mimetic achievements" (1984, 390). The place in Habermas's thought for a source of the bonding/binding power among language users is precisely the flash in which postauratic selves, without being blinded by the fascination of aura, are confronted by their own creativity in linguistic, intersubjective understanding—that which calls to the present its link to the prehistory of language, as a mimesis of the cosmos. But of course, modern experience is no mimesis of the cosmos, but rather, of intersubjectivity itself, the encounter *in* language with the other which at once brings speakers together, but also recognizes the otherness of the other in the sense that language never encompasses all that may be. Dews writes:

> If we understand the notion of mimesis as evoking the human ability to reach out across the non-identity between persons and things, without crushing this non-identity, then Benjamin's philosophical fable . . . [of the] play of correspondences between macro- and microcosm which dominated the human life-cycle . . . expresses a hope which is equally implicit in

> Habermas's theory of communicative action. (Habermas 1992g, 37–38)

A link to prehistory on an auratic model turns now to the *determinate* history of subjects and peoples, of community, in other words, but as an achievement, as recollection and positive reconstruction.

Postauratic selves encounter one another and build solidarity in the event of understanding. In everyday linguistic experience (and not just art!)[32] there is the potential to realize that primordial shudder in the presence of the absolutely other, manifested now only in the postauratic dialectic that is language in its historically effective, cognitive, and semiotic utility. The Benjaminian notion of the "thought-image" captures this aspect of intersubjectivity:

> It's not that what is past casts its light on what is present, or what is present its light on what is past; rather, image is that wherein what has been comes together in a flash with the now to form a constellation. In other words, image is dialectics at a standstill . . . and the place where one encounters them is language. (1999i, 462)

VI. Habermas's Benjaminian Experience

It remains in this chapter to take up directly the question of how the mimetic experience of communication in Benjamin speaks to, or from *within*, Habermas's depiction of communicative action and the question of motivation in modernity. Habermas knows, of course, that Benjamin's theory that relates experience to a mimetic theory of language operates through the thought-figure of *dialectics at a standstill* in an age of postauraticism, or, as Habermas puts it, in "images [which] arise from the secret communication between the oldest semantic potential of human needs and the conditions of life generated by capitalism" (1988, 117). Furthermore, Habermas recognizes the risk for modernity's potential nihilism in its overcoming of aura: "Without the influx of those semantic energies with which Benjamin's rescuing critique was concerned, the structures of practical discourse . . . would necessarily become desolate" (123). The question for Habermas is how precisely to "enlist the services" of Benjamin's concept of experience in a way that does not sacrifice Enlightenment by way of messianic shock, leaving history defenseless against Fascistic manipulation, but that likewise does not surrender to the advance of instrumental reason that would negate the potential of the postauratic power of experience to invigorate and inaugurate meaning for identity and community.

Habermas's usual approach to questions aesthetic is to assume that the aesthetic may be subsumed under the category of art within the tripartite division of human knowledge and activity—the separation of art from morality and from science—which, following Max Weber, characterizes the modern condition.[33] Typical in Habermas is this statement: "Explosive experiences of the extraordinary have migrated into an art that has become autonomous" (1992e, 51). His exoteric self-explication posits communicative rationality as an activity of reason, not feeling, of persons coming together in understanding something in the world, that, when actualized, produces the *Bindungseffekt* of agreement. This agreement is rational because parties to the conversation accept one another's claims only on the basis of weighing the reasons proffered in support. Weighing those reasons on what scales? As discussed earlier, participants consider and make judgments regarding the truthfulness, rightfulness, and sincerity of validity claims; these three values, respectively, correspond to objective truth, intersubjective rightness and expressive feeling.

To complicate Habermas's account, I have considered in detail the process of Meadian role-switching that for Habermas is the explicit technique of coming to mutual understanding. As we saw above, each party to the conversation does not merely suspend his or her automatic clinging to his or her own position, for rational thought already entails a pantomimetic adoption of the others' viewpoints, so as to gauge what one's own response might be. The experience of such a process is not dizzying insofar as the mimetic, communicating subject is not thrown adrift. Rather, the determinate form of role-switching, of playing, gives one an exquisite sense of being *as* another, in light of and adding to the memory-images/thought images made articulate by employing the nonsensuous archive that is language. As Gadamer (1986, 119) says of mimetic art: "Every [mimetic] representation finds its genuine fulfillment simply in the fact that what it represents is emphatically there." To understand dialogue as an art, as inheriting from the sphere of aesthetics its affective, mimetic mode, is to acknowledge that participants bring into being that which is imitated in the imitation. In the speech situation, what is made real in the mimetic substitution of oneself in the other's position is, precisely, one's own position with respect to what is being discussed. The art of self-making that Mead had given to the *I* must, in Habermas's model, shift to the process of intersubjectivity itself: Communicative action is an affective act in articulate form, communicability as intersubjectivity.

In this respect, Habermas's claim for modernity's internal differentiation is misleading insofar as the three types of rationality specific to each of the three institutional domains—art, science, and morality—do not confine the force of communicative action to any one of them. This is particularly so if we accept that the unforced force of the better argument as an *aesthetic* task takes up its articulate form in the modern condition, as Benjamin claims, as part and parcel of the demise of aura in the age of mechanical reproduction. There is *no* reason to accept that art is autonomous in the way Habermas claims *if* we accept Benjamin's idea that, to the contrary, autonomous art withers, yielding its bonding/binding force—the unforced force of aura—to the active mimetic participation in the nonsensuous archive that is language. Aesthetic force migrates into the everyday, which can include art, of course, but will not be restricted there. If we are to consider the question of motivation, it is perfectly reasonable to ask of an everyday affectivity how a theory of communicative action might take its motivational bearings from itself. For us moderns, all activity stands as potentially communal-making/bonding in the way ritually spurred aura once animated community, which is to say, as a genuinely political force.

One important observation analysts must make in moving from Benjamin's worldview to Habermas's is to accept that Benjamin, by and large, concentrates on how a subject might achieve dialectical insight via a mimetic faculty; he is less attentive to the *intersubjective* aspect of reaching understanding. Habermas's theoretical advance is to insist on a structure in the activity of communication that, like Benjamin's thought-image, preserves otherness and difference while shaking the ground in a shock that can help to form, affirm, or dissolve identity and tradition. Benjamin's emphasis on a postauratic experience that links up primordial semantic energies with the immediate shock of the transmission of understanding naturally finds a successor in Habermas, who rigidly poses the procedure of discussion in terms of its internal, geometrical coordination (ego, alter, and neuter). What Habermas typically leaves aside in his discussion of procedure, but that is otherwise not at all absent from the experience of communication, is, of course the orienting, affective power of *communicability* in a postauratic sense. Agamben puts it this way:

> If what human beings had to communicate to each other were always and only something, there would never be politics properly speaking, but only exchange and conflict, signals and answers. But because what human beings have to communicate to each other is above all a pure communicability (that is, language), politics then arises as the communicative emptiness in which the human face emerges as such.[34]

Despite himself, Habermas will occasionally gesture in this direction. For example, he interprets Benjamin's concept of *aura* as "the mystery of complex experience" and he suggests that "[t]he auratic appearance can occur only in the intersubjective relationship of the I with its counterpart, the alter ego" (Habermas 1988, 107). In this rather too quick and never repeated turn of phrase, we can see that Habermas claims aura *for* intersubjectivity; aura translated in an intersubjective idiom is *Bindungseffekt*, the bonding/binding power that inheres in the event of understanding. Is understanding that which brings humans together into the mystery of what postauratic language is, a dialectics at a standstill, a still (and fundamentally ambiguous, original) moment among the force fields of semantic truth, objective truth, subjective truth, and historical realization? If so, it would be for this reason that Habermas can write: "the authority of the sacred is converted over to the binding force of normative validity claims that can be redeemed only in discourse" (1987a, 93–94).

As argued in Chapter 3, Habermas, appropriating Mead, quite clearly articulates the interactive, *mimetic* structure of communication necessary to procure mutual understanding, that which bridges speakers while leaving their relative autonomy intact in an act of mimetic role-switching. The consequence is startlingly Benjaminian insofar as it poses precisely a postauratic interchange:

> if . . . the self is part of a relation-to-self that is performatively established when the speaker takes up the second-person perspective of a hearer toward the speaker, then this self is not introduced as an *object*, as it is in a relation of reflection, but as a subject that forms itself through participation in linguistic interaction and expresses itself in the capacity for speech and action. (1992b, 25)

The aim of role-switching and substituting perspectives as participants in discussion for the purpose of understanding something is precisely to *creatively form* oneself as an effect of depersonalization. It is the "capacity" for speech and action, for "communicativity itself," which humanizes as the realization of intersubjectivity. In communicative action, although it is true that the grammatical separation in the *exchange* of utterances remains intact, the attachment of those formal pronouns to the selves who employ them shakes or slides. The intersubjective experience of understanding brings speaking subjects under the priority of the nonsensuous archive of memory-images in their immediate application to experience, in their pragmatic application to the problem or subject matter at hand.

When explaining the production of self-consciousness as an *effect* of dialogue (rather than of introspection, as in a philosophy of consciousness, or *a priori*, as in the natural law tradition), Habermas calls on Mead's article "The Social Self." Habermas writes:

> the "me" that is accessible in the performative attitude *does* present itself as the exact memory of a spontaneous state of the "I," which can, moreover be authentically read from the reaction of the second person. The self that is given for me through the mediation of the gaze of the other upon me is the "memory image" of my ego, such as it has just acted in the sight of an alter ego and face to face with it. (1992a, 172)

Habermas maintains that this Meadian " 'memory image' " of the I is *through the reaction of the other* made manifest. Although I would argue that Habermas is wrong here, that this does *not* actually occur in Mead (because in Mead the *I never* appears—not in the *me*, nor in the face of the other, although by saying it Habermas effectively disowns Mead's empty *I*),[35] that objection is beside the point. What we should notice in Habermas's clever misreading is the rhetorical parallel between Mead's "memory-image" and Benjamin's "thought-image." In the passage just cited, Habermas's "self" is the "memory-image" conjured in the specular "face-to-face." Benjamin (1999h, 723–24) writes in "Thought Figures," that "speech is not simply the expression but also the making real of thought. In the same way that running is not just the expression of the desire to reach a goal, but also the realization of that goal." Speech well-said "redounds not to [the speaker's] benefit, but solely to the benefit of what he wants to say." Language performatively, mimetically reproduces thought-being as nonsensuous similarity, as significant signs. Habermas, in shifting the scene of the production of thought from language itself to its intersubjective use, carries the mimetic play of language and its bonding/binding energy to the interaction of participants. In the history of Critical Theory, we detect here the shift from the "face" to the "face-to-face." The *effectiveness* of self-appearance here is simply a transposition of Benjamin's postauratic account of the procreative power of language *into* an intersubjective paradigm.

Such participatory and self-procreative speech places the inner self as so many interpellations of our thought-images. In a subjectivistic register, Benjamin writes:

> The so-called inner image of oneself that we all possess is a set of pure improvisations from one minute to the next. It is determined, so to speak, entirely by the masks that are made available to it. The world is an arsenal of such masks. But the

> impoverished and desolate human being seeks out the image as a disguise within himself. For we are generally lacking in internal resources. This is why it makes us so happy when someone approaches us with a whole boxful of exotic masks, offering us the more unusual kinds, such as the mask of the murderer, the magnate, or the round-the-world sailor. We are fascinated by the opportunity of looking out through these masks. We see the constellations, the moments in which we really were one or another of these things, or all of them together. We yearn for this game with masks as a kind of intoxication. . . . (1999a, 271)

In Benjamin, private "inner images" resonate with the truth that masks signify, namely, that we are constitutive of so many disguises, pantomimetic play. Pantomimetic play promises a dialectical intoxication. To actually put on a mask is to double reflectively one's self in the roles of others, and to be intoxicated by the labyrinth of multiple interpretations of who we have been, are, and will be, now.

Habermas, in shifting the scene of the production of thought from the subjective to the intersubjective, carries the mimetic play of language and its bonding/binding energy to a more highly organized and specialized differentiation of the interaction among participants. Habermas's project precisely maps a geometry of intersubjective relations wherein each encounters the other in his or her respective individuatedness, and *simultaneously*, as a participant in a process of coming to understanding, and thereby forms him or herself and the other as the result of having together experienced the *same* historical event. Within the nonviolent, but anarchic confines of communicative action, individuation and sociation are a product of rational-mimetic reconstruction in the process of interactive work. Thus,

> [t]he performative attitude we have to take up if we want to reach an understanding with one another about something gives every speaker the possibility (which certainly has not always been put to use) of employing the "I" of the illocutionary act in such a way that it becomes linked to the comprehensible claim that I should be recognized as an individual person who cannot be replaced in taking responsibility for my own life history. (Habermas 1992f, 144)

For Benjamin, modern consciousness has developed an ability to *resist* the euphoria of the shock. Hence, consciousness reduces shock to a mere moment of the integration of thought. We might call it "dialectical detox." The integration of shock into experience (*Erfahrung*) takes place *affirmatively* and through conscious effort, through positive acts of remembrance, which is to say, reconstruction: the reconstruction of a life, of a biography, of shared history. This is nothing other than Habermas's notion that a post-conventional self is formed ideally as a product of will, but the will of an ego with an "intersubjective core,"[36] that is, a mimetic dialectic pulsating within. A Kantian concept of subjective will is no longer available as the last retreat of autonomy and self-determination. In communicative action, it is intersubjective mimesis which subtends the affective bond of understanding in articulate form. To take "responsibility for my own life history" can only mean to find disclosed intersubjectivity already and always as one's core and potentially at one's disposal.

VII. Conclusions

Given this analysis of Benjamin's theory of experience, and its by-and-large unacknowledged operation within the proceduralism of Habermas's theory of communicative action, what may we conclude about the question of "our" modern deficit of motivation and meaning? We can say first off, that the *source* of motivation exists nowhere else but in the dialogical activity of speech itself. Just as Habermas insists that the modern epoch "*has to create its normativity out of itself*" (1987b, 7), so too motivation. However, the source and site of motivation is by no means anymore registered (for "us" moderns) in a religious idiom, nor even as a psychological condition. Motivation belongs to the province of language itself, in the mimetic play of linguistified intersubjectivity, a figure ultimately of reason as belonging. Motivation if it is to exist must be *enacted*, and it arises as the unforced force within participation. (We look for but do not find motivation *prior to* action; we find it instead reconstructively, emerging from action itself.) This moment of mimetic nonviolence in understanding is potentially, of course, subject to abuse, but the clinging only to a theory of *justification*—which Habermas places in the post hoc architecture of defense elaborated in principle (U)—indicates a posture of retreat, based principally in fear and doubt.

Habermas writes that there is an "internal relation of meaning and validity. We understand a sentence if we know how to justify its truth, as well as the action-relevant consequences incurred in case of our accepting it as true" (1999, 437). Given my argument above, validity is not internal to understanding except insofar as validity too is given over to the dialectics at a standstill of intersubjectivity: in the mimetic play of understanding, validity can only mean that one has successfully taken up the others' views in order to determine one's own. It does not mean that one stands as an objective viewer testing claims in discourse; it means that as a role-switching participant, one accepts the others' claims for what they may be, as legitimate given the other's historico-ethical position. It may be that (U) is necessary as a strategic-political test to be applied to the outcomes of communicative action, but it is not (U), but communicative action itself that answers the question of meaning and motivation in modernity.

Apart from the dynamics of procedural justification, communicative *understanding* proceeds fearlessly and affectively, if illiberally, for it admits into it language as a nonsensuous correspondence *among* participants in the play of significant symbols, of *Erlebnis* within the temporality of *Erfahrung*. This is Habermas's paradoxical attempt to admit a glimmer of premodernity into postauratic subjects, but within the protective shell of speech norms. For this reason, Habermas admits that mere knowledge of normative rightness does not guarantee its exercise. Attention to procedural principles can help safeguard from manipulation that moment of nonviolence—now made determinate in language—which lies at the heart of the mimetic bond of communicative action, the center of the revitalization of tradition and production of the new. Yet, without the bonding effect in intersubjectivity, the rationalized semantics and pragmatics of speech would be empty of the *pneuma* that Weber, Benjamin, and Habermas cling to against the tide of total disenchantment.

Coda

Habermas and the Affective Bond of Understanding

> We can explain what a fact is only with the help of the truth of a statement of fact, and we can explain what is real only in terms of what is true. Being, as Tugendhat says, is veritative being. Since the truth of beliefs or sentences can in turn be justified only with the help of other beliefs and sentences, we cannot break free from the magic circle of our language.
>
> —Jürgen Habermas (1998c, 357)

> Experience is communicative experience.
>
> —Jürgen Habermas (1995b, 107)

> [I]ntersubjective understanding, because it is a communicative experience, cannot be carried out in a solipsistic manner. Understanding [Verstehen] a symbolic expression fundamentally requires participation in a process of reaching understanding [Verständigung].
>
> —Jürgen Habermas (1984, 112)

As should be clear from the course of my argument, the opposition between mimesis and reason is sensible only in a metaphysical light. In *The Cambridge Companion to Habermas*, Strong and Sposito argue that "Habermas's thought should require that he retain the postmodernists as other and not seek to eliminate them as enemies" (1995, 269). Within postmetaphysical thinking, Habermas need not treat the postmoderns as enemies, nor retain them as other, for their insights get taken up into his own sublation insofar as communicative action is intersubjective, inexorably temporal, and therefore continually integrating, disintegrating, and reconstituting itself. In posing their view in the way they do, Strong and Sposito, as well as many friendly and unfriendly readers alike, miss how Habermas's figure of communicative action attempts to preserve while transcending the opposition between mimesis and reason. Since Plato, the philosophical tradition is replete with the use of the rhetorical tactic that denigrates mimesis (as irrational) only to recommend covertly *another* form of (rational) mimesis considered more significant, more defensible, more legitimate—because, within this tradition, mimesis is a figure that cannot be resisted. The common misconception trusts too much in Habermas's polemics against mimesis, and so remains blind to how Habermas deploys pantomimesis himself.

If we push Habermas's thought more explicitly in the direction it implicitly leads us, given his appropriations of Platonic mimesis, Meadian mimesis, and Benjaminian mimesis, communicative action carries within it the tension between mimesis and reason in a new, temporal model of immanent distance preserved as intersubjectivity in the linguistification of the sacred, the shock of *Erlebnis* deflated in the articulate now of prosaic, intersubjective *Erfahrung*. It is a risky philosophical gambit to be sure because this process of reaching understanding destabilizes from within the (false) sense of security proffered by adherence to speech norms, yet it is what the critique, avowal and creative renewal of meaning in this world requires. Pantomimesis is the mode of communicative action, producing in its course the articulate, affectual bond among speakers who are transformed in the experience. The unforced force felt in this bond of understanding is communicative action's offering to the problem of meaning and motivation in modernity.[1]

Benjamin (1999b) provides an extremely helpful rendering of the affect I have in mind, so long as, consistent with Habermas's project, we attenuate its monumentality and release its meaning-horizon from a strictly religious idiom: He tells us of a dream where he finds himself in front of the Notre Dame Cathedral, but "too close." His intimate proximity renders him "overwhelmed" by a "yearning," a desire for that which he already has, to be right there, in front of Notre Dame. How is it that his being there has not yet satisfied his yearning to be there? How is it that his desire is only heightened and made more convoluted? Benjamin describes it thusly: "It was the blissful yearning that has already crossed the threshold of image and possession, and knows only the power of the name—the power from which the loved one lives, is transformed, ages, rejuvenates itself, and imageless, is the refuge of all images" (269). The power inherent in mimetic communication is such as to allow in its light what may happen next. The authority granted by mimetic contact—what I am arguing occurs in the event process of communicative action—is such that it stands, now, outside of processes of legitimation or discursive tinkering, but of course deploying as its medium the linguistic and justificatory manner of our bearing. Such authority, not anymore in the *name* but in articulate intersubjectivity, *requires* speech acts for its production, but what follows is the promise that community might be made of it.

I detailed earlier (Chapter 4, Section IV, especially nt. 27) Benjamin's fascination with citation. Citation is a curious form of speaking as oneself and as another at the same time while negating and transcending the authority of oneself and the other, both. It is a condition fraught with the uncertainty of authority: He who invokes another as authority is himself the author while denying it at the same time, and what gets quoted is no longer itself, rent from its original context and brought to purposes foreign to its original inscription. Citation, in other words, is mimetic speech, and to do it justice, a consciousness adequate for the author and reader, interlocutors and audience, requires the proper level of analysis—not a toggling between the cite and he who cites, but rather intersubjectivity and the destabilizing and restabilizing effects of temporal experience. The shared rendering of experience into meaning is Habermasian speech properly understood. As in Benjamin's citation of a text, Habermasian speech destabilizes authority, while putting the common bond of making meaning together a matter of establishing authority anew.

In his theses on history, Benjamin writes that "only a redeemed mankind is granted the fullness of its past—which is to say, only for a redeemed mankind has its past become citable in all its moments. Each moment it has lived becomes a *citation à l'ordre du jour*. And that day is Judgment Day" (2003, 390). Judgment is nothing if not closure, or at least a certain closure, even if it may, too, be an opening. But the ultimate closure is divine judgment, and all events of judgment take as their model the form of divine judgment, when, again, as Benjamin writes, all past moments become citable in their fullness. Judgment Day, when we stand before God and we give account of ourselves, and in grace, we are taken up into the divine embrace, or in terror we are cast elsewhere. In death and with the divine, a universalizing clarity falls on a life as it has been lived. From this vantage of a (Judeo-Christian) death and possible redemption or damnation, the condition of our mortality, its temporality, is revealed for what it is, a fiction. In death, the fiction of becoming ceases. The indeterminacy of human experience is revealed as a condition of our all-too-human mortality, now overcome. The question of authority and its moral judgment is solved, negated even, by a theology that fantasizes of a totalizing, epiphanic experience in the afterlife.

Of course Benjamin makes prosaic the scene of God's final judgment. His is not the fantasy of judgment day in the afterlife that Nietzsche (1967, 48) condemns (as a cover for *ressentiment*, where the self-servingly pious passively wait out this life for justice, that is, revenge in the next). Instead, Benjamin turns divine judgment into a citation of the day, a working brief, a daily injunction to discern the presence of the past, to work through past horror to find our humanity. In offering up the image of experiencing "the fullness of [mankind's] past . . . citable in all its moments," Benjamin retains a theological impulse, but *for* action *now*. The stitching together of the mimesis of citation and the anti-mimesis of citation (again, that what I cite is what I say and at the same time what speaks through me, leaving me involved with but strangely absent from the utterance and the experiencing of its meaning) works at the level of transformation: It reveals the abyss that stands between the fullness of now and the future we might act to realize. Thus, he says, it inaugurates the " 'state of emergency' " that "is not the exception but the rule. We must attain to a conception of history that accords with this insight. Then we will clearly see that it is our task to bring about a real state of emergency, and this will improve our position in the struggle against fascism" (2003, 392). Benjamin hopes that a domesticated redemptive closure, modeled on the fantasy of divine judgment, might reinvigorate political struggle.

Habermas cannot straightforwardly endorse this temporal foreclosure (e.g., the fullness of the past citable now) as a modernist philosophy's thought-image. It is not our station to preach a redemptive anamnesis. In Habermas's view, where a public philosophy does use such metaphors as "redemption" and the like, it "makes religious experience a mere *citation*" (1992h, 233, emphasis added). And this notion of "citation" should be understood precisely. Where Plato divided speech (see Chapter 2, Section IV) into three manners—simple narrative, mimetic, and mixed modes—the "citation" in a postmetaphysical, intersubjective paradigm strings all three manners together and resists any single reading of the performance: We speak as another, yet allow that other to speak; we use scare quotes, thereby acknowledging our own authorial role; and, the citation calls from out of its own world, but cannot hope to do it justice. Citation is a palimpsest, something like Benjamin's dialectics at a standstill, yet the effect is more indeterminate, that of intersubjectivity. It produces the shock of insight employing the articulate resources of the past for a determined purpose now, but it remains fundamentally open to interpretive contestation, and remains in essence fragmented even as it takes the form of a wish for authority.

When Habermas claims that he can *merely cite* religious experience, in so doing, he puts himself and his reading public into a properly critical mode of uptake and aesthetic production both. Yes, he is intending to reap the *semantic* potential from religious idioms, but he also animates its inchoate potential, that which can bring new meaning into our present moment.

To be sure, Strong and Sposito rightly criticize Habermas where Habermas himself clings to the equation of subjectivity and authentic expression. I, too, have questioned herein Habermas's stubborn clinging to a discourse of Kantian autonomy when his own appropriation of Mead's intersubjective ego suggests a different path: The metaleptic figure of a self-binding will must give way to the *intersubjective* recapitulation of meaning, that which in the event of dialogic understanding with respect to a given subject matter, stills momentarily the process of its own becoming in the thought-image of political becoming. The experience of "unforced force" signals an affective submission in a trans-subjective and aesthetically productive register.

The paradigm shift to a temporal model of intersubjectivity, in fact, puts Habermas's late discourse ethics at some remove from his theory of communicative action. Where communicative action is the opening of articulate intersubjectivity, discourse ethics analytically filters communication for a specific, democratic, ethical imaginary. Given democratic values, this makes good sense, but communicative action does not in itself preserve democratic values so much as it might produce that for which democratic values matter.[2] What a self comes to realize in the circuit of pantomimesis is its constitutive linguistic intersubjectivity, not the normative rightness or wrongness of its claims, nor the truth in either its subjective or collective expression. Mimesis is the granting of authority, apart from the question of legitimacy. In his most postmetaphysical work, Habermas gestures toward a rethinking of affect and the aesthetic theorizing which attends to the experience of communicative intersubjectivity, even if he himself has not (yet?) performed this task. The radical and hopeful streak in critical theory, the promise of communicative action, is placed by Habermas in the linguistic reception and production of meaning, of intersubjectivity as the medium of modern experience and action. The temporal dimension of intersubjective experience can deliver moral images of our world, such as "discourse ethics," which may then be brought to bear on action, but only for those to whom such images belong. The universalization of such images remains a political project, answering to the vividness of shared experience in the bond of understanding, the mimesis in communicative action.

Notes

Notes to Preface

1. Havelock, for one, calls *mimesis* "the most baffling of all words in [Plato's] philosophic vocabulary" (1963, 20). Mimesis is translated typically as *imitation*, but the word form carries many other connotations, discussed in more detail below. The best extended discussion of mimesis in ancient Greece is Sörbom 1966.

2. See Beiner 1997, 98.

3. See Warren 1995.

Notes to Introduction

1. It is Nancy Fraser, both a critic and follower of Habermas, who has posed this distinction most sharply, between a politics of distribution and a politics of recognition, where a political philosophy of *recognition* is being carried out by, among others, Axel Honneth (who turns to Hegel and George Herbert Mead) and Charles Taylor (who traces a notion of authenticity to Rousseau, Herder, and the Romantic tradition). See Fraser 1997, chap. 1; Honneth 1996; and, Taylor 1995 and 1989. For a critique of the sharp separation between a politics of redistribution and recognition, see Young 1997b.

2. On whether universalism is itself a coherent category, see Benhabib 2002, as well as Horkheimer's (1972) pivotal essay "Traditional and Critical Theory."

3. This characterization roughly denotes how MacIntyre (1984) and Rorty (1984, 1985, 1989) discuss the moral universe: Hermeneutic grounding within ethno-homogenous groups precludes a viable concept of interethnic morality.

4. See Benhabib 2002.

5. Significantly, Habermas (1993a, vii) renames with more precision his discourse ethics as a discourse *morality*. Morality and ethics often are conflated. For Habermas, an "ethic" belongs to a particular group as its ideal way of life; "morality," to the contrary, answers to what is equally good for all. An ethic does not aim to be universal, although each typically finds itself the best among the lot. A morality, in Habermas's view, aims to be universal in its application, always referring any practice back to a principle that demands that all affected by that practice might participate in its legitimation.

6. We can observe this, for example, in his discussion of the stages of human moral development, where, he says, "action based on concrete duties [is viewed from the perspective of a higher level of moral consciousness as] contrasted with autonomy as something *merely* heteronomous" (1990, 169). This suggests that autonomous judgment wins a place for itself beyond heteronomy.

7. See Cascardi 1992, 269–74.

8. See Critchley 2002, chap. 6.

Notes to Chapter 1

1. See Gadamer 1984; Wellmer 1971, 41–51, 1998; R. Bernstein 1996.

2. Adorno (1992, 216) describes very well this modern crisis of representation: "As in emancipated film, thought uses a handheld camera. . . . This shakeup in the relationship of the subject to what he wants to say alters the idea of truth itself. And with this, presentation, which except for Nietzsche had long been neglected in academia, becomes essential to the matter at hand again for the first time."

3. This is not to minimize the difficulties of establishing just whose opinion deserves a hearing, the nature of the relevant publics, and indeed, counterpublics, and the terms and style of engagement. To the contrary, it raises those issues as fundamental to moral thinking. (See Habermas 1989, and among the responses and more recent contributions: Warner 2002; Fraser 1997; Benhabib 1992.)

4. See for example, Flax 1992; Lyotard 1984; and Wellmer 1991.

5. Locke 1980, §6. Habermas recommends that we "abandon . . . [t]he assumption of an abstract equality of interest among individual persons who are conceived, on the model of possessive individualism, as standing in a relation of ownership to themselves" (1993a, 64), with reference to his essay of 1973, "Labor and Interaction." Furthermore: "From the standpoint of the theory of intersubjectivity, autonomy does not signify the discretionary power of a subject who disposes of himself as his own property but the independence of a person made possible by relations of reciprocal recognition that can exist only in conjunction with the correlative independence of the other" (1993a, 43).

6. The extra-rational sentiment, we might say, is the all-too-convenient elision of the distance between the actual producer who invests his labor in his work product and the lord of the domain who takes credit for the product, and enjoys the profit therefrom. Locke of course lauds those who produce, but he does so without noticing the social inequities this position would indict. It is a fuller appreciation of the historicality of reason's enactment that a critical theory of reason needs to build into reason itself. As Wallerstein (1983) says of capitalism, there *is* no capitalism in general, there is only *historical* capitalism; or, as MacIntyre says of morality: there is no morality in general, just moralities of various times and places. So, too, for reason. Locke's account of reason was not, however, self-consciously historical; reason was unreflectively posited as a gift from God. Because of this, the social injustice in the organization of production did not appear to Locke as a problem of his conception of reason, but of inadequate reason on the part of the

morally weak or underdeveloped. Thus, he might offer pity or punishment for the unreasoning, but those deemed rational and industrious shall emerge blameless for the unintended consequences of their striving.

7. See Benhabib 1984.

8. For his discussion of the priority of the right over the good, see Habermas 1993a, 92–105.

9. With this I want to make plain that those who read Habermas without appreciating the ways in which he has attempted to place the productive work of aesthetics under the heading of communication have missed something crucial. It is a modernization theory that allows Habermas to make this move, one that he appropriates in general from his Marxist–Weberian synthesis, but one that very specifically arises from a positive valuation and appropriation of Walter Benjamin's thesis regarding modernity's reification of the occulted relation between words and things, as shown in Chapter 4.

10. See Horkheimer 1974, or Rorty 1979.

11. It is Habermas's supposed insensitivity to a "constitutive other" that spurs Strong and Sposito (1995) to their criticism of Habermas. They have a point, but in my view, Habermas *relocates* the tension with the "other"; for postmetaphysics, we look instead to those actual tensions among, on the one hand, determinate, articulate forms, and on the other, the lifeworld, which acts as the "sedimented" repository of authority and past judgments that, when not explicitly thematized, act with an often unrecognized force. As Derrida admits on occasion, the postmodern attention to constitutive difference belongs not to postmodernism itself, but to a postmodern critique of metaphysical thinking. Strong and Sposito rightly point out that "[i]ntersubjectivity does not, for Habermas, appear to require a tension with that of which I cannot speak" (280), but as I try to show throughout, the temporality of intersubjectivity in articulate form is not thereby assimilable to the figure of Hegelian reconciliation.

12. See Sörbom (1966, 11–40) on the Greek word group *mimeisthai*, and the discussion, initiated by Herman Koller's 1954 *Die Mimesis in der Antike: Nachahmung, Darstellung, Ausdruck*, as to the various early usages of mimesis. The starting point for understanding mimesis is to reject the far too narrow definition of mimesis as *copying*, where copying may be likened to a photoreproduction. The thinning down over time conceptually of *mimesis* to a technical *copying* covers over without removing the philosophical and experiential questions presented by the production of and engagement with a mimetic double that is both the same as and other than its original.

13. Aristotle inaugurates this positive tradition by defining successful tragedy as *mimesis praxeōs*, the imitation of an action, or better, the staged reperformance of an action: "Tragedy is an imitation in the form of action [*mimesis praxeōs*] . . . enacted by the persons themselves and not presented through narrative, by means of pity and fear bringing about the purgation [catharsis] of such emotions" (1967, §9 and §49). Aristotle classifies as *mimetic* art not only (successful) performance of tragedy but also the practice of writing tragedy, epic, and comedy as well as the composing of dithyrambs and most music with the flute and lyre. (1967, 1447:14–16.)

14. See Taussig (1993, 254) who relies on Adorno for conceptual support.

15. On music, see Halliwell 2002, 159 and chap. 8; on dance, Plato 1997b, 1460–1.

16. See Green 2003.

17. This explains why Hobbes insists that it is immoral to act against the Sovereign up until the moment when the Sovereign fails to protect the lives of citizens. A citizen obeys rationally, in standard Hobbesian terms, because disobedience would result in one's death by the State. Individuals make the simple calculation that they prefer life to death. And yet are citizens in a state of perpetual calculation? No, and why not? Because Hobbes wishes to close the gap—via mimesis qua incorporation—between citizen and sovereign, such that there is an identity, as between an author and his agent. The fantasy of mimetic identity preempts disobedience from the get-go, which is why Leviathan is less a Commonwealth bound by fear than a mimetic republic supposed as already identical to itself. The fear-awe citizens feel before the Sovereign is a carryover affect of their Godlike work of creating the Sovereign. Just as one would not commit suicide, one would not in advance suspect that the Sovereign would kill a citizen—when the Sovereign puts the citizen's life in danger, the mimetic compact is shown up for what it is, a fantasy of identity between citizen and state.

18. One caveat and a clarification: I am not here speaking of the other mode of political founding that Hobbes discusses, conquest or acquisition. Where a conquered people submits, political mimesis on the model I am describing is obviated. As Bhabha (1984) argues, mimesis *as a technique* performed by colonialists on a subjected people slips into mockery—mimicry—where the process of disciplining the subjected people (through the imposition of law, manners, education, etc.) shores up all the more the rift between the two groups while paradoxically, in the same movement, destabilizing the authority of the colonists to set the terms of status. Fanon (2004, 239), of course, advocates more than simply a "grotesque and generally obscene emulation." He takes the anti-mimetic route: turn away from "reflection" of the European colonialists, and instead, "innovate [for] we must be pioneers [to] make a new start, develop a new way of thinking, and endeavor to create a new man."

19. See Pye 1984. I am indebted to Paul Axelrod on this issue.

20. Rousseau's Platonism shows up both in his diagnosis (mimesis gone wild) and his cure (disciplined mimesis). Rousseau (1973) ends his "Discourse on the Origins of Inequality," with the diagnosis of the ills of civilization as mimesis gone wild: "the savage lives within himself, while social man lives constantly outside himself, and only knows how to live in the opinion of others, so that he seems to receive the consciousness of his own existence merely from the judgment of others concerning him" (116). Rousseau reads this out-of-mind experience as the price paid by civilization, a corruption of original nature that tragically cannot be regained, a distraction of our vital powers and a distancing from a natural sense of what matters, and an immersion in the protean, shifting values of ungrounded and rootless social valuation. Unsurprisingly, undisciplined mimesis will find its cure in a disciplined mimesis, namely the social contract and patriotism. Mimesis rightly construed provides the affective binding power of social integration. In his "Discourse on Political Economy," Rousseau (1973) proposes that citizens "might

at length come to identify themselves in some degree with this greater whole [the State], to feel themselves members of their country, and to love it with that exquisite feeling which no isolated person has save for himself; to lift up their spirits perpetually to this great object, and thus to transform into a sublime virtue that dangerous disposition which gives rise to all our vices" (148). This is not an elimination of mimesis but a focusing and disciplining of it via collective identification. For Rousseau patriotism sublates (individualistic) mimetic rivalry into communal, political love, an act that consummates the self-love of the State. The point here is that mimesis can be both integrative and disintegrative, and that Plato sets the table for the tradition of political philosophy in tracking the play of mimesis as both sickness and cure to the human condition.

21. Gadamer (1998) refers to this tendency as the "flight to the logoi."

22. See Scott 1991.

23. Here I am thinking of a group of contemporary theorists who might loosely be called a school, oriented by an ethos of engagement, generosity, and respect toward others, and an appreciation for the feeling of *wonder* in strange and delightful encounters. It would include William Connolly, Jane Bennett, Romand Coles, Stephen K. White, Morton Schoolman, Tracy Strong, and others. Foucault's notion that power is ubiquitous and works itself out in thought and truth regimes lends itself to a program of generalized tenderness toward those who would fall through the grid of reason, left behind by modernity's self-conception, and therefore represent resistance incarnated (e.g., criminals and the insane), but also any abjected quasi-category constituted as such by the "normal." For example, Coles's "concern [with Habermas's project] is with the way the transcendent, inexhaustible, cacophonous, tragic, and aporetical aspects of truth are conceptually devitalized and their effects on discursive processes correspondingly weakened in Habermas's account. The result is a weakening of our openness to the future, our openness to the world and others" (2000, 559). This approach finds an unusual cross-section of philosophical support from both Nietzsche and J.S. Mill, who both wish to preserve idiosyncratic individuals from the tyranny of the (moralizing) majority. Both Nietzsche's asocial Übermensch as well as Mill's genius-individual signify "others" who deserve protection from the overwhelming, magical force of mimetic conformity reified in social custom. In these nineteenth-century lines of argument, the genius "other" needs escape not from *ratio* but from tradition. As Benhabib and Bohman have (separately) argued, a moral concern for "others" *in general* evades the task of moral accounting. The often unacknowledged parallel between this new school and the traditional liberal concern for protecting the genius within society raises the old question of demarcating the "harm" that warrants or demands social or political intervention.

24. See Strong and Sposito 1995.

25. This is very much the way Bakhtin's *Rabelais and his World* has been enlisted for his defense of the carnivalesque and laughter. (Although many look to Bakhtin as an antidote to Habermas's rationality, I would rather follow Hirschkop [2004] in stressing their complementarity.)

26. Habermas explicitly argues to keep analytically separate the techniques of persuasion used by literature on the one side and philosophy on the other. (See Habermas 1992f, and "On leveling the Genre Distinction between Philosophy and

Literature" in Habermas 1987b.) Bohman argues, correctly I believe, that "[b]y attempting to limit disclosure to art, Habermas also sees disclosure as a *type* of communication rather than as a *level* of reflective communicative practice" (1997, 208). This error of separating philosophy from art as *types* as opposed to *levels* of discourse gets stuck in the dispute between romanticism and classicism. The shift to a communicative paradigm pushes past this dispute, and where aesthetic expression and art are concerned Habermas resists the shift despite himself because he does not wish to deflate the moral status of rational discourse *against* aesthetic revelation.

27. There is some textual evidence that Plato himself viewed the political power of his writing in poetic terms, and his poetry as political. In *Timaeus*, Socrates reflects on his creation, the *Republic*, and says that his "feelings are like those of a man who gazes on magnificent-looking animals, whether they're animals in a painting or even actually alive but standing still, and who then finds himself longing to look at them in motion or engaged in some struggle or conflict that seems to show off their distinctive physical qualities" (1997d, 19c–d). We have here the *Republic* characterized as a painting or as containing living simulacra, aesthetic images he'd like to see come to life in political combat. Socrates then playfully suggests a singing contest, boasting that citizens of his Republic shall sing better and higher praises to his city than others would of theirs.

28. . . . albeit to prepare "the way for a positive notion of enlightenment which will release it from entanglement in blind domination" (1969, xvi).

29. See Bubner 1988, 14.

30. Adorno too resisted idealism in its Hegelian totalizing form. See Osborne 1989.

31. On the Frankfurt School's position within Western Marxism, see Buck-Morss 1977; Jay 1973; Therborn 1996.

32. Habermas's shift of historical materialism from a "production paradigm" to a the paradigm of communication pursues exactly this agenda. See "Excursus on the Obsolescence of the Production Paradigm," in Habermas 1987b.

33. Jay (1984b, 216) writes that by the 1940s, "the failure of the working-class movement to prevent Fascism, the horrors of the concentration camps, and the devastation of Hiroshima [were] interpreted as emblematic of capitalism's dogged power to survive, [and on this basis] the Frankfurt School lost virtually all hope for the realization of normative totality either in the immediate or in the distant future." Horkheimer would later write, "The vision of instituting justice and freedom in the world which underlay Kant's thought has been transformed into the mobilization of nations. With each revolt that followed in the wake of the great revolution in France, it seems, the humanistic elements atrophied while nationalism thrived. In this century it was socialism itself that orchestrated the supreme farce of perverting the pledge to humanity into an intransigent cult of the state" ("*Die Aktualität Schopenhauers*," *Gesammelte Schriften* [Frankfurt, 1986], 7:136, quoted in Habermas 1993a, 139).

34. See Weber 1946. Cf. Bennett 2001.

35. Walter Benjamin in his last writings famously contends: "There is no document of civilization which is not at the same time a document of barbarism" (1968d, 256).

36. The significance of mimesis is drawn out even more explicitly in Adorno's unfinished, posthumously published *Aesthetic Theory*, where resistance to the tyranny of reason is sought in the mimetic impulse behind avant-garde art. There, and in Adorno's *Negative Dialectics*, a nonidenticality in art is posited as capable of putting the lie to the modern spirit and its institutional Frankenstein, a totally administered world. See Wolin 1992, chap. 3.

37. To this extent, Horkheimer and Adorno's analysis of cultic mimesis follows Freud's account of *transference* between a hypnotist and his patient in Freud, for a hypnotist must not work directly on the conscious attention of the analysand. Conscious attention is a barrier rather than an aid to the hypnotic connection. For Freud, "the hypnotist avoids directing the subject's conscious thoughts towards his own intentions, and makes the person upon whom he is experimenting sink into an activity in which the world is bound to seem uninteresting to him; but at the same time the subject is in reality unconsciously concentrating his whole attention upon the hypnotist, and is getting into an attitude of *rapport*, of transference on to him" (1959, 74). Where intentional concentration is applied, hypnosis fails. One must forget that one is being hypnotized for hypnosis to work. This paradoxical thought-figure of "unconscious concentration" is lifted from the Freudian scene of hypnosis and applied by Adorno to a naturalistic *mimesis*. (See Borch-Jacobsen 1988, 228–31; and "Hypnosis in Psychoanalysis" in 1992.)

38. "Only consciously contrived adaptation to nature brings nature under the control of the physically weaker. The *ratio* which supplants is not simply its counterpart. It is itself mimesis: mimesis unto death. The subjective spirit which cancels the animation of nature can master a despiritualized nature only by imitating its rigidity and despiritualizing itself in turn. Imitation enters into the service of domination inasmuch as even man is anthropomorphized for man" (1969, 57). The "mimesis unto death" of science is a perverse mantra that signifies that a scientific approach to self-knowledge can only arrive at the moment of death, that is, at a deathlike self-reconciliation, an unconscious self-possession, as inanimate nature. Of course, not only would this science violate its method of controlled alienation, it also would experience itself as itself without knowledge of same, and so this would be worthless in the terms of science. This display of the paradox of the impossibility of self-knowledge is not only a criticism of a Hegelian idealism and a positivistic empiricism; it also, like Rousseau's rendering of civilized man, repudiates the possibility of a willful return to a state of nature.

39. Cahn emphasizes in his analysis that the concept Adorno links to mimesis is *anschmiegen*, which means snuggling up, as a figure to its mold: "For him [Adorno] mimesis is 'a process of making oneself similar to the environment' (*macht sich der Umwelt ähnlich*) and in it 'the outside serves as a model onto which the inside *molds itself*' (anschmiegen), but this does not imply, as his translator believes [Cahn is referring to Cumming's translation of *Dialectic of Enlightenment*], that 'mimesis is an imitation of the environment' " (1984, 31). Mimesis for Adorno is a matter of intimate correlation, not correspondence (i.e., it is *not* a Cartesian correspondence between reality and its representations). See also the terrific discussion by Huyssen (2000) of Adorno's mimesis in relation to Art Spiegelman's graphic novel, *Maus*. For Huyssen, *Maus* successfully epitomizes (in its images, its voicings, and its

temporality) the attempt to mimetically represent the necessarily failed prospect of recapturing the experience of the holocaust. *Maus* is a mimesis that sidles up to its object while preserving the ineradicable distance from it.

40. Jay Bernstein adds, "To be true to itself, then, art must turn against itself, against its autonomy, and hence against the processes of societal differentiations which have deprived it of substantiality" (1989, 50).

41. Adorno typically has music in mind, for music is a medium without concepts, but the problem that art represents as a dialectic between the conceptual and the nonconceptual is especially foregrounded in his literary criticism. See, for example, his essay (1991) on Samuel Beckett. The editors to Adorno's collected works tell us he had intended to dedicate his unfinished *Aesthetic Theory* to Beckett. See also Hohendahl 1997.

42. The obverse of this is the *organized* control of mimesis. This mimesis of mimesis (as the forced return of the repressed) is the technique of fascism.

43. Menke provides the following formulation: "In the process of [aesthetic,] mimetic reenactment, we reach behind the already formed figures of meaning back to the dynamics, force, and energy of their formation; in this way, we experience aesthetically meaning *in statu nascendi*" (1998, 98). And this retroaction is "internal to understanding," not its other.

44. I don't in this brief sketch tackle the question of history. Let me just indicate that Adorno does not advocate a mimesis that simply exits history. Adorno was deeply critical of, for example, Dilthey's concept of *Erlebnis*, a mode of experience beyond history. Adorno was too much of a historical materialist to accept the theory of genius, that inspired artists produce on the basis of talent that emanates unadorned from nature. I take up the notion of a mimesis *in* history below.

45. *Zur Metakritik der Erkenntnistheorie*, 148, quoted in Cahn 1984, 36.

46. Habermas's most extended critiques of Adorno's position occur in 1984, 366–92, and 1987b, chap. 5.

47. See Morris 1997 and 2001; Coles 1995; J. Bernstein 1989; Sevilla 1997; Schoolman 2005.

48. See, for example, Menke 1998; Gebauer and Wulf 1995, chap. 22; among Wellmer's many essays on Adorno, see "Adorno, Modernity, and the Sublime," in 1998; Cahn 1984.

49. I use the word *myth* not as a falsehood, but in the sense that Lincoln (1999) develops as ideology in narrative form.

50. See d'Entrèves and Benhabib (eds.) 1997.

51. See, for example, Kateb 2000.

52. See Habermas 1993b.

53. Cf. Dallmayr 1997, 71–74.

54. I use "autonomy" here in the traditionally understood Kantian sense, in that autonomy does not signal freedom without license but rather reason's subordination to the moral law. As an aside and a forewarning, I would note that Kant in *Groundwork for the Metaphysics of Morals* describes autonomy as an experience of *submission* on the basis of *respect*. A conscientious and considered reason is necessary for moral action, which is why for Kant "[i]mitation has no place at all in moral matters" (1993, 21). Yet, it is at least a question to what extent a submission to

law on the basis of respect is a matter of choice, and therefore properly moral action as Kant defines it: "The immediate determination of the will by the law [the categorical imperative], and the consciousness thereof, is called respect, which is hence regarded *as the effect of the law upon the subject*" (14, nt. 14, emphasis added). The key phrase here: "is hence regarded as." Autonomy describes a *substitution* of one's undisciplined will and unfocused reason for "good will" as determined by law. However, Kant tells us that respect is *an effect of law upon the subject.* Respect, then, we must pretend, does not *originate* in the subject; it originates in the law. Law is the actor, and law acts to awe the subject, interjecting respect inside of the subject's mind, as it were. That the *affective* (as *respect*) should *originate* in law, as law's power radiating outward, requires additional explanation from Kant: "Respect is properly regarded as an object of neither inclination nor fear, although it has at the same time something *analogous to both*" (14, nt. 14, emphasis added). This power radiating from law finds a direct correspondence to what Habermas later will attribute to the "unforced force" of the better argument; its model *by analogy,* in Kant's own words, is bodily inclination, or fear. At this early point in the present analysis, I can pose the issue as a question: if autonomy is supposed to stand opposed to mimesis, how then can the guarantee for moral action reside in an experience (of respect) that overawes subjectivity? I would argue that the Kantian bid to oppose reason to mimesis *already* is *infected,* as it were, with the language of mimesis in that a subject must lose itself to the law that stands *as if* the law resided outside of the subject. This fantasy that the law is self-originating, and the willful forgetting that the law, in fact, originates elsewhere, is, to put a name on it, the "origin trick," outright metalepsis. Habermas's reworking of rationality *inherits* the logic of this self-deception regarding the independent status of the concept (law), its instantiation (via metalepsis), and its mode of power (mimesis). As Adorno has written in a different context: "To represent the mimesis it supplanted, the concept has no other way than to adopt something mimetic in its own conduct, without abandoning itself" (1973, 15).

55. On the "aesthetic sphere," briefly, Habermas takes up Weber's rendering of Kant's three *Critiques* into a tripartite division of epistemic and institutional labor in modern thinking. The argument goes: Under conditions of modernization and secularization, three separate spheres of thinking and activity formerly held in a unity by religion emerge in the modern age: science, morality and aesthetics. Underlying this tripartite division is the loss of legitimate anchoring in other-worldly sources of truth or fate, and so the new and modern problem of the *legitimacy* of authority develops. Each of the three spheres of knowledge contains a separate type of rationality appropriate to its ends, which produces and answers to its own standards of legitimacy, and within each sphere specialists and institutions develop that undergo learning processes. The differentiation of knowledge spheres is both a blessing and a curse, as it were, because the progress of modernization comes at the cost of an increased decoupling of expert spheres from everyday life. The already disenchanted life of secular humans suffers a further loss of meaning because vital life-fulfilling activities are increasingly either farmed out or taken over by others who are experts in that field. On this model, Habermas places aesthetics *on par* with the other two spheres of knowledge/power. However, Habermas's *solution* to

the ills of modernity rests on his theory of communicative rationality as the crucible of reconciliation of differentiation, which, as I will argue throughout, emphasizes the *morally* normative elements of speech *over* its aesthetic elements. In his account, the aesthetic aspects of speech reduce to a pejorative status of perlocution and manipulation. Hence, within Habermas's overall project of uncovering from the ashes of religion's demise its secular resurrection in communicative rationality, aesthetic experience is bequeathed a decidedly insignificant and sometimes dangerous role, at least in most of Habermas's *exoteric* formulations of this problem.

56. I use these terms as a deliberate spin on Walter Benjamin's concept of "profane illumination" which Benjamin used to characterize the deliberate production of insight. See, for example, Benjamin 1978, and Chapter 4, this volume.

57. See, however, Ingram 1995, chap. 7, as well as Ingram 1997 where he brings together Lyotard and Habermas on this essential issue of aesthetic rationality. See also his fine treatment of this theme in 1991. On Habermas and aesthetics, see Duvenage 2003.

Notes to Chapter 2

1. As Habermas puts it, "Horkheimer and Adorno made the really problematic move; like historicism, they surrendered themselves to an uninhibited scepticism regarding reason, instead of weighing the grounds that cast doubt on this scepticism itself" (1987b, 1). Katznelson (2000, chap. 2) locates another alternative to such skepticism in the work of Arendt and Karl Polanyi.

2. Cf. Dews 1995a.

3. See Habermas (1987b) on modern time-consciousness and Kompridis 2006. Harvey (1989, 10) similarly invokes Baudelaire's formulation as the exemplar of modernity's self-consciousness.

4. George Herbert Mead, the principal source for Habermas's theory of the subject (as discussed in Chapter 3) also is supremely modern in this sense of holding to a particular time-consciousness. As Mead writes: "Past and future are actually oriented in the present. It is the import of the present that we desire, and we can find it only in the past that the present's own unique quality demands and in that future to which it alone can lead. In a sense every unexampled present creates the past that is logically demanded for its explanation. It is the fathomless wealth of the perceptual present that was veiled to Hegel's eyes" (1964, 335). Again: "All history is the interpretation of the present" (1964, 298).

5. See Chapter 1. To be sure, Adorno warns that any positivistic, appropriative mimetic procedure will betray itself: "When men try to become like nature they harden themselves against it" (Horkheimer and Adorno 1969, 180). Note that Habermas's contention that Adorno incoherently advocates a mimesis with nature is in dispute. Recently, critics have emphasized in Adorno's theorizing the priority of the *object*, arguing that this move releases Adorno from a metaphysics of the subject. See, for example, Morris 1997; D. Cook 2001. Indeed, Habermas is quite aware that Adorno does not simply advocate mimesis with nature (or art) as a panacea; to the contrary, such a mimesis is terrifying. (See Habermas 1984,

382, nt. 52.) Adorno validates a primordial mimesis in the same way that Rousseau validates the life of the savage in his *Discourse on Inequality*: we cannot return to *that* state of nature, to *that* mimesis. Nonetheless, Habermas wishes to underline that Adorno's mimesis with the nonidentical already signals a kind of rationality that stands *behind* our conjuring of it, and that has been covered over by conceptualizing reason as strictly an instrumental faculty, opposite to a mimesis with nature. How could mimesis even present itself to us moderns if we had instrumental reason and naught else to combat its ills? An *other* kind of rationality is, in Habermas's view, insufficiently recognized by Adorno, and it is this conceptual limitation that explains Adorno's cultural pessimism, positing a cul-de-sac of subjectivity as the inescapable condition of modern life.

6. See Chapter 1, nt. 55.

7. Habermas's position against the metaphysically inflated truth-claims of philosophers remains consistent through to his later work. He argues for example to limit the role of the philosopher to properly that of speech participant and "interpreter on behalf of the lifeworld" (1990, 18–19), rather than as an objective arbiter of truth and justice. Why should this be the case? Because philosophers are not seers, but adept analysts. They should not smuggle into generalized statements parochial biases: "In view of the morally justified pluralism of life projects and life-forms, philosophers can no longer provide on their own account *generally binding* directives concerning the meaning of life. In their capacity as philosophers, their only recourse is to reflective analysis of the procedure through which ethical questions *in general* can be answered" (1993a, 75). See McCumber 1988.

8. This myth of mimesis with the cosmos appears in Plato's *Phaedrus*. It is Aristotle who reports that, following the Pythagorean notion of a mimetic relationship between humans and cosmos, between number and cosmos, "Plato changed the [Pythagorean] name [of this relationship from] imitation to participation" (Arist., *Metaph.* 987B). See Castelli 1991, chap. 3. This subtle substitution of participation for imitation has the result that Plato's use of mimesis tends to conflate or alternate among imitation (as literal, pictorial or bodily citation), participation (in the divine or the political) and (passive or active, mindful or mindless) possession. This is not so much a problem of Plato's indecision so much as the ambiguity of the dialectical quality of mimetic activity. The mimesis complex is so rich in part because of its siting at the intersection of self-identical entities whose boundaries shift in the contact. Mimetic contact can alter the doer or other participants in the doing, so we have a game where potentially all of the relevant variables are in motion at once. Hence, for example, Gadamer's attraction to the concept of play as a model for the ontology of human being in *Truth and Method*.

9. Rousseau 1973, *Social Contract*, chap. 7.

10. See nt. 8; see also, for instance, the list of uses of mimesis in Plato spelled out in Gebauer and Wulf 1995, 35–37, which includes the production of similarity, representing a true model, the emulation of a model, simulation, a transformative capacity, infection.

11. Plato's model of de-individuation and conformity to a god reappears in Nietzsche's early theory of artistic creation in *The Birth of Tragedy*.

12. Cf. Levinas 1969, 111–14.

13. The significance of memory is again signaled in the last section of *Phaedrus* where Plato condemns writing for its debilitating effect on memory. (Plato [1997c, Book VI] requires of philosophers that they possess a good memory.) When writing cribs for memory, the soul needn't capture the imprint of what is taught, mistakenly fetishizing the imitation as the real—true memory is always participation (which writing preempts). (At the limit, however, as Derrida (1981, 104–9) emphasizes, if one's aim is *total* memory, to live *immediately* in the Forms, then memory itself loses the temporal and spatial distance that makes it operable. This dream-death would depend for its completion on the hypnotic power of mimetic reconciliation. (This argument is in conversation with Augustine's notion of time and divine reconciliation in *Confessions*, Book XI.) Thus, as Gadamer reminds us, following Plato: Gods have no need for philosophy. It is humans who must live off of memory—it is the best we mortals can do. And, later, for Derrida: "It is from the site of death as the place of my irreplaceability, that is, of my singularity, that I feel called to responsibility. In this sense only a mortal can be responsible" (1995, 41).

14. See Taylor 1989, chap. 6.

15. See also, on the separation of soul and body: *Phaedo,* 82d–84b.

16. . . . because, following Agamben's reading of Benjamin, what we communicate ultimately is not any particular meaning but communicativity itself, and like the spirit animating Benjamin's storyteller, the flame requires a wick. To foreshorten my argument (see Chapter 4), we might say that "mimesis" stands for the mode of becoming itself, a mode which nonetheless, to appear, requires being, like a flame needs a wick, or *Geist* requires a host. Even with the desacralization of everything, potentiality requires an object; the affective power of becoming requires a vehicle and (at the least) a moment of stillness, usually understood as such in positive reconstruction. Given the linguistic turn in philosophy, Habermas's answer: communicative action and understanding.

17. Aristotle follows Plato in this view, and even naturalizes a mimetic faculty: "As to the origin of the poetic art as a whole, it stands to reason that two operative causes brought it into being, both of them rooted in human nature. Namely (1) the habit of imitating is congenital to human beings from childhood (actually man differs from the other animals in that he is the most imitative and learns his first lessons through imitation), and so is (2) the pleasure that all men take in works of imitation" (1967, Sec. 6, 1448b3–10).

18. By way of contrast, and in reference to my discussion in Section I of this chapter, note the metaphor of the *stamp* used by Descartes: "God, in creating me, put this idea in my nature in much the same way as an artisan imprints his mark on his work. Nor is it necessary that this mark be something different from the work itself. From the very fact that God has created me, it is very credible that he has made me, in some sense, in his own image and similitude, and that I conceive this similitude, in which the idea of God is contained, by the same faculty by which I conceive myself" (1951, 49). Here we see a purified *cogito,* absented from all influence but that of the God, created as a "similitude" of God. In this sense we can underline the continuity (and not the rupture) between Descartes's modern philosophy and Platonic divine mimesis. Likewise, John Locke founds his theory of human nature in his *Second Treatise of Government* on man as God's

workmanship (chap. 1, §6), with reason figured both as the working out of God's will, and as man's faculty for knowing and realizing.

19. See Young 1996.

20. Interestingly, Plato's own form of writing, the philosophical dialogue, is not included in this typology. On this ambiguity, see Derrida 1981, Melberg 1995, chap. 1.

21. The poet's resistance to identity is perhaps surprisingly similar to Socrates's own claim to ignorance in *Apology*. Socrates's is a resistance to mimesis by way of the continuously examined life. Poets peddle mimesis (while proliferating models for others) without the critical self-examination, according to Plato, but the poet's own mode to the side, can their art nevertheless stimulate a critical attitude? For what purpose is Sophocles's *Antigone* taught in liberal arts programs today?

22. Aristotle, unlike Plato, does *not* morally condemn the theater, though he nevertheless *shares* with Plato this same theory of successful acting. Aristotle's famous definition of tragedy (see Chapter 1, nt. 13) depends on affectual identification and transformation. Aristotle's mimetic theory of acting does not ultimately rest on plot, which is to say, on logos. He even suggests that the specular aspect of the mimesis can be ignored; hearing the voices of the actors should suffice to produce the tragic effect. The audience should identify with characters on stage *so that they pass through what stands before them, right to the real which is affect itself.* Viewers/listeners leave behind the situated identification of the emplotted actors, *and feel affect unfettered by the human details.* In this way fiction becomes real. Its truth lies in the experience of affect. The similarity to Plato's mimesis should be evident; its ahistoricality is what really distinguishes the transcendental orientation of the ancients from postmetaphysical revisions. (See Schmidt 2001.)

23. Specifically, speech-acts find governance in a reflective procedure in reference to an undistorted, ideal speech situation, measured strictly in terms of its accordance with three validity claims: truth, rightness, and truthfulness (1990, 58). An earlier formulation stipulated *four* validity claims: sincerity, intelligibility, justifiability, and truthfulness (Habermas 1979, 2, 65). However, *intelligibility* drops out of the picture so the norms can better suit the tripartite directionality of action and judgment: a) to objective facts in the world, b) to intersubjective, social relations, or c) to private experience.

24. See also Honneth 1995, 102. Habermas (1973) appropriates the distinction between "work" and "interaction" from the early writings of Hegel.

25. Contrary to Arendt's claim, but also motivated by its worry, that intimacy or compassion eliminates the plurality requisite for politics by closing the gap between subjects that both predicates and spurs action, Habermas's model of sincere interlocution hopes to *retain* the respective subject positions of each speaker. See Arendt 1966, 81, and 1958 *passim*.

26. See Austin 1962, 108–9. Ricoeur (1973, 94) characterizes perlocution as *stimulus*: "the perlocutionary action is precisely what is the least discursive in discourse. It is the discourse as stimulus. It acts, not by my interlocutor's recognition of my intention, but energetically, by direct influence upon the emotions and the affective dispositions."

27. See also Habermas 1984, 278.

28. Habermas's use of this concept *aura* signals the parallel between his own narrative of the advent of the modern *Bindungseffekt* and Walter Benjamin's narrative with respect to the dissemination and transposition of *aura* in the transition from traditional to modern art techniques. See Benjamin 1968b, and Chapter 4, this volume.

29. This is nothing other than Max Weber's conclusion of his famous essay "Science as a Vocation": "It is not accidental that our greatest art is intimate and not monumental, nor is it accidental that today only within the smallest and intimate circles, in personal human situations, in *pianissimo,* that something is pulsating that corresponds to the prophetic *pneuma*, which in former times swept through the great communities like a firebrand, welding them together" (1946, 155). The "prophetic *pneuma*" is God's breath, the spirit that enraptures and makes holy those who are inspired. I return to this issue in Chapter 4 with reference to Walter Benjamin.

30. See Chapter 1, nt. 54.

31. See Chapter 3.

32. See Wagner and Zipprian 1991.

33. Habermas has attempted in general to relegate affective dispositions to the sphere of the expressive, aesthetic, and noncognitive. He thereby hopes to exorcize the private from communicative action proper. Even though Habermas tells us that communicative action depends in part on meeting the norm of "sincerity," that is, authentic expression, the justificatory procedure of offering reasons does not hearken back to "expression" because no public test could be sufficient, not so long as aesthetic expression is given a purely subjective, that is, private rendering. What needs doing here is not so much a reinvigoration of subjective aesthetics, but rather, an account of aesthetics that answers to the demands of the intersubjective paradigm shift, a postsubjectivistic aesthetics. The question then becomes: What happens to the status of the "aesthetic"? For one attempt to think through this question, see the collected essays in Carroll 2001.

34. See Chapter 3, nt. 3.

35. On further developments, see Habermas 1998a, 41; Coles 2000, 546.

36. See, for example, Habermas 1985a, 154, 1993a, 31, or 1998c, 367.

37. See Dodds 1951, 79.

38. It is at this point of sacrifice that Hobbesian mimesis balks. See Chapter 1, nt. 17.

39. When pressed, Habermas does speak in an interview of "moral feelings," but solely as an external spur to the necessity of making moral judgments, not as internal to understanding itself. Without compassion we are blind to moral problems, he says. Yet what is the source of compassion? It is not Rousseauian nature. Habermas's brief remarks do not address this issue directly, but it seems clear that for Habermas feelings take their place strictly within the interiority of the subjective. Hence, he can write uncritically: "empathy—the ability to project oneself across cultural distances into alien and at first sight incomprehensible conditions of life, behavioral predispositions, and interpretive perspectives—is an emotional prerequisite for ideal role-taking, which requires everyone to take the perspective of all others" (1993a, 174–75). Yet Habermas cannot mean what he says. It is a category mistake to recruit the concept of "empathy" as an "emotional prerequisite" for communicative action.

Such a view would require a philosophy of subjective consciousness that Habermas has rejected by accepting the degree zero of an intersubjective self. (See Chapter 3.) Recall Gadamer's criticism of empathy in Dilthey and in Husserl. In formulating empathy as a condition of *epistemology*, as Habermas does here, he has put the interiority of self-consciousness as primary, but *that* move is precisely denied in any anti-psychologistic account of the subject (Gadamer 1989, 250). Indeed, Habermas himself writes: "To my mind, Gadamer's convincing critique of the empathy theory of the young Dilthey has blocked this retreat once and for all" (1990, 28). Dean characterizes Habermas's confusion over empathy "more as some sort of motivational supplement than a constitutive component of intersubjective relationships" (1995, 220). I would say that where in Habermas "empathy" is a supplement, he fails the intentions of his paradigm shift to intersubjectivity. (In a related vein, it is significant that Rorty [2002] chooses "sympathy" and not "empathy" as the sentiment of choice to guide humanity toward an international rights regime.)

40. I discuss in Chapter 4 Habermas's enlistment of Benjamin's theory of experience in language.

Notes to Chapter 3

1. Some notions of autonomy imply self-sufficiency with respect to needs and desires in forming and satisfying a life plan. These notions of autonomy belong to the discourses of self-realization and self-determination. (See Di Stefano 1996.) In these respects, Habermas does speak to the reconstructive production of a biography, and in some places, of a context-free, autonomous ego. (See my discussion in Section VII of this chapter.) Over the course of his work, however, Habermas comes to (exoterically) restrict his notion of autonomy to the capacity for moral reasoning, where moral judgment aims to take account of what is good not only with respect to one's own needs and lifeplan, but what is good for all. He writes: "An autonomous will is one that is guided by practical reason. Freedom in general consists in the capacity to choose in accordance with maxims; but autonomy is the self-binding of the will by maxims we adopt on the basis of *insight*. Because it is mediated by reason, autonomy is not just one value alongside others. . . . A procedure that operationalizes the moral point of view of impartial judgment is neutral with respect to arbitrary constellations of values but not with respect to practical reason itself [which takes as its guide the] intuition[:] Nobody can be free at the expense of anybody else's freedom" (1998b, 99–101). Again: "With Kant, we refer to the capacity for binding one's own will on the basis of moral insight as freedom of will (*Willensfreiheit*), or autonomy" (1998d, 311). See Habermas 1990, 37; Hinchman 1996.

2. In a similar vein, Aristotle famously writes: "The man who is isolated, who is unable to share in the benefits of political association, or has no need to share because he is already self-sufficient, is no part of the city, and must therefore be either a beast or a god" (1995, 1253a18).

3. Habermas's latest formulation of the *results* of communicative action differentiates between strong agreement *(Einverständnis)* and a weaker form of

understanding: "*Agreement* in the strict sense is achieved only if the participants are able to accept a validity claim for the *same* reasons, while *mutual understanding* (*Verständigung*) can also come about when one participant sees that the other, in light of her preferences, has good reasons in the given circumstances for her declared intention—that is, reasons that are good *for her—without having to make these reasons his own in light of his preferences.* Actor-independent reasons permit a stronger mode of reaching understanding than actor-relative reasons" (1998d, 321).

4. Young, for one, is quite direct in opposing this notion of *reversibility* in practice and principle: "one person cannot adopt another person's perspective because he cannot live another person's history" (1997a, 352). She develops as an alternative a theory of moral respect in communication based on the recognition of irreducible *difference* rather than on mutual understanding—as if the "recognition of irreducible difference" and "mutual understanding" differ in principle. I believe that Gadamer's formulation of *understanding* can remove the sting from Young's objections, where to understand means to understand *differently*. To insist that "one person cannot adopt another person's perspective because he cannot live another person's history" begs the question of what it means to live one's *own* history. One of the commitments of the linguistic turn in critical theory is that experience arrives in articulate form. For experience to be articulate is for it to be publicly accessible. The circuit of publicity invalidates the trumping power of authenticity. Young's insistence that reversibility means identicality is wrong in two ways: First, it wrongfully denies that a person takes up his or her own history in language. If a person takes up his history in articulate form, then nothing in principle can stop anyone from understanding another. Second, it holds the bar too high for what counts as understanding. If two people can only understand one another if, in fact, they are one person, then understanding in principle is denied. Political theory must work with a weaker form of understanding. Young (1990, 232) herself supports such a view ("the subject is a heterogeneous process" who always exceeds him or herself), but constructs a strawman when denying this position to her purported opponents. Benhabib is also critical of "reversibility" where the notion of reversibility presumes a disembodied or disembedded ego. She wishes to distinguish between "substitutionalist" and "interactive" universalism. The first makes the mistake of posing an asymmetrical opposition, where *men's* (and not women's) experience is assumed to stand for *human* experience. Interactive universalism, in contrast, "acknowledges the plurality of modes of being human, and differences among humans, without endorsing all these pluralities and differences as morally and politically valid" (1992, 153).

5. Herbert Blumer is the principal representative of this school, but Peter Berger and Thomas Luckmann, in their famous *The Social Construction of Reality*, also claim Mead as a principle inspiration. Habermas (1987a, 138–40) distances his own appropriation of Mead from this tradition by arguing that their analyses reduce communicative action to questions of social psychology, while his own appropriation of Mead broaches not only social psychology but also questions of social integration and cultural reproduction.

6. Habermas is not alone in emphasizing Mead's significance in Western philosophy as the turning point to intersubjectivity. Tugendhat (1986, 219) writes:

"Aside from Heidegger, George Herbert Mead is the only philosopher I know of who has attempted to free the relation of oneself to oneself from the conception of a reflexive relation. He thereby sought to extricate it from the traditional subject–object model, and to reconceptualize it in a structurally new way." This conclusion is also held by Honneth (1994): "Even today, [Mead's] writings contain the most suitable means for reconstructing the intersubjectivist intuitions of the young Hegel within a postmetaphysical framework. Mead clearly has more in common with the Hegel of the Jena period than just the idea of a social genesis of ego-identity. And the agreement between their political-philosophical approaches is not limited to their criticisms of the atomism of social contract theory. . . . Mead also aims to make the struggle for recognition the point of reference for a theoretical construction in terms of which the moral development of society is to be explained" (1996, 71).

7. See Leys 1994; Joas 1997, 99ff; Borch-Jacobsen 1992.

8. Deploring the closed circle of the Absolute, Mead writes: "Life is a happening; things take place; the novel arises; and our intelligence shows itself in solving problems. . . . The collapse of absolute idealism lies in the fact that everything is all accomplished in the Absolute. All that is to take place has already taken place in the Absolute. But our life is an adventure. . . . The realization of emergence in philosophy, the large acceptance of pluralism which you see, is involved in the assumption that the novel can appear by saying it is an enlarging of our finite imperfect experience" (1936, 508). Additionally, insofar as the concept of the Absolute negates with a preemptive move the importance of the concept of "emergence," it depends on a concept of the human subject only to abrogate its impact: "The grandiose undertaking of Absolute Idealism . . . failed because it left the perspective of the finite ego hopelessly infected with subjectivity and consequently unreal. . . . It recognized the two dominant forces of modern life, the creative individual and creative science only to abrogate them as falsifications of the experience of the absolute ego" (1932, 161).

9. It is necessary to indicate that the reliability of Mead's most well-known work, *Mind, Self, Society*, as well as his *Movements of Thought in the Nineteenth Century*, cannot always be assured. These volumes are collections of classnotes, reportedly taken down verbatim from Mead's lectures and arranged by editors, his former students. Many of Mead's significant published essays are collected in *Selected Writings*, and an extremely useful archive of his written work and notes (as well as that of many of his fellow travelers and followers) can be freely accessed at URL: http://www.brocku.ca/MeadProject/inventory5.html

10. Interestingly, this formulation, developed by Mead beginning in his 1903 article "The Definition of the Psychical," mirrors that of W.E.B. Du Bois who, also in 1903, famously reckons the American Negro's problem as one of "double consciousness": "It is a peculiar sensation, this double-consciousness, this sense of always looking at one's self through the eyes of others, of measuring one's soul by the tape of a world that looks on in amused contempt and pity" (1986, 364). Where Mead speaks of recognition of socially constituted selves, Du Bois works on the interruption of this circuit of recognition and its consequences. Both writers in this pragmatist mode are working to domesticate and anthropomorphize the circuit of recognition in Hegel's Master-Slave dialectic of *The Phenomenology of*

Spirit. Both were students at Harvard and then at the University of Berlin. Mead was at Harvard from 1887 to the spring 1889; Du Bois, from fall 1888 to 1892. At Harvard, both took classes from the Hegelian idealist Josiah Royce, as well as George Palmer. Although Mead did not attend William James's classes, he lived in James's home, and Du Bois who did take classes with James was frequently a guest in James's home. (Miller 1973, xii–xiv; Wolters 2002, 16.) Mead was in Berlin for spring 1889 through autumn 1891; Du Bois was in Berlin from 1892 to 1894. At the University of Berlin Mead studied under Wilhelm Dilthey; Du Bois did not study with Dilthey, but attended nevertheless, in Posnock's (1988, 180) words, "in the midst of a Hegelian revival."

11. This formulation recurs in his article "The Social Self": "The self which consciously stands over against other selves thus becomes an object, an other to himself, through the very fact that he hears himself talk, and replies. The mechanism of introspection is therefore given in the social attitude which man necessarily assumes toward himself, and the mechanism of thought, insofar as thought uses symbols which are used in social intercourse, is but an inner conversation" (1964, 146).

12. Hegel: "Self-consciousness is faced by another self-consciousness; it has come *out of itself*. This has a twofold significance: first, it has lost itself, for it finds itself as an *other* being; secondly, in doing so it has superceded the other, for it does not see the other as an essential being, but in the other sees its own self" (1977, 111).

13. Dews 1999, 102–10.

14. Tugendhat (1986) draws the parallels between Heidegger and Mead. Habermas writes, "Pragmatism [has] highlighted . . . the phenomenon described in an ontological fashion by Heidegger as 'being-ahead-of-oneself' in a 'thrown projection.' The anticipatory character of understanding is universal; the moments of projection and discovery complement each other in *all* cognitive activities" (1993a, 30). Mead's own account of temporality falls under his concept of "emergence." See Mead's (1932) lecture "Emergence and Identity."

15. I have found nothing to indicate that Mead was familiar with the writings of V.N. Volosinov (which may or may not have been penned by Mikhail Bakhtin). Volosinov in roughly the same time period writes explicitly against Dilthey, and, paralleling Mead, argues for an "objective psychology," arguing that "experience exists even for the person undergoing it only in the material of signs. . . . [and] the semiotic material of the psyche is preeminently the word—*inner speech*. . . . it is the word that constitutes the foundation, the skeleton of inner life. Were it to be deprived of the word, the psyche would shrink to an extreme degree. . . . Orientation in one's own soul (introspection) is in actuality inseparable from orientation in the particular social situation in which the experience occurs" (1986, 28–29, 37).

16. Joas (1997, 230, nt. 61) notes that a full treatment of complementary themes in Freud and Mead is yet to be written. Dews's (1999) essay on Lacan and Mead is perhaps a step in that direction. Habermas differentiates Mead from Freud insofar as Freud investigates the "psychodynamic facets" of depersonalization and the internalization of norms, whereas Mead looks to the "*sociocognitive conditions of internalization*" (1990, 154).

17. To adumbrate the parallels I'll draw between Mead and Benjamin (Chapter 4), note that Benjamin writes: "Awakening is the exemplary case of remembering: the weighty and momentous case, in which we succeed in remembering the nearest (most obvious)" (1999i, 907).

18. This view originated with Mead's friend and fellow pragmatist John Dewey.

19. It is on the basis of the significance given here to interpretation that I will frequently use the term *intersubjective*, as it better captures Mead's argument where he himself uses the term *objective*.

20. Mead calls such latent responses "tendencies," as in: "the individual who is stimulating others to response is at the same time arousing in himself the tendencies to the same reactions" (1964, 286). He also uses the careful phrase "congenital tendency," as in "Human behavior, or conduct, like the behavior of lower animal forms, springs from impulses. An impulse is a congenital tendency to react in a specific manner to a certain sort of stimulus, under certain organic conditions. Hunger and anger are illustrations of such impulses. They are best termed 'impulses,' and not 'instincts,' because they are subject to extensive modifications in the life-history of individuals" (1934, 337). By figuring "congenital tendency" as "impulse" capable of modification via learned experience, Mead attempts to split the difference between nature and nurture, giving the dominant role to the latter without negating the former. In one of his last major essays, he breaks from this fence-sitting giving total priority to nurture: "In man even the immediate impulse that lies above the automatisms is the response of a self, and a self-experience is possible only insofar as the individual has already taken the attitude of the other" (1964, 397). Mead can distinguish as two separate stages automatic behavior from responsive behavior, but he cannot ultimately explain how to get from the first stage to the second, nor why the truths uncovered by reflection in the second stage sometimes revert to the status of the first, to habit. Habermas's focus on "reconstructive" sciences potentially removes the teleology implied in Mead's framework.

21. Recall here that Aristotle in his *Poetics* attributes an imitative faculty in children to nature, and refers to this imitative faculty as the origin of the imitative arts: "As to the origin of the poetic art as a whole, it stands to reason that two operative causes brought it into being, both of them rooted in human nature. Namely (1) the habit of imitating is congenital to human beings from childhood (actually man differs from the other animals in that he is the most imitative and learns his first lessons through imitation), and so is (2) the pleasure that all men take in works of imitation" (1967, Sec. 6, 1448b3–10). Mead shares the view with Aristotle *and* Plato that imitation in children is fundamental, but hopes to differentiate a mindless imitation from conscious imitation, the rational working out of mimetic activity.

22. Mead: "Imitation as the mere tendency on the part of an organism to reproduce what it sees or hears other organisms doing is mechanically impossible; one cannot conceive an organism as so constructed that all the sights and sounds which reach it would arouse in the organism tendencies to reproduce what it sees and hears in those fields of experience" (1934, 60).

23. Cf. on tribal rationality, see Henry 2000. Mead here simply follows Adam Smith who similarly equates primitive backwardness with animality and Africa with unconscious mimesis as their mode of interaction (Smith 1976, 16).

24. It goes without saying that following a rule implies also recognizing rule violations, yet Mead does not thematize rule-breaking, and does not make it internal to the process of understanding.

25. This "pro-duction" signals the bridge between poiesis and praxis, where praxis is *intentional* and *willed* action—the acceptance of a doer behind the deed—and *poiesis* describes the pro-duction of being from non-being without conscious intentionality. See Agamben 1999, chap. 8, which reads through Heideggerian/Arendtian glasses Aristotle's distinction between poiesis and praxis in *Nicomachean Ethics*.

26. See nt. 20.

27. See Allison 2001, chap. 12.

28. Planty-Bonjour (1983, 23–24) writes: "It is through desire that a man becomes a thing. . . . Hegel found out that making is that kind of activity by which an agent by producing something produces himself. Making is not only a transitive action, but has all the characteristics of an immanent action. Hegel assigns to *poiesis* what Aristotle assigns only to *praxis*: to be an end in itself. Insofar as, by making, the subject made himself a thing, it follows that action is not a mere *Entausserung* [alienation] but it is also a true *Entfremdung* [estrangement]. Hegel means by that the great ambiguity of the nature of making, also of work in the modern economy. If making is no longer as Aristotle believed, the activity of an unfree man, it is nevertheless not that of a free man either, the activity by which man may realize himself entirely."

29. Mead: "When we use the term 'recognition,' . . . what we generally mean is that the character of the object that is a stimulus to its recognition is present in our experience" (1934, 85).

30. This is indeed what is at stake in many, many explorations of generalized mimesis, from Freud's *Group Psychology and the Ego* to Fritz Lang's film *M*.

31. To be sure Mead tries to make room for a self critical of itself, and in his essay of 1913, "The Social Self," he attributes the self-critical attitude to "another 'me' criticising, approving, and suggesting, and consciously planning, i.e., the reflective self" (145). This would make the total structural positions not two, but three: an *I*, a socialized *me* (which can be fragmented into multiple roles), and a reflective *me*. However, this last term, the reflective self, what he calls an "inner response to his [own] action," that is, a response to the meaning of his multiple *me's* determined socially, "may [appear] in the role of another—we present his arguments in imagination and do it with his intonations and gestures and even perhaps with his facial expression." Thus the *reflective me* can take the form of the mimetic doubling of another within the self. This however would be a *me* that is *not* free of socialization: thus, the self-evaluative modes of "criticizing, approving, suggesting and consciously planning" would appear to one in the voice of another. Mead suggests no other non-mimetic form for this *reflective me*, and so Mead is unable to distinguish this so-called *reflective me* from the overdetermined, socialized me. At this point in the development of his theoretical apparatus, he might have dropped the *I* from his account of the self in recognition of the fact that criticism can arise within a self, for example, via the importation of those fissures, healthy

and otherwise, within society. This path, however, Mead does not take. Instead, in his later lectures of 1927 and 1930 collected in *Mind, Self, Society,* this notion of a reflective *me* has been dropped, and the reflective function given over to the *I*. Cf. Aboulafia 2001.

32. See also Mead 1964, 287–88.

33. See Chapter 1, nt. 54.

34. Think here of Emerson's memorable provocation: "imitation is suicide."

35. Dews (1999) argues that both Mead and Lacan, and generally speaking, any theory of self that contains a figure of the *unconscious*, where the self is not transparent to him or herself, must entail a structural division within the self. In Mead's work, this rupture is construed as a dialectic *between subjectivity and intersubjectivity*. Dews believes that he can use this insight to undercut the tenor of Habermas's paradigm shift from subjectivity to intersubjectivity. I believe what this shows is that Habermas at this point wisely cuts ties with Mead.

36. See also Agamben 1999, chap. 10.

37. See Pensky 1989.

38. Habermas's emphasis on intersubjectivity as the substance or way of the subject's own interiority shows up also (1992e, 144) in his discussion of Kierkegaard, where he writes that the "I alone can performatively lay claim to being recognized as an individual in my uniqueness," and yet, the I as a "capsule of absolute inwardness [is inadequate; we must instead] follow Humboldt and George Herbert Mead in grafting it onto the medium of a language that crosses processes of socialization and individuation with each other."

39. Frank (2002), a staunch defender of a metaphysical *I*, in fact strongly criticizes Habermas for forcing the I to disappear into language.

40. Cf. Finlayson 1999.

Notes to Chapter 4

1. See Chapter 3, Section V.

2. See Habermas 1993b.

3. See Introduction, nt. 3.

4. See, for example, Dews 1995b, 207. Habermas argues in 1982 that "the [priority] of historically situated morality (*Sittlichkeit*) against an abstractly universal morality (*Moral*) [is] false" (1982, 253). Just one year later, however, he reverses himself: "Because morality is always embedded in what Hegel called ethical life (*Sittlichkeit*), discourse ethics is always subject to limitations, though not limitations that can devalue its critical function or strengthen the skeptic in his role as an advocate of a counterenlightenment" (1990, 99). See, however, Siep (1983, 153) who concludes that "one cannot accuse Hegel of eliminating conscience and responsibility [because conscience] cannot be placed beyond all intersubjective standards for examination." This would suggest that Habermas is addressing merely a pseudo-problem in Hegel.

5. See also Gutmann and Thompson 2002. From a very different perspective, Dean (2002) criticizes as "Habermasochism" the apparently compulsive drive toward universal, undistorted speech as a cure for distorted speech. On Dean's

reading, public life is plagued already by too much talk. Communication only produces more communication, whether distorted or no, and can't therefore recoup that which instrumental rationality has squandered. Habermas's notion of "communicative rationality," for Dean, is merely the *ideology* of a "communicative capitalism."

6. See Chapter 2, Section II.

7. See Habermas 1984, 249–50; but, see also Lukes 1982.

8. This *integrative* role of communication works at the intersubjective level of dialogic interaction, in what Habermas identifies as rationality's three core expressions: knowledge, action, and speech—"It is more probably the case that the structure of discourse establishes an interrelation among the entwined structures of rationality (the structures of knowledge, action, and speech) by, in a sense, *bringing together* the propositional, teleological, and communicative roots [of each of the three structures]. According to such a model of *intermeshed* core structures, discursive rationality owes its special position not to its foundational but to its integrative role" (1998d, 308–9).

9. In a later formulation, Habermas will admit that communicative rationality is not in competition with religion, and is agnostic to religion's viability: "As long as no better words for what religion can say are found in the medium of rational discourse, it [communicative reason] will even coexist abstemiously with the former, neither supporting it nor combating it" (1992f, 145). We should read this apparently accommodating view as *also* saying that once rational discourse *can* say what religion says better than religion, then religion as such would wither away. As Strong and Sposito (1995, 267) suggest, for Habermas, "[r]eligion is no longer a modern alternative, for when God is dead the religious mode becomes monstrous." This formulation of "religion as monstrous" may capture Habermas's modernist tendencies, but he is very clear to argue (Habermas 1992h) that philosophy may only *cite* religious exuberance, while religion can deploy it. Habermas's intention for the theory of communicative rationality is to imagine a nondogmatic mode of dialectical thought for postauratic subjects. It is not so much that communicative rationality *can* exist side by side the institutions of religion—of course it *does*, and indeed, it continues to harvest "semantic potentials" in religious law, practice and belief. The issue rather is that Habermas, when he follows Benjamin, writes in a Marxist and messianic mode, for a future yet to come, for a new kind of political and postreligious subject, where communicative rationality itself motivates postconventional selves to normative action. For now, however, Habermas contends we belong to a postsecular moment, where the rise of high capitalism has been uncoupled from a corresponding secularization. No *necessary* causal force leads from one to the other, and in fact, religious belief is enjoying an apparent renaissance (Habermas c. 2009).

10. See Cascardi 1992, chap. 5.

11. See Benjamin 1968c, 156ff.

12. Jay writes: "Adorno shared his friend's [Benjamin's] hostility to *Erlebnis*, a term which had been extolled by the irrationalist 'philosophers of life' [e.g., Dilthey,] in Germany because of its alleged spontaneity and freedom from overly intellectual reflection. More recent thinkers like the existentialists were no less guilty of privileging a pseudo-immediacy through what Adorno called their

'jargon of authenticity.' In both cases, a philosophy that wanted to break through the stultifying confines of rationality and tradition to grasp human existence in its naked form had unwittingly duplicated the irrationality and uprootedness of modern social experience" (1984a, 74–75).

13. See Benjamin 1999c. Already in Benjamin's (1918) early "On the Program of the Coming Philosophy," he argues that Kant relegates experience to the temporally ephemeral, and in doing so, improperly allows himself to ignore the effect experience necessarily has on knowledge. See Lindroos 2001, 22. This is precisely Mead's view of educated instinct, as we saw above. Where Habermas holds onto "intuition" as a precognitive form, he returns behind the advances Mead and Benjamin had already made.

14. See Jay 2005, chap. 8.

15. Page numbers in this section refer to this text.

16. See Andrew Benjamin 1999.

17. Benjamin writes: "Experience of the aura thus rests on the transposition of a response common in human relationships to the relationship between the inanimate or natural object and man. The person we look at, or who feels he is being looked at, looks at us in turn. To perceive the aura of an object we look at means to invest it with the ability to look at us in return. This experience corresponds to the data of [Proust's] *mémoire involontaire*" (1968c, 188). It is the phenomena of involuntary memory—that which overcomes us in the shock of a moment which absorbs us in its historicality—which we moderns, like Proust, can only "synthetically," or artificially try to achieve. As Benjamin would write a year later: "What withers in the age of mechanical reproduction is the aura of the work of art" (1968b, 221).

18. Baudrillard will later refer to the television "news item" in a similar manner. Consumption, he writes, is "[t]he denial of the real on the basis of an avid and repeated apprehending of its signs" (1998, 34).

19. Hansen (1999, 310) writes, "The decline of experience, '*Erfahrung*' in Benjamin's emphatic sense, is inseparable from that of memory, as the faculty that connects sense perceptions of the present with those of the past and thus enables us to remember both past sufferings and forgotten futures."

20. Ricoeur (1985, 28), for one, writes: "And yet . . . and yet. . . . Perhaps new modes will be invented, are being born. . . . For we have no idea of what a culture would be where no one any longer knew what it meant to narrate things." To the contrary, the destruction of experience is the starting point for Agamben's analysis in *Infancy and History*.

21. This point is made very clear in the lecture on Bataille in Habermas 1987b. For his own criticism of the Surrealists, see Habermas 1997, 40–42.

22. Ingram (1995, 318ff) makes a closely related point, that to emphasize the epiphanic power of poetic illumination and/or profane illumination is to weaken in a salutary way the "discursive rigidity" in Habermas's communicative rationality.

23. "In Baudelaire," Benjamin writes, "the price for which the sensation of the modern age may be had: the disintegration of the aura in the experience of shock." Baudelaire had "given the weight of an experience (*Erfahrung*) to . . . the nature of something lived through (*Erlebnis*)" (1968c, 194).

24. Proust's innovation in how the past comes to realize itself in the present is through the experience of involuntary memory. Proust's remembrance was an active (not a passive), synthetic reconstruction of a life spurred by a chain of memory which acted on its own, as it were. See Benjamin 1999a, but also 1968c and McCole 1993, 259–60.

25. Ely writes that the specific anticonceptual character of Benjamin's images play the "foil to the German (Northern) industrial and administrative development. Thus Positano, Capri, and even Naples [i.e., those locales where Benjamin would vacation with compatriots Adorno, Ernst Bloch, Siegfried Kracauer, Alfred Sohn-Rethel, et al.] became topoi for the concrete localization of the mimetic and montage images to which instrumental reason was opposed. Image-concepts such as 'the fair [*Jahrmarket*],' the 'continuum' and the 'standstill' of history's movement, 'cliff-madness' [*Felsenwahn*] 'colportage,' 'mass ornament,' 'constellation,' and 'correspondence' are not (abstract) concepts but material symbols and montage composites" (Ely 1998, 195).

26. See Chapter 3, Section VII.

27. To indicate what he has in mind, in addition to the fact that much of the *Arcades Project* is a compendium of citations arrayed like a cityscape, note the tension between the following two notes: "Michelet—an author who, wherever he is quoted, makes the reader forget the book in which the quotation appears" (1999i, 468); and: "The events surrounding the historian, and in which he himself takes part, will underlie his presentation in the form of a text written in invisible ink. The history which he lays before the reader comprises, as it were, the citations occurring in this text, and it is only these citations that occur in a manner legible to all. To write history thus means to *cite* history. It belongs to the concept of citation, however, that the historical object in each case is torn from its context" (476). In the first instance, the choice citation becomes exemplary and stands apart from and outshines any new context that is supposed to animate it. In the second, the citation betrays its original context that had made it exemplary by presuming to stand for the whole while rising beyond it, seeking permanence beyond its original constellation of meaning. We see here the tension between mimesis and anti-mimesis in the cross-purposes of immanence and transcendence. We select a citation because it speaks better than we might in our own voice, demanding it speak for us, though the mimicry is half-hearted for its voice betrays us and itself in being both amenable to our purposes and therefore out of sorts with itself. What emerges, in fact, is something new, but not so utterly new that it surpasses without remainder the fraught condition of its rebirthing.

28. No film-maker simply turns on the camera and microphones and lets them roll without interruption. The rare exception which proves the rule: Andy Warhol's exceedingly boring film of a man sleeping through the night, or consider film from a security camera at an all-night gas station. These are less films than they are recordings in real time. Thus, they are not examples of mimesis. They occupy the dead zone between life and art. The recent Danish Dogme film-making movement holds as its ideal unmanipulated filming, but in execution it cannot but stage its actors and plot its narrative (i.e., it remains theater).

29. See Gebauer and Wulf 1995, chap. 21.

30. Cf. Wohlfarth 1989.

31. See Habermas 1987b, 220, where he essentially reiterates his position from 1972 (1988, 124).

32. This view—that insisting on the "autonomy" of the aesthetic risks its ghettoization as *art*—finds accord in Dewey, for whom the aesthetic may resonate in any experience. For the suggestion that we might reconstruct Habermas's aesthetics on the basis of Dewey's aesthetics, see Langsdorf 2002; Kompridis 1994. See also McCumber 1989, chap. 21.

33. See Chapter 1, nt. 55.

34. Agamben continues: "It is precisely this empty space that politicians and the media establishment are trying to be sure to control, by keeping it separate in a sphere that guarantees its unseizability and by preventing communicativity itself from coming to light. This means that an integrated Marxian analysis should take into consideration the fact that capitalism (or whatever other name we might want to give to the process dominating world history today) not only was directed to the expropriation of productive activity, but was also and above all directed to the alienation of language itself, of the communicative nature of human beings" (2000, 94–95).

35. See Chapter 3.

36. Habermas writes: "The ego, which seems to me to be given in my self-consciousness as what is purely my own, cannot be maintained by me solely through my own power, as it were for me alone—it does not 'belong' to me. Rather, this ego always retains an intersubjective core because the process of individuation from which it emerges runs through the network of linguistically mediated interactions" (1992a, 170).

Notes to Coda

1. Bohman (1994) writes, too, in a mode that attempts to domesticate disclosure as an event which *a posteriori* answers to public deliberation: "First, disclosure is . . . an act of expression that opens up new possibilities and restores the plasticity of the cultural world necessary for learning and change. Second, disclosures are not disclosures of truth; they are prior to truth and concern what makes truth possible, in the sense that they make possible both true and false statements about the world and ourselves. Disclosures are not self-justifying or self-verifying, but require public reflection to test them. . . . The ultimate test for reflection on disclosure is the practical question of how we should live" (94–95).

2. Bennett in her defense of "enchantment" as part and parcel of the modern condition makes this apology: "there is no way to guarantee that an aesthetic disposition will produce or even incline toward goodness, generosity, or social justice. Affect can join narcissism, beauty can serve violence, and enchantment can foster cruelty. These links are not inevitable, however, and an affective ethics does not automatically lead to frivolity, violence, or cruelty. It is also important to recall, as the critics often fail to do [although Habermas does not] that even rationality-based morality cannot determine what its ethical effects will be" (2001, 148).

Bibliography

Aboulafia, Mitchell. 2001. *The Cosmopolitan Self: George Herbert Mead and Continental Philosophy.* Urbana, IL: University of Illinois Press.

Adorno, Theodor. 1973 [1966]. *Negative Dialectics.* Trans. E. B. Ashton. New York: Continuum.

———. 1991 [1961] "Trying to Understand *Endgame*." In *Notes to Literature, Volume I*, edited by Rolf Tiedemann. Trans. Shierry Weber Nicholsen. New York: Columbia University Press.

———. 1992 [1965]. "The Handle, the Pot, and Early Experience." In *Notes to Literature, Volume II*, edited by Rolf Tiedemann. Trans. Shierry Weber Nicholsen. New York: Columbia University Press.

Agamben, Giorgio. 1999 [1994]. *The Man Without Content.* Trans. Georgia Albert. Stanford: Stanford University Press.

———. 2000. *Means without End: Notes on Politics.* Minneapolis, MN: University of Minnesota Press.

———. 2007 [1978]. *Infancy and history: On the Destruction of Experience.* Trans. Liz Heron. London: Verso.

Allison, Henry E. 2001. *Kant's Theory of Taste: A Reading of the* Critique of Aesthetic Judgment. Cambridge: Cambridge University Press.

Anderson, Perry. 1983. *In the Tracks of Historical Materialism.* London: Verso Press.

Arendt, Hannah.1958. *The Human Condition.* Chicago: University of Chicago Press.

———. 1961. "What is Authority?" In *Between Past and Future: Six Exercises in Political Thought.* New York: Viking Press.

———. 1966. *On Revolution.* New York: Viking Press.

Aristotle. 1967. *Poetics.* Trans. Gerald F. Else. Ann Arbor: University of Michigan Press.

———. 1995. *The Politics.* Trans. Ernest Barker, Revised by R. F. Stalley. Oxford and New York: Oxford Press.

Austin, J.L. 1962. *How to Do Things with Words*, 2nd ed. Edited by J.O. Urmson and Marina Sbisà. Cambridge, MA: Harvard University Press.

Bakhtin, M.M. 1986. "The Problem of Speech Genres" (1952–53) in *Speech Genres & Other Late Essays.* Trans. Vern W. McGee and Edited by Caryl Emerson and Michael Holquist. Austin, TX: University of Texas Press.

Balibar, Etienne. 1991. "Citizen Subject." In *Who Comes After the Subject?*, edited by Eduardo Cadava, Peter Connor and Jean-Luc Nancy. Trans. James B. Swenson, Jr. London: Routledge.

Baudrillard, Jean. 1998 [1970]. *The Consumer Society: Myths and Structures*. London: Sage Publications.

Beiner, Ronald. 1997 [1984]. "Rescuing the Rationalist Heritage." In *Philosophy in a Time of Lost Spirit: Essays on Contemporary Theory*. Toronto, Buffalo and London: University of Toronto Press.

Benhabib, Seyla. 1984. "Epistemologies of Postmodernism: A Rejoinder to Jean-François Lyotard." *New German Critique* 33 Autumn 103–26.

———. 1992. *Situating the Self: Gender, Community and Postmodernism in Contemporary Ethics*. New York: Routledge.

———. 2002. *The Claims of Culture*. Princeton, NJ: Princeton University Press.

Benjamin, Andrew. 1999. "Tradition and Experience: Walter Benjamin's *Some Motifs in Baudelaire*." In *The Problems of Modernity: Adorno and Benjamin*, edited by Andrew Benjamin. London: Routledge.

Benjamin, Walter.1968a [1936]. "The Storyteller: Reflections on the Works of Nikolai Leskov." In *Illuminations: Essays and Reflections*, edited with an Introduction by Hannah Arendt. Trans. Harry Zohn. New York: Schocken Books.

———. 1968b [1936]. "The Work of Art in the Age of Mechanical Reproduction." In *Illuminations: Essays and Reflections*, edited with an Introduction by Hannah Arendt. Trans. Harry Zohn. New York: Schocken Books.

———. 1968c [1939]. "On Some Motifs in Baudelaire." In *Illuminations: Essays and Reflections*, edited with an Introduction by Hannah Arendt. Trans. Harry Zohn. New York: Schocken Books.

———. 1968d [c.1940]. "Theses on the Philosophy of History." In *Illuminations: Essays and Reflections*, edited with an Introduction by Hannah Arendt. Trans. Harry Zohn. New York: Schocken Books.

———. 1978 [1929]. "Surrealism." In *Reflections: Essays, Aphorisms, Autobiographical Writings*, edited with an Introduction by Peter Demetz. Trans. Edmund Jephcott. New York: Schocken Books.

———. 1996a [1916]. "On Language as Such and the Language of Man." In *Selected Writings, Volume I, 1913–1926*. Trans. Edmund Jephcott. Cambridge, MA: Belknap Press.

———. 1996b [1918]. "On the Program of the Coming Philosophy."*Selected Writings, Volume I, 1913–1926*. Trans. Mark Ritter. Cambridge, MA: Belknap Press.

———. 1996c [1921]. "Critique of Violence." In *Selected Writings, Volume I, 1913–1926*. Trans. Edmund Jephcott. Cambridge, MA: Belknap Press.

———. 1999a [1929] "On the Image of Proust." In *Selected Writings, Volume 2, 1927–1934*. Trans. Rodney Livingstone. Cambridge, MA: Belknap Press.

———. 1999b [1929] "Short Shadows (1)." In *Selected Writings, Volume 2, 1927–1934*. Trans. Rodney Livingstone. Cambridge, MA: Belknap Press.

———. 1999c [1931/32] "Experience." In *Selected Writings, Volume 2, 1927–1934*. Trans. Rodney Livingstone. Cambridge, MA: Belknap Press.

———. 1999d [1932]. "The Handkerchief." In *Selected Writings, Volume 2, 1927–1934*. Trans. Rodney Livingstone. Cambridge, MA: Belknap Press.

———. 1999e [1933]. "On the Mimetic Faculty." In *Selected Writings, Volume 2, 1927–1934*. Trans. Edmund Jephcott. Cambridge, MA: Belknap Press.

———. 1999f [1933]. "Doctrine of the Similar." In *Selected Writings, Volume 2, 1927–1934.* Trans. Michael Jennings. Cambridge, MA: Belknap Press.

———. 1999g [1933]. "Experience and Poverty." In *Selected Writings, Volume 2, 1927–1934.* Trans. Rodney Livingstone. Cambridge, MA: Belknap Press.

———. 1999h [1933]. "Thought Figures." In *Selected Writings, Volume 2, 1927–1934.* Trans. Rodney Livingstone. Cambridge, MA: Belknap Press.

———. 1999i. *The Arcades Project.* Trans. Howard Eiland and Kevin McLaughlin. Cambridge, MA: Belknap Press.

———. 2003 [1940]. "On the Concept of History." In *Selected Writings, Volume 4, 1938–1940.* Trans. Harry Zohn. Cambridge, MA: Belknap Press.

Bennett, Jane. 2001. *The Enchantment of Modern Life: Attachments, Crossings, and Ethics.* Princeton, NJ: Princeton University Press.

Bernstein, Jay M. 1989. "Art Against Enlightenment: Adorno's Critique of Habermas." In *The Problems of Modernity: Adorno and Benjamin*, edited by Andrew Benjamin. London: Routledge.

———. 1997. "The Causality of Fate: Modernity and Modernism in Habermas." In *Habermas and the Unfinished Project of Modernity: Critical Essays on The Philosophical Discourse of Modernity*, edited by Maurizio Passerin d'Entrèves and Seyla Benhabib. Cambridge, MA: MIT Press.

———. 1999. "Adorno on Disenchantment: The Scepticism of Enlightened Reason." In *German Philosophy Since Kant*, edited by Anthony O'Hear. Cambridge: Cambridge University Press.

Bernstein, Richard J. 1996. "What is the Difference that Makes a Difference? Gadamer, Habermas, and Rorty." In *Hermeneutics and Modern Philosophy*, edited by Brice R. Wachterhauser. Albany: SUNY Press.

———. 1998. "Community in the Pragmatic Tradition." In T*he Revival of Pragmatism: New Essays on Social Thought, Law, and Culture*, edited by Morris Dickstein. Durham, NC: Duke University Press, 1998.

Bhabha, Homi. 1984. "Of Mimicry and Man: The Ambivalence of Colonial Discourse." *October* 28: 125–33.

Bohman, James. 1994. "World Disclosure and Radical Criticism." *Thesis Eleven* 37: 82–97.

———. 1997. "Two Versions of the Linguistic Turn." In *Habermas and the Unfinished Project of Modernity: Critical Essays on The Philosophical Discourse of Modernity*, edited by Maurizio Passerin d'Entrèves and Seyla Benhabib. Cambridge, MA: MIT Press.

Borch-Jacobsen, Mikkel. 1988. *The Freudian Subject.* Trans. Catherine Porter. Stanford, CA: Stanford University Press.

———. 1992. *The Emotional Tie: Psychoanalysis, Mimesis, and Affect.* Trans. Douglas Brick, et al. Stanford, CA: Stanford University Press.

Bowie, Andrew. 1999. "German Philosophy Today: Between Idealism, Romanticism, and Pragmatism." In *German Philosophy Since Kant*, edited by Anthony O'Hear. Cambridge: Cambridge University Press.

Bowring, Finn. 1997. "Communitarianism and Morality: In Search of the Subject." *New Left Review* 222:93–113.

Bubner, Rüdiger. 1988. *Essays in Hermeneutics and Critical Theory*. Trans. Eric Matthews. New York: Columbia University Press.

Buck-Morss, Susan. 1977. *The Origin of Negative Dialectics: Theodor W. Adorno, Walter Benjamin, and the Frankfurt Institute*. New York: The Free Press.

Cahn, Michael. 1984. "Subversive Mimesis: Theodor W. Adorno and the Modern Impasse of Critique" In *Mimesis in Contemporary Theory: An Interdisciplinary Approach*, edited by Mihai Spariosu. Philadelphia and Amsterdam: John Benjamins Publishing Company.

Carroll, Noël. 2001. *Beyond Aesthetics: Philosophical Essays*. Cambridge: Cambridge University Press.

Cascardi, Anthony. 1992. *The Subject of Modernity*. Cambridge: Cambridge University Press.

Castelli, Elizabeth A. 1991. *Imitating Paul: A Discourse of Power*. Louisville, KY: Westminster/John Knox Press.

Coles, Romand. 1995. "Identity and difference in the ethical positions of Adorno and Habermas." In *The Cambridge Companion to Habermas*, edited by Stephen K. White. Cambridge: Cambridge University Press.

———. 2000. "Of Democracy, Discourse, and Dirt Virtue: Developments in Recent Critical Theory." *Political Theory* 28 (4): 540–64.

Cook, Deborah. 2001. "Adorno, ideology and ideology critique." *Philosophy & Social Criticism* 27: 1–20.

Cook, Gary A. 1993. *George Herbert Mead: The Making of a Social Pragmatist*. Urbana: University of Illinois Press.

Coole, Diana. 1997. "Habermas and the Question of Alterity." In *Habermas and the Unfinished Project of Modernity: Critical Essays on The Philosophical Discourse of Modernity*, edited by Maurizio Passerin d'Entrèves and Seyla Benhabib. Cambridge, MA: MIT Press.

Critchley, Simon. 2002. *On Humour*. London: Routledge.

Dallmayr, Fred. 1997. "The Discourse of Modernity: Hegel, Nietzsche, Heidegger and Habermas." In *Habermas and the Unfinished Project of Modernity: Critical Essays on The Philosophical Discourse of Modernity*, edited by Maurizio Passerin d'Entrèves and Seyla Benhabib. Cambridge, MA: MIT Press.

Davis, Charles. 1992. "Pluralism, Privacy, and the Interior Self." In *Habermas, Modernity, and Public Theology*, edited by Don S. Browning and Francis Schüssler Fiorenza. New York: Crossroad.

Dean, Jodi. 1995. "Discourse in Different Voices." In *Feminists Read Habermas: Gendering the Subject of Discourse*, edited by Johanna Meehan. London: Routledge.

———. 2002. *Publicity's Secret: How Technoculture Capitalizes on Democracy*. Ithaca, NY: Cornell University Press.

d'Entrèves, Maurizio Passerin and Seyla Benhabib, eds. 1997. *Habermas and the Unfinished Project of Modernity: Critical Essays on The Philosophical Discourse of Modernity*. Cambridge, MA: MIT Press.

Derrida, Jacques.1981 [1972]. "Plato's Pharmacy." In *Dissemination*. Trans. Barbara Johnson. Chicago: University of Chicago Press.

———. 1995. *The Gift of Death.* Trans. David Wills. Chicago: University of Chicago Press.

———. 2000. "Performative Powerlessness: A Response to Simon Critchley." *Constellations* 7(4): 466–68.

Descartes, René. 1951 [1641]. *Meditations on First Philosophy*. Trans. Laurence J. Lafleur. Upper Saddle River, NJ: Prentice-Hall.

Dews, Peter. 1995a. "Adorno, Poststructuralism, and the Critique of Identity" (1986). In *The Limits of Disenchantment: Essays on Contemporary European Philosophy.* London: Verso Press.

———. 1995b. "Morality, Ethics and 'Postmetaphysical Thinking.'" In *The Limits of Disenchantment: Essays on Contemporary European Philosophy.* London: Verso Press.

———. 1999. "Communicative Paradigms and the Question of Subjectivity: Habermas, Mead and Lacan." In *Habermas: A Critical Reader*, edited by Peter Dews. London: Basil Blackwell Publishers.

Di Stefano, Christine. 1996. "Autonomy in the Light of Difference." In *Revisioning the Political: Feminist Reconstructions of Traditional Concepts in Western Political Theory*, edited by Nancy J. Hirschmann and Christine Di Stefano. Boulder, CO: Westview Press.

Dodds, E.R. 1951. *The Greeks and the Irrational.* Berkeley: University of California Press.

Dryzek, John S. 2001. "Legitimacy and Economy in Deliberative Democracy." *Political Theory* 29(5): 651–69.

Du Bois, W.E.B. 1986 [1903]. *The Souls of Black Folk.* In *Writings*, edited by Nathan Huggins. New York: The Library of America.

Duvenage, Pieter. 2003. *Habermas and Aesthetics: The Limits of Communicative Reason.* Cambridge: Polity Press.

Ely, John. 1998. "Intellectual Friendship and the Elective Affinities of Critical Theory." *The South Atlantic Quarterly* 97(1): 137–224.

Fanon, Frantz. 2004. *The Wretched of the Earth.* Trans. Ichard Philcox. New York: Grove Press.

Finlayson, Gordon. 1999. "Does Hegel's Critique of Kant's Moral Theory Apply to Discourse Ethics?" In *Habermas: A Critical Reader*, edited by Peter Dews. London: Basil Blackwell Publishers.

Flax, Jane. 1992. "The End of Innocence." In *Feminists Theorize the Political*, edited by Judith Butler and Joan Scott. New York: Routledge.

Foucault, Michel. 1979. *Discipline and Punish: The Birth of the Prison.* Trans. Alan Sheridan. New York: Vintage Books.

Frank, Manfred. 2002. "Self-consciousness and Self-knowledge: On Some Difficulties with the Reduction of Subjectivity." Trans. Bruce Matthews. *Constellations* 9 (3): 390–408.

Fraser, Nancy. 1997. *Justice Interruptus: Critical Reflections on the "Postsocialist" Condition.* London: Routledge.

Freud, Sigmund. 1959 [1921]. *Group Psychology and the Analysis of the Ego.* Trans. James Strachey. New York: W.W. Norton.

———. 1961 [1930]. *Civilization and its Discontents*. Trans. James Strachey. New York: W.W. Norton.

Gadamer, Hans-Georg. 1984. "The Hermeneutics of Suspicion." In *Hermeneutics: Questions and Prospects*, edited by Gary Shapiro and Alan Sica. Amherst, MA: University of Massachusetts Press.

———. 1986. "Poetry and Mimesis" (1972). In *The Relevance of the Beautiful and Other Essays*. Trans. Nicholas Walker. Edited with an Introduction by Robert Bernasconi. Cambridge: Cambridge University Press.

———. 1989 [1960]. *Truth and Method*. Trans. Joel Weinsheimer and Donald G. Marshall. New York: Continuum.

———. 1992 [1961]. "The Philosophy and Religion of Judaism." In *Hans-Georg Gadamer on Education, Poetry, and History*, edited by Dieter Misgeld and Graeme Nicholson. Trans. Lawrence Schmidt and Monica Reuss. Albany: SUNY Press.

———. 1998. *The Beginning of Philosophy*. New York: Continuum.

Gasché, Rodolphe. 1988. "Saturnine Vision and the Question of Difference: Reflections on Walter Benjamin's Theory of Language." In *Benjamin's Ground: New Readings of Walter Benjamin*, edited by Rainer Nägle. Detroit, MI: Wayne State University Press.

Gebauer, Gunter and Christoph Wulf. 1995. *Mimesis: Culture, Art, Society*. Trans. Don Reneau. Berkeley: University of California Press.

Green, Michael. 2003. "Justice and Law in Hobbes." In *Oxford Studies in Early Modern Philosophy, Volume I*, edited by Daniel Garber and Steven Nadler. Oxford: Clarendon Press.

Gutmann, Amy and Dennis Thompson. 2002. "Deliberative Democracy Beyond Process." *The Journal of Political Philosophy* 10: 153–74.

Habermas, Jürgen. 1971 [1968]. *Knowledge and Human Interests*. Trans. Jeremy J. Shapiro. Boston: Beacon Press.

———. 1973 [1971]. "Labor and Interaction: Remarks on Hegel's Jena *Philosophy of Mind*." In *Theory and Practice*. Trans. John Viertel. Boston: Beacon Press.

———. 1974. "On Social Identity." *Telos* 19:91–103.

———. 1979 [1976]. *Communication and the Evolution of Society*. Trans. Thomas McCarthy. Boston: Beacon Press.

———. 1982. "A Reply to My Critics." In *Habermas: Critical Debates*, edited by John B. Thompson and David Held. Cambridge, MA: MIT Press.

———. 1984 [1981]. *The Theory of Communicative Action, Volume One; Reason and the Rationalization of Society*. Trans. Thomas McCarthy. Boston, MA: Beacon Press.

———. 1985a [1983]. "Remarks on the Concept of Communicative Action." In *Social Action*, edited by Gottfried Seebaß and Raimo Tuomela. Dordrecht: D. Reidel Publishing Company.

———. 1985b. "A Philosophico-Political Profile." Interview by Perry Anderson and Peter Dews. *New Left Review* 151:75–105.

———. 1985c. "Questions and Counterquestions." In *Habermas and Modernity*, edited by Richard J. Bernstein. Cambridge, MA: MIT Press.

———. 1987a [1981]. *The Theory of Communicative Action, Volume Two; Lifeworld and System: a Critique of Functionalist Reason*. Trans. Thomas McCarthy. Boston, MA: Beacon Press.

———. 1987b [1985]. *The Philosophical Discourse of Modernity: Twelve Lectures*. Trans. Frederick G. Lawrence. Cambridge, MA: MIT Press.

———. 1988 [1972]. "Walter Benjamin: Consciousness-Raising or Rescuing Critique." In *On Walter Benjamin: Critical Essays and Recollections*, edited by Gary Smith. Cambridge, MA: MIT Press.

———. 1989 [1962]. *The Structural Transformation of the Public Sphere: An Inquiry into a Category of Bourgeois Society*. Trans. Thomas Burger with Frederick Lawrence. Cambridge, MA: MIT Press.

———. 1990 [1983]. *Moral Consciousness and Communicative Action*. Trans. Christian Lenhardt and Shierry Weber Nicholsen. Cambridge, MA: MIT Press.

———. 1991 [1986]. "A Reply." In *Communicative Action: Essays on Jürgen Habermas's* The Theory of Communicative Action, edited by Axel Honneth and Hans Joas. Trans. Jeremy Gaines and Doris L. Jones. Cambridge: Polity Press.

———. 1992a [1988]. "Individuation through Socialization: On George Herbert Mead's Theory of Subjectivity." In *Postmetaphysical Thinking: Philosophical Essays*. Trans. William Mark Hohengarten. Cambridge, MA: MIT Press.

———. 1992b [1988]. "Metaphysics after Kant." In *Postmetaphysical Thinking: Philosophical Essays*. Trans. William Mark Hohengarten. Cambridge, MA: MIT Press.

———. 1992c [1988]. "Philosophy and Science as Literature?" In *Postmetaphysical Thinking: Philosophical Essays*. Trans. William Mark Hohengarten. Cambridge, MA: MIT Press.

———. 1992d [1988]. *Postmetaphysical Thinking: Philosophical Essays*. Trans. William Mark Hohengarten. Cambridge, MA: MIT Press.

———. 1992e [1988]. "Themes in Postmetaphysical Thinking." In *Postmetaphysical Thinking: Philosophical Essays*. Trans. William Mark Hohengarten. Cambridge, MA: MIT Press.

———. 1992f [1988]. "The Unity of Reason in the Diversity of Its Voices." In *Postmetaphysical Thinking: Philosophical Essays*. Trans. William Mark Hohengarten. Cambridge, MA: MIT Press.

———. 1992g. *Autonomy and Solidarity: Interviews with Jürgen Habermas* (Rev. ed.). Edited and with an Introduction by Peter Dews. London: Verso Press.

———. 1992h. "Transcendence from Within, Transcendence in this World." In *Habermas, Modernity, and Public Theology*, edited by Dons S. Browning and Francis Schüssler Fiorenza. New York: Crossroad Publishing Company.

———. 1993a [1991]. *Justification and Application: Remarks on Discourse Ethics*. Trans. Ciaran P. Cronin. Cambridge, MA: MIT Press.

———. 1993b [1991]. "On the Pragmatic, the Ethical, and the Moral Employments of Practical Reason." In *Justification and Application: Remarks on Discourse Ethics*. Trans. Ciaran Cronin. Cambridge, MA: MIT Press.

———. 1996a [1992]. *Between Facts and Norms: Contributions to a Discourse Theory of Law and Democracy*. Trans. William Rehg. Cambridge, MA: MIT Press.

———. 1996b. *Autonomy and Solidarity: Interviews with Jürgen Habermas*. Edited by Peter Dews. London: Verso Press.

———. 1997 [1980]. "Modernity—An Unfinished Project." In *Habermas and the Unfinished Project of Modernity: Critical Essays on The Philosophical Discourse of*

Modernity, edited by Maurizio Passerin d'Entrèves and Seyla Benhabib. Cambridge, MA: MIT Press.

———. 1998a [1996]. "A Genealogical Analysis of the Cognitive Content of Morality." In *Inclusion of the Other: Studies in Political Theory*, edited by Ciaran Cronin and Pablo De Greiff. Trans. Ciaran Cronin. Cambridge, MA: MIT Press.

———. 1998b [1996]. " 'Reasonable' versus 'True,' or the Morality of Worldviews." In *Inclusion of the Other: Studies in Political Theory*, edited by Ciaran Cronin and Pablo De Greiff. Trans. Ciaran Cronin. Cambridge, MA: MIT Press.

———. 1998c [1996]. "Richard Rorty's Pragmatic Turn." In *On the Pragmatics of Communication*, edited by Maeve Cooke. Trans. Maeve Cooke. Cambridge, MA: MIT Press.

———. 1998d [1996]. "Some Further Clarifications of the Concept of Communicative Rationality." In *On the Pragmatics of Communication*, edited by Maeve Cooke. Trans. Maeve Cooke. Cambridge, MA: MIT Press.

———. 1999. "Hermeneutic and Analytic Philosophy. Two Complementary Versions of the Linguistic Turn?" In *German Philosophy Since Kant*, edited by Anthony O'Hear. Cambridge: Cambridge University Press.

———. [no date. ———. 2009]. "A Postsecular World Society? On the Philosophical Significance of Postsecular consciousness and the multicultural World Society." An Interview with Jürgen Habermas by Eduardo Mendieta. Trans. Matthias Fritsch. http://blogs.ssrc.org/tif/wp-content/uploads/2010/02/A-Postsecular-World-Society-TIF.pdf. Accessed February 14, 2010.

Halliwell, Stephen. 2002. *The Aesthetics of Mimesis: Ancient Texts and Modern Problems*. Princeton: Princeton University Press.

Hansen, Miriam Bratu. 1999. "Benjamin and Cinema." *Critical Inquiry* 25(2): 306–43.

Hartman, Geoffrey H. 1999. "Benjamin in Hope." *Critical Inquiry* 25(2): 344–52.

Harvey, David. 1989. *The Condition of Postmodernity: An Enquiry into the Origins of Cultural Change*. Oxford: Basil Blackwell.

Havelock, Eric A. 1963. *Preface to Plato*. Cambridge, MA: Belknap Press.

Hegel, G.W.F. 1977. *Phenomenology of Spirit*. Trans. A.V. Miller. Oxford: Oxford University Press.

Henry, Michel. 1991. "The Critique of the Subject." In *Who Comes After the Subject?* edited by Eduardo Cadava, Peter Connor and Jean-Luc Nancy. Trans. Peter T. Conner. London: Routledge.

Henry, Paget. 2000. "Myth, Language, and Habermasian Rationality: Another Africana Contribution." In *Perspectives on Habermas*, edited by Lewis Edwin Hahn. Chicago: Open Court.

Hinchman, Lewis. 1996. "Autonomy, Individuality, and Self-Determination." In *What is Enlightenment? Eighteenth-Century Answers and Twentieth-Century Questions*, edited by James Schmidt. Berkeley: University of California Press.

Hirschkop, Ken. 2004. "Justice and drama: on Bakhtin as a complement to Habermas." In *After Habermas: New Perspectives on the Public Sphere*, edited by Nick Crossley and John Michael Roberts. Oxford; Blackwell Publishing.

Hobbes, Thomas. 1994 [1668]. *Leviathan*. Edited by Edwin Curley. Indianapolis, IN: Hackett Publishing.

Hohendahl, Peter Uwe. 1997. "Adorno: The Discourse of Philosophy and the Problem of Language." In *The Actuality of Adorno: Critical Essays on Adorno and the Postmodern*, edited and with an Introduction by Max Pensky. Albany: SUNY Press.

Honneth, Axel. 1995 [1976]. "From Adorno to Habermas: On the Transformation of Critical Social Theory." In *The Fragmented World of the Social: Essays in Social and Political Philosophy* (1990), edited by Charles W. Wright. Albany: SUNY Press.

———. 1996 [1994]. *The Struggle for Recognition: The Moral Grammar of Social Conflicts*. Trans. Joel Anderson. Cambridge, MA: MIT Press.

Horkheimer, Max. 1972. *Critical Theory: Selected Essays*. Trans. Matthew J. O'Connell, et al. New York: Seabury Press.

———. 1974 [1947]. *The Eclipse of Reason*. New York: Continuum.

Horkheimer, Max and Theodor Adorno. 1969 [1944]. *Dialectic of Enlightenment.* Trans. John Cumming. New York: Continuum.

Huyssen, Andreas. 2000. "Of Mice and Mimesis: Reading Spiegelman with Adorno." *New German Critique* 81: 65–82.

Ingram, David. 1991. "Habermas on Aesthetics and Rationality: Completing the Project of Enlightenment." *New German Critique* 53 (Spring/Summer) 67–103.

———. 1995. *Reason, History, and Politics: The Communitarian Grounds of Legitimation in the Modern Age.* Albany: SUNY Press.

———. 1997. "The Subject of Justice in Postmodern Discourse: Aesthetic Judgement and Political Rationality." In *Habermas and the Unfinished Project of Modernity: Critical Essays on The Philosophical Discourse of Modernity*, edited by Maurizio Passerin d'Entrèves and Seyla Benhabib. Cambridge, MA: MIT Press.

Jay, Martin.1973. *The Dialectical Imagination: A History of the Frankfurt School and the Institute of Social Research, 1923–1950.* Boston: Little Brown and Company.

———. 1984a. *Adorno.* Cambridge, MA: Harvard University Press.

———. 1984b. *Marxism and Totality: The Adventures of a Concept from Lukács to Habermas.* Berkeley: University of California Press.

———. 1985. "Habermas and Modernism." In *Habermas and Modernity,* edited by Richard J. Bernstein. Cambridge, MA: MIT Press.

———. 1997. "Mimesis and Mimetology: Adorno and Lacoue-Labarthe." In *The Semblance of Subjectivity,* edited by Tom Huhn and Lambert Zuidervaart. Cambridge, MA: MIT Press.

———. 2005. Songs of Experience: Modern American and European Variations on a Universal Theme. Berkeley: University of California Press.

Joas, Hans. 1997 [1980]. *G.H. Mead: A Contemporary Re-Examination of His Thought.* Trans. Raymond Meyer. Cambridge, MA: MIT Press.

Kant, Immanuel. 1951. *Critique of Judgment*. Trans. J.H. Bernard. London: Hafner Publishing Co.

———. 1993 [1785]. *Grounding for the Metaphysics of Morals*. Trans. James W. Ellington. Indianapolis: Hackett Publishing Company, Inc.

Kateb, George. 2000. "Aestheticism and Morality." *Political Theory* 28(1): 5–37.

Katznelson, Ira. 2000. *Desolation and Enlightenment: Political Knowledge After Total War, Totalitarianism and the Holocaust*. New York: Columbia University Press.

Koczanowicz, Leszek. 1999. "The choice of tradition and the tradition of choice: Habermas' and Rorty's interpretation of pragmatism." *Philosophy and Social Criticism* 25(1): 55–70.

Kompridis, Nikolas. 1994. "On World Disclosure: Heidegger, Habermas, and Dewey." *Thesis Eleven* 37: 29–45.

———. 2006. *Critique and Disclosure: Critical Theory between Past and Future*. Cambridge, MA: MIT Press.

Langsdorf, Lenore. 2002. "Reconstructing the Fourth Dimension: A Deweyan Critique of Habermas's Conception of Communicative Action." In *Habermas and Pragmatism*, edited by Mitchell Aboulafia, Myra Bookman and Catherine Kemp. London: Routledge.

Levinas, Emmanuel. 1969 [1961]. *Totality and Infinity: An Essay on Exteriority*. Trans. Alphonso Lingis. Pittsburgh: Duquesne University Press.

Leys, Ruth. 1994. "Mead's Voices: Imitation as Foundation; or, the Struggle against Mimesis." In *Modernist Impulses in the Human Sciences, 1870–1930*, edited by Dorothy Ross. Baltimore: Johns Hopkins University Press.

Lincoln, Bruce. 1999. *Theorizing Myth: Narrative, Ideology, and Scholarship*. Chicago: University of Chicago.

Lindroos, Kia. 2001. "Scattering Community: Benjamin on experience, narrative and history." *Philosophy and Social Criticism* 27(6): 19–42.

Locke, John. 1980 [1690]. *The Second Treatise of Government*. Indianapolis: Hackett Publishing Company.

Lukes, Steven. 1982. "Of Gods and Demons: Habermas and Practical Reason." In *Habermas: Critical Debates*, edited by John B. Thompson and David Held. Cambridge, MA: MIT Press.

Lyons, John D. 1982. "Subjectivity and Imitation in the *Discours de la Méthode*." *Neophilologus* 66: 508–24.

Lyotard, Jean-François. 1984 [1979]. *The Postmodern Condition: A Report on Knowledge*. Trans. Geoff Bennington and Brian Massumi. Minneapolis: University of Minnesota Press.

MacIntyre, Alasdair. 1984. *After Virtue: A Study in Moral Theory* (2nd Ed.). Notre Dame, IN: University of Notre Dame Press.

Marx, Karl. 1988. *Economic and Philosophic Manuscripts of 1844*. Trans. Martin Milligan. New York: Prometheus Books.

McCarthy, Thomas. 1993. "The Idea of a Critical Theory and Its Relation to Philosophy" In *On Max Horkheimer: New Perspectives*, edited by Seyla Benhabib, Wolfgang Bonß, and John McCole. Cambridge, MA: MIT Press.

McCole, John. 1993. *Walter Benjamin and the Antinomies of Tradition*. Ithaca, NY: Cornell University Press.

McCumber, John. 1988. "Philosophy as the Heteronomous Center of Modern Discourse: Jürgen Habermas." In *Philosophy and Non-Philosophy Since Merleau-Ponty*, edited by Hugh J. Silverman. London: Routledge.

———. 1989. *Poetic Interaction: Language, Freedom, Reason*. Chicago: University of Chicago Press.

Mead, George Herbert. 1932. *The Philosophy of the Present*. Edited by Arthur E. Murphy. Chicago: University of Chicago Press.

———. 1934. *Mind, Self, Society from the Standpoint of a Social Behaviorist*. Edited by Charles W. Morris. Chicago: University of Chicago Press.

———. 1936. *Movements of Thought in the Nineteenth Century*. Edited by Merritt H. Moore. Chicago: University of Chicago Press.

———. 1964. *Selected Writings*. Edited by Andrew J. Reck. Indianapolis: Bobbs-Merrill Company, Inc.

Melberg, Arne. 1995. *Theories of Mimesis*. Cambridge: Cambridge University Press.

Menke, Cristoph. 1998 [1988]. *The Sovereignty of Art: Aesthetic Negativity in Adorno and Derrida*. Trans. Neil Solomon. Cambridge, MA: MIT Press.

Miller, David L. 1973. *George Herbert Mead: Self, Language, and the World*. Austin: University of Texas Press.

Morris, Martin. 1997. "The Paradigm Shift to Communication and the Eclipse of the Object." *The South Atlantic Quarterly* 96(4): 755–87.

———. 2001. *Rethinking the Communicative Turn: Adorno, Habermas, and the Problem of Communicative Freedom.* Albany: SUNY Press.

Nietzsche, Friedrich. 1967 [1887]. *On the Genealogy of Morals: A Polemic.* Trans. Walter Kaufmann and R.J. Hollingdale. New York: Vintage.

———. 1989 [1873]. "On Truth and Lying in an Extra-Moral Sense." In *Friedrich Nietzsche on Rhetoric and Language,* edited, translated, and with an Introduction by Sander L. Gilman, Carole Blair, David J. Parent. New York: Oxford University Press.

Osborne, Peter. 1989. "Adorno and the Metaphysics of Modernism: The Problem of a 'Postmodern' Art." In *The Problems of Modernity: Adorno and Benjamin,* edited by Andrew Benjamin. London: Routledge.

Pensky, Max. 1989. "On the Use and Abuse of Memory: Habermas, 'Anamnestic Solidarity,' and the *Historikerstreit*." *Philosophy and Social Criticism* 15: 351–80.

Planty-Bonjour, Guy. 1983. "Hegel's Concept of Action as a Unity of Poiesis and Praxis." In *Hegel's Philosophy of Action,* edited by Lawrence S. Stepelevich and David Lamb. Atlantic Highlands, NJ: Humanities Press.

Plato. 1938. *Ion.* In *Phaedrus, Ion, Gorgias, and Symposium, with passages from the Republic and Laws.* Trans. Lane Cooper. London: Oxford University Press.

———. 1973. *Phaedrus.* In *Phaedrus and The Seventh and Eighth Letters*. Trans. Walter Hamilton. Harmondsworth: Penguin Books.

———. 1997a. *Crito.* In *Plato: Complete Works,* edited by John M. Cooper. Trans. G.M.A. Grube. Indianapolis: Hackett Publishing Company.

———. 1997b. *Laws.* In *Plato: Complete Works,* edited by John M. Cooper. Trans. G.M.A. Grube. Indianapolis: Hackett Publishing Company.

———. 1997c. *Republic.* In *Plato: Complete Works,* edited by John M. Cooper. Trans. G.M.A. Grube. Revised by C.D.C. Reeve. Indianapolis: Hackett Publishing Company.

———. 1997d. *Timaeus.* In *Plato: Complete Works,* edited by John M. Cooper. Trans. G.M.A. Grube. Revised by C.D.C. Reeve. Indianapolis: Hackett Publishing Company.

Posnock, Ross. 1998. "Going Astray, Going Forward: Du Boisian Pragmatism and Its Lineage." In *The Revival of Pragmatism: New Essays on Social Thought, Law, and Culture,* edited by Morris Dickstein. Durham, NC: Duke University Press.

Pye, Christopher. 1984. "The Sovereign, the Theater, and the Kingdome of Darknesse: Hobbes and the Spectacle of Power." *Representations* 8 (Autumn): 84–106.

Ricoeur, Paul. 1973. "The Model of The Text: Meaningful Action Considered as a Text." *New Literary History* 5(1): 91–117.

———. 1985 [1984]. *Time and Narrative*. Vol. 2. Trans. Kathleen McLaughlin and David Pellauer. Chicago: University of Chicago Press.

———. 1992. *Oneself as Another*. Trans. Kathleen Blamey. Chicago: University of Chicago Press.

Rorty, Richard. 1979. *Philosophy and the Mirror of Nature*. Princeton, NJ: Princeton University Press.

———. 1984. "Solidarity or Objectivity?" In *Post-Analytic Philosophy*, edited by John Ranchman and Cornel West. New York: Columbia University Press.

———. 1985. "Postmodern Bourgeois Liberalism." In *Hermeneutics and Praxis*, edited by Robert Hollinger. Notre Dame, IN: University of Notre Dame Press.

———. 1989. *Contingency, Irony, and Solidarity*. New York: Cambridge University Press.

———. 2002. "Human Rights, Rationality, and Sentimentality." In *The Politics of Human Rights*, edited by The Belgrade Circle. London: Verso Press.

Rousseau, Jean-Jacques.1973. *The Social Contract and Discourses*. Trans. G.D.H. Cole. Rutland, VT: Everyman.

Schmidt, Dennis J. 2001. *On Germans and Other Greeks: Tragedy and Ethical Life*. Bloomington: Indiana University Press.

Schoolman, Morton. 2005. "Avoiding 'Embarrassment': Aesthetic Reason and Aporetic Critique in *Dialectic of Enlightenment*." *Polity* 37(3): 335–64.

Scott, Joan W. 1991. "The Evidence of Experience." *Critical Inquiry* 17(4): 773–97.

Sevilla, Sergio. 1997. "Critical Theory and Rationality." *boundary* 2 24 (1): 29–78.

Siep, Ludwig. 1983. "The '*Aufhebung*' of Morality in Ethical Life." In *Hegel's Philosophy of Action*, edited by Lawrence S. Stepelevich and David Lamb. Atlantic Highlands, NJ: Humanities Press.

Smith, Adam. 1976 [1776]. *An Inquiry into the Wealth of Nations*. Edited by E. Cannan. Chicago: University of Chicago Press.

Sörbom, Göran. 1966. *Mimesis and Art: Studies in the Origin and Early Development of an Aesthetic Vocabulary*. Svenska Bokförlaget, Bonniers: Uppsala.

Strong, Tracy B. and Frank Andreas Sposito. 1995. "Habermas' Significant Other." In *The Cambridge Companion to Habermas*, edited by Stephen K. White. Cambridge: Cambridge University Press.

Taussig, Michael. 1993. *Mimesis and Alterity: A Particular History of the Senses*. London: Routledge.

Taylor, Charles. 1989. *Sources of the Self: The Making of the Modern Identity*. Cambridge, MA: Harvard University Press.

———. 1995. "The Politics of Recognition." In *Philosophical Arguments*. Cambridge, MA: Harvard University Press.

Therborn, Göran. 1996. "Dialectics of Modernity: On Critical Theory and the Legacy of Twentieth-Century Marxism." *New Left Review* 215: 59–81.

Tugendhat, Ernst. 1986 [1979]. *Self-Consciousness and Self-Determination*. Trans. Paul Stern. Cambridge, MA: MIT Press.

Vološinov, V.N. 1986 [1929]. *Marxism and the Philosophy of Language*. Trans. Ladislav Matejka and I.R. Titunik. Cambridge, MA: Harvard University Press.

Wagner, Gerhard and Heinz Zipprian. 1991. "Intersubjectivity and Critical Consciousness: Remarks on Habermas's Theory of Communicative Action." *Inquiry* 34(1): 49–62.

Wallerstein, Immanuel. 1983. *Historical Capitalism*. London: Verso.

Warner, Michael. 2002. "Publics and Counterpublics." *Public Culture* 14 (1) 49–90.

Warren, Mark E. 1995. "The Self in Discursive Democracy." In *The Cambridge Companion to Habermas*, edited by Stephen K. White. Cambridge: Cambridge University Press.

Weber, Max. 1946 [1919]. "Science as a Vocation." In *From Max Weber: Essays in Sociology*. Translated and edited by H.H. Gerth and C. Wright Mills. New York: Oxford University Press.

———. 1958. *The Protestant Ethic and the Spirit of Capitalism*. Trans. Talcott Parsons. New York: Charles Scribner's Sons.

Wellmer, Albrecht. 1971 [1969]. *Critical Theory of Society*. Trans. John Cumming. New York: Herder and Herder.

———. 1991. *The Persistence of Modernity: Essays on Aesthetics, Ethics, and Postmodernism*. Trans. David Midgley. Cambridge, MA: MIT Press.

———. 1998 [1993]. *Endgames: The Irreconcilable Nature of Modernity*. Trans. David Midgley. Cambridge, MA: MIT Press.

Wilson, Elizabeth. 1992. *The Sphinx in the City: Urban Life, the Control of Disorder, and Women*. Berkeley: University of California Press.

Wohlfarth, Irving. 1989. "On Some Jewish Motifs in Benjamin." In *The Problems of Modernity: Adorno and Benjamin*, edited by Andrew Benjamin. London: Routledge.

Wolin, Richard. 1992. *The Terms of Cultural Criticism: The Frankfurt School, Existentialism, Poststructuralism*. New York: Columbia University Press.

Wolters, Raymond. 2002. *Du Bois and His Rivals*. Columbia: University of Missouri Press.

Young, Iris Marion. 1990. *Justice and the Politics of Difference*. Princeton, NJ: Princeton University Press.

———. 1996. "Communication and the Other: Beyond Deliberative Democracy." In *Democracy and Difference: Contesting the Boundaries of the Political*, edited by Seyla Benhabib. Princeton, NJ: Princeton University Press.

———. 1997a. "Asymmetrical Reciprocity: On Moral Respect, Wonder, and Enlarged Thought." *Constellations* 3(3): 340–363.

———. 1997b. "Unruly Categories: A Critique of Nancy Fraser's Dual Systems Theory." *New Left Review* 222: 147–60.

Index

www.ingramcontent.com/pod-product-compliance
Lightning Source LLC
LaVergne TN
LVHW101627040926
847296LV00026B/118
9781438437408